Personal Shorthand "80"

CARDINAL SERIES

80-LESSONS, BOOKS 1 & 2 COMBINED

Book 1, 40 Lessons — Theory
**Book 2, 40 Lessons — Speed Building
and Transcription**

NO. 241180

0885

ISBN 0-89420-221-9

PERSONAL SHORTHAND

BOOK 1

BOOK 2

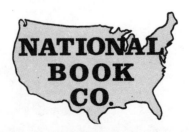

NATIONAL BOOK CO.

Personal Shorthand

CARDINAL SERIES

BOOK 1

CARL W. SALSER
C. THEO. YERIAN

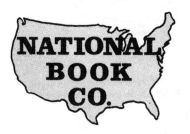

No. 241050

NATIONAL BOOK COMPANY
A Division of
Educational Research Associates
A Nonprofit Educational Research Corporation
333 SW Park Avenue
Portland, Oregon 97205

Personal Shorthand

CARDINAL SERIES
BOOK 1

ISBN 0-89420-106-9

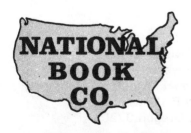

Graphics/Production	John Kimmel
Typesetting	Type Craft

PREFACE

TO THE STUDENT:

It is good to know that already you are equipped with the main ingredient for learning PERSONAL SHORTHAND ... The ENGLISH ALPHABET.

PS theory makes use of *only* the 26 letters of our native alphabet. You will not be asked to use *any* symbols foreign to longhand letters. There are no curves, angles, or unnatural joinings; no plus signs, minus signs, hyphens, quotation marks, parentheses, etc., used to represent phonetic and syllabic combinations.

Moreover, YOU PUNCTUATE AND CAPITALIZE JUST AS YOU DO IN LONGHAND: and YOU WRITE IN THE SAME STYLE AND SIZE AS YOU NOW WRITE IN LONGHAND.

PS, the only *truly* alphabetic shorthand, is fulfilling a long-felt need for a more easily learned and less time consuming notetaking system. It is the product of many years of patient research and development by authors who have had much experience with both alphabetic and nonalphabetic shorthands. They are bringing you a readily and easily learned notetaking skill that will serve you most adequately and efficiently as a commercial and/or personal-use skill.

An important thing to remember is that a *personal-use* objective for PS can readily be turned into a job-level goal, with little additional time and study.

There is no need to take two years of your time to develop an efficient notetaking skill. One semester/term will suffice for personal use; one year will provide sufficient time in which to develop notetaking and general stenographic/secretarial skills required in the office.

Shorthand has played an important role, down through the centuries, dating back approximately 3,000 years to clay tablets and papyrus. Symbol shorthands (geometric and cursive characters) have dominated the shorthand scene until recent years. Because of a changing world and technological improvements of every conceivable type, symbol shorthands have found themselves challenged by many emerging non-symbol, so-called "alphabetic" shorthand systems. However, these systems, *with the exception of PS,* are represented by a combination of *symbols* and *alphabetic* characters; thus, the learning difficulties created by the symbols have not been eliminated completely. Indeed, in the opinion of many experts, a combination or "hybrid" system (using both symbols and letters of the alphabet) is as difficult to learn (if not *more* so) than an all-symbol system.

PERSONAL SHORTHAND has tenaciously adhered to a completely alphabetic concept; and, by doing so, has gained wide acceptance as an "all-purpose" notetaking system. PS is "at home" on the typewriter, as well as with pen or pencil. Everything you need to write PS is on the regular typewriter keyboard!

CARDINAL SERIES

This book is Part 1 of the three-book "Cardinal Series" in Personal Shorthand. It is designed to provide the following: Theory, Personal Notetaking Techniques, and an Introduction to Transcription.

Part 2 will provide: Speedbuilding and Transcription Techniques, Vocational Applications, and Special Vocabularies.

Part 3 will provide: Advanced Speedbuilding and Transcription Techniques, Secretarial Procedures, Technical Vocabularies, and a Reference Guide.

TEXTBOOK FEATURES

Purposefully, the six basic theory rules are presented in the first lesson. They can be covered very quickly. Constant review of the rules throughout the text will serve to strengthen your knowledge of them.

Lessons 2 and 3 present the BRIEF FORMS ... common words which comprise 40-60 percent of normal office dictation. Sentences within each lesson provide concentrated practice on specific Brief Forms.

Lesson 4 provides additional drill on Brief Forms and the theory rules.

Lessons 5 through 8 provide the phonetic abbreviations which make it possible to increase further the speed of writing. Ample opportunity is provided for practice.

Lesson 9 presents some recommended shortcuts for common word beginnings (prefixes). Their use further increases the speed of writing.

Lesson 10 presents some special words which call for careful attention to pronunciation. Remember, all shorthand systems require writing by sound (phonetic), and this is the case with PS ... only in a less complicated manner. Believe it or not, you will have covered all of the PS theory in the first ten lessons of this textbook!

Lessons 11 to 40 provide systematic "review" and pretty much follow the same organizational pattern for the purpose of *automatizing* PS writing skills. The lessons are characterized generally by concentrated theory review materials, reading and writing practice, Brief Form letters, and notetaking/transcription pointers.

Beginning on Page 163, there are 56 longhand articles and letters (Section 1) to be used for oral or copy dictation. They are marked off in 20-word (28 syllables) groupings for timing purposes.

Beginning on Page 174, there are 25 letters and articles (Section 2) written in PS. These provide convenient speed reading and copy practice.

Beginning on Page 182, there are PS Theory References (Section 3), which will enable you to "double-check," when necessary, without having to thumb through pages in the forepart of the book.

The Authors

TABLE OF CONTENTS

STUDY SUGGESTIONS

1. Remember, you need not change your normal manner of writing. You should strive, however, for *neatness* and *clarity* of writing.
2. Select a quiet place in which to study and practice. Use the same time and place if possible. Do not be tempted to "break into" your study routines for other purposes. Work diligently and as rapidly as you can learn. One hour of concentrated effort is worth more than three hours of "lackadaisical" practice.
3. Your reading rate should increase gradually as you gain confidence in your understanding of PS. Soon you will approach your longhand reading rate. This is to be expected. Strive to recognize words more and more rapidly.
4. Although theory principles are important and make writing and reading easier, you need not be a "slave" to them. It is better to achieve a steady, flowing type method of writing, instead of "hesitating" while groping for specific rule interpretation and application. It is recommended that notes be reviewed for rule violation and incorrectly written or omitted PS characters. Practice writing these until they can be written smoothly and correctly. It is the reduction of time *between* PS words that really contributes to the increase in writing speed.
5. It is recommended that you do not write longhand or PS "interpretations" in your textbook, even if it is your property. Use a straight edge to place alongside or underneath words or sentences to be translated into longhand or PS. Develop and maintain the habit of moving along as rapidly as possible in the interpretative process. If a PS word is not readily readable in a sentence, look ahead until another word is recognized. This may assist you to identify the word you had to pass by.
6. Begin early to build "word-carrying" power. For instance, read a longhand sentence completely before beginning to translate it into PS; then write your notes as quickly as you can. You will find that your "word-carrying" ability will increase steadily. This ability is desirable, especially when taking oral dictation.
7. Develop early the habit of *thinking* PS for new and little-known words. PS will open to you a new world of opportunities for recording information in abbreviated form. This will assist you to develop "vocabulary power," as well as correct pronunciation. This is the logical place to recommend that you consult a well-known dictionary when in doubt concerning the proper pronunciation of a word. Learn how to read vowel markings, recognize the "schwa," develop pride in pronouncing words correctly, etc. Remember: YOU CAN WRITE ANYTHING IN PS THAT YOU CAN PRONOUNCE!
8. It is recommended that you keep a record of the types of mistakes you make frequently, not for the purpose of dwelling on them, but for the purpose of eliminating them as quickly as possible. Begin each study period with a review of frequent errors, and you'll be surprised how quickly they become a thing of the past. Design an easily located symbol to identify your errors; a colored pen is helpful.
9. You don't have to wait for your teacher to give you a test; prepare tests of your own, and be sure to place emphasis on your "trouble spots." Also, be sure that you make your test cover everything to date.
10. The Brief Forms, as you know, represent commonly used words and need to become completely "automatized." Practice these over and

over again. You will notice that several are grouped to make meaningful combinations when recited. For instance, make a question out of "j" by asking the question, "Just gentlemen?" "N" becomes, "When not in, no know information!" Etc.

11. As with any other skill where instant recall or response is necessary, consistent and repetitious practice is very important. Write words and combinations of words, especially those that may cause you to hesitate, a sufficient number of times to eliminate the hesitation and uncertainty. Just remember how capable athletes have to do the same thing many, many times, some more than others, perhaps, in order to become proficient in their respective skills. Meaningful repetition, even though a bit "boring" at times, will help you to become a better PS writer.

12. Notetaking pointers begin in Lesson 16. Many useful ideas are presented for making your personal-use notetaking more practical and efficient. Pay close attention to what they say. You may want to discuss some of the "pointers" with your teacher.

13. In addition to learning to read PS notes rapidly, spend considerable time *transcribing*. Use the typewriter, if you have developed that skill; otherwise in longhand ... all the time paying particular attention to spelling and punctuation. Your teacher will counsel with you regarding this type of activity.

14. It is recommended that you equip yourself with *two* notebooks ... one for outside practice work and one for class time. A free-flowing ballpoint pen (medium or fine point) is recommended for writing. Pencil or felt pen create undesirable "drag" on the writing surface. It is a good idea to have a second ballpoint handy, if the one in use runs out of ink.

15. Keep your notebook in a comfortable writing position. This means that your forearm is on the desk surface and remains there throughout the writing time. The free hand should be used to move the notebook when necessary in order to keep it in the correct writing position. If this type of writing stance is maintained, notetaking will be less tiring, your posture will be more attractive, and the PS notes will be more legible and easily read.

16. Pronunication of the same word may vary, depending upon the part of the country in which you find yourself. New Englanders may pronounce the word "law" as "lawr." In every case, however, it should be written as it is spelled and marked in standard dictionaries.

17. Commonly used and well-known longhand "abbreviations," if shorter than the PS words, should be used when taking dictation. You be the judge.

18. A regular stenographic notebook (spiral binding) is recommended. Use your own judgment concerning whether you write down one column at a time or completely across the page. Remember, use the nonwriting hand to keep the pad in an effective writing position.

19. Recordings in cassette form have been prepared to provide instructional assistance throughout this textbook. If your school has purchased them, your teacher will devise a procedure by which you can make effective use of them. They will talk to you through the theory in very much the same manner that would be used by a teacher. They can be useful especially for "make-up" and "review" purposes.

Personal Shorthand

1.1 In learning PS (PERSONAL SHORTHAND), there are no special "symbols" to master, since PS uses nothing but the 26 letters of the longhand alphabet; nor is there any prescribed way that individual letters must be written; no costly "unlearning" of established habit patterns.

1.2 Remember that PS—unlike other so-called ABC, alphabetic, or abbreviated longhand, shorthand, or notetaking systems—uses only the 26 letters of the longhand alphabet and does not require that letters of the alphabet be written in some *specific* or *unnatural* manner. In short, write all letters as it is *natural* for you to write them, although you are urged to write as neatly as possible, simply for the sake of readability.

1.3 In PERSONAL SHORTHAND (PS),*capital* letters may be handled in one of two ways: They may be written in the normal manner; or capitalizing may be ignored entirely, since most PS writers have no trouble remembering (when transcribing) that the initial letter in each sentence should be capitalized and that proper nouns (names of people, cities, organizations, etc.) should be capitalized.

1.4 PS can be *typed*, just as it is written with pen or pencil. When typing PERSONAL SHORTHAND, letters can be capitalized in the normal way or (as in longhand) simply ignored. It should be emphasized that PS can be typed without *any* changes or modifications whatsoever. This is possible because—again —PERSONAL SHORTHAND uses nothing but the 26 letters of the alphabet—no strange symbols, dashes, dots, curves, etc.

1.5 In PERSONAL SHORTHAND (PS) theory, emphasis is on simplicity, above all else. For this reason, even *punctuation marks* are used exactly as they are in longhand. *Paragraphing* may be indicated by a single diagonal line or, if you prefer, you may indent as you do in longhand.

1.6 For the purpose of review, let's consider the following questions once more: (1) PERSONAL SHORTHAND employs nothing but the ___2 6___ letters of the longhand alphabet; (2) PS does not require that letters of the alphabet be written in any _Strange_ or unnatural way; (3) in taking PS notes, capital letters can be written in the normal manner or completely _ignored_; (4) and punctuation marks in PS are expressed in exactly the same way they are in _longhand_.

1.7 There are six Basic Theory Rules for PERSONAL SHORT-HAND. Once you have learned these well, you will have mastered an important part of the system.

1.8

> **RULE NO. 1. Never write a *silent* vowel. The English language has thousands of silent vowels that actually contribute *no* sound whatsoever. Try to avoid writing these. For example: The word *kite* would be written *kit*; the word *late*, *lat*, etc.**

1.9 Applying this principle, how would you write these words in PS:

size _siz_	vote _vot_	bite _bit_
note _not_	gate _gat_	goat _got_

1.10

> **RULE NO. 2. Even sounding vowels within a word should be omitted, unless they have the long sound of *a, i, o, u,* or *oo*. Normally the long sound of *e* is assigned *automatically* to *any preceding consonant*.**

1.11 Listen carefully for the long sounds of *a, i, o, u, oo,* and e, as illustrated in the words *bay, bite, note, fuse, move,* and *heat.*

1.12 Remember: Except in the case of a double *ee* combination or when the preceding consonant is representing some phonetic unit *other than its own basic sound* (such as *c* representing *ch*), *the sound of long e* is automatically assigned to any *preceding* consonant.

1.13 Note: Treat *half-long* vowels as you would *short* vowels and omit them.

1.14 Applying Rule No. 2, how would you write these words:

fate _fat_	site _sit_	coat _cot_	sit _st_
fuse _fus_	hot _ht_	neat _nt_	move _mov_

1.15

> RULE NO. 3. Always write a *sounding* vowel whenever it occurs at the very *beginning* of a word. True, as your skill and confidence increase, you will find some shortcuts that will enable you to avoid writing certain initial vowels; but the rule is still a very valid one; and you are never wrong (and always safer) when you write *beginning vowels*. Based on Rule No. 3, then, the word *acre* would be written *acr*; the word *abate*, *abat*; *estate*, *estat*.

1.16 Applying this principle, how would you write these words:

ate *a+*	ease *eS*	even *evn*
eat *e+*	east *eSt*	acute *acut*

1.17

> RULE NO. 4. If a word contains a *double* vowel, write only *one* of these. Therefore, in a word like *broom*, we keep one of the two *o's* and throw the other away. The word *book* would be written *bok* and the word *deep*, simply *dep*.

1.18 Applying this rule, how would you write these words:

food *fod*	moon *mon*	feet *fet*
vacuum *vcum*	reel *rel*	beet *bet*

1.19

> RULE NO. 5. Omit all *silent consonants* (just as we omit silent or non-long vowels); and if a word contains *double consonants*, write only one. There are thousands of silent consonants in the English language, which contribute nothing at all to the sound of a word. Do *not* write these. Also, remember to handle *double consonants* just as you would handle *double vowels* - keep one and discard one. For example: The words *right, planner,* and *ball* would be written, *rit, plnr,* and *bl.*

1.20 How should we write these words:

grapple *grpl*	office *ofc*	light *lit*
knight *nit*	hymn *hm*	little *litl*

1.21

> **RULE NO.6.A** *sounding vowel* at the end of a word should
> be *written,* except for the *short i* sound of the *letter y,*
> which we tend to pronounce like a *long e.* This *short i*
> sound of the *letter y* therefore should be assigned
> *automatically* to the preceding consonant. For example:
> The word *salary* should be written *slr,* with the *short i*
> sound of the *letter y* being carried by the *r.* All other *ter-
> minal* sounding vowels should be written, including the
> *long i* sound.

1.22 Applying this principle, how would you write these words:

academy acdm	*wary* wr	*starry* str
secretary scrtr	*area* ar	*mania* mana

1.23 Review. Keeping in mind the *long a* sound, write these words:

bake bak	*tame* tam	*grate* grat
irate irat	*graze* graz	*late* lat

1.24 Review. Keeping in mind the *long i* sound, write these words:

bide bid	*nice* nic	*side* sid
advice advic	*glide* glid	*apply* apli

1.25 Review. Keeping in mind the *long o* sound, write these words:

code cod	*alone* alon	*close* clos
elope elop	*froze* froz	*hose* hos

1.26 Review. Keeping in mind the *long u* sound, write these words:

huge hug	*accuse* acuz	*few* fu
view vu	*bugle* bugl	*cue* cu

1.27 Review. Keeping in mind the *long oo* sound, write these words:

moon mon	*move* muv	*group* grup
soup sup	*grew* gru	*fruit* frat

1.28 Review. Keeping in mind Rule No. 2, having to do with the
automatic assignment of the *long e* sound to any *preceding
consonant* (except in the case of a double *ee* combination),
write these words:

heat ht	*beat* bt	*treat* trt
neat nt	*feet* fet	*seat* st

1.29 Review. There are many words that contain vowel "combinations" which—regardless of how they *look*—provide *long
vowel sounds.* For example: The *ia* combination in the word
dial provides a *long i* sound, which we write; but the *short* (non-

long) *a* sound we eliminate. *Dial* is therefore written *dil.*

1.30 Keeping this principle in mind, write these words:

eaves *evs*   type *tip*   trial *tril*
heap *hp*   hue *hu*   sleigh *sla*

1.31 Review. Applying Rules 1, 2, and 3, write these words:

erase *eras*   eclipse *eclps*   paper *papr*
isolate *isolat*   elevate *elvat*   feign *fan*

1.32 Review. Applying Rule No. 4, write these words:

need *ned*   broom *brom*   book *bok*
boot *bot*   deer *der*   deep *dep*

1.33 Review. Applying Rule No. 5, (referring to silent and double consonants), write these words:

fight *fit*   isle *il*   kneel *nel*
add *ad*   right *rit*   supple *spl*

1.34 Review. Though relatively few words in the English language *end* with a *sounding vowel*, any *sounding vowel* at the end of a word should be *written*, except the *short i* sound of the letter y (which we tend to pronounce *long e*). This vowel sound may be carried by the preceding consonant, automatically. Therefore, as covered in Rule 6, the word *academy*, would be written *acdm*. Applying this same principle, write these words:

vary *vr*   honey *hn*   accrue *acru*
funny *fn*   baggy *bg*   glue *glu*
obey *oba*   debut *dabu*   canoe *cnu*

1.35 Now, let's try writing the following words in PERSONAL SHORTHAND. Use the six Basic Theory Rules as introduced in this lesson. Review these rules over and over again. Write these words:

flavor *flavr*   line *lin*   zest *zst*
allure *alr*   boat *bot*   ample *ampl*
wood *wod*   gnarl *nrl*   hue *hu*

1.36 Using your six Basic Theory Rules, write these words in PS: (you always are free to use a standard abbreviation with which you are thoroughly acquainted—*ave.* for *avenue*, etc.— provided you can read it back with ease.) Write these words:

bright *brit*   alter *altr*   temperature *tmp.*
better *btr*   paid *pd.*   honeymoon *hnmon*
view *vu*   weighed *wad*   boulevard *blvd.*

1.37 Using your six Basic Theory Rules, write the following words in PS: (Special Note: At all times, treat *half-long vowels* as you would *short vowels*.)

over *Ovr*   state *stat*   peak *pk*
binocular *bnclr*   cover *cvr*   hassle *hsl*
note *not*   scholastic *sclstc* moody *mod*

1.38 Using your six Basic Theory Rules, write these words in PS:

bake *bak*   litter *ltr*   additive *adtv*
add *ad*   peddle *pdl*   pony *pon*
took *tok*   capitol *cptl*   struggle *strgl*

1.39 Using your six Basic Theory Rules, write these words in PS:

nook *nok*   used *usd*   obey *ob*
tennis *tns*   sales *sls*   eagle *egl*
workday *wrkda*   easy *ez*   knife *nif*

1.40 Using your six Basic Theory Rules, write these words in PS:

value *vlu*   puzzle *pzl*   knobby *nb*
coat *cot*   eat *et*   loamy *lom*
physical *fscl*   gourmet *gorma*   oscillator *oslatr*

1.41 Using your six Basic Theory Rules, write these words in PS:

slave *slav*   list *lst*   suite *swt*
mate *mat*   sweet *swt*   retinue *rtnu*
balloon *blon*   rarely *rrl*   poorly *porl*

Personal Shorthand

CARDINAL SERIES

2.1 *Numbers* in PS are written as they are in *longhand*. There is nothing special about them and no special way in which they must be written (except that they should be written with care).

2.2 Because of the frequency with which they are written, *Days of the Week* are represented by their initial letters, with the exception of *Sunday* and *Tuesday,* which are expressed by *Sn* and *Tu. Monday, Wednesday, Thursday, Friday* and *Saturday* therefore are written M, W, T, F, and S. Of course, lower case letters may be used in place of capitals, if you prefer.

2.3 In PERSONAL SHORTHAND, *Months of the Year* also are represented by their initial letters, except for *January, Jn; March, Mr; July, Jy;* and *August, Ag.* Of course these, too, can be written with small letters only: *jn, mr, jy,* and *ag.* Again: All *other* months are expressed by initial letters.

2.4 BRIEF FORMS. Some words occur so often in the English language that there is no reason at all for writing them in full, even phonetically. In fact, there are some 100 words that comprise well over 50 per cent of our general vocabulary. The words that we shall study at this point are the most important of the high-frequency (or most-used) words in the English language. These are represented by *single letters.* For example:

2.5 The letter *a* represents the words *a, an, and, at, about.*
The letter *b* represents the words *be, by, buy, been, but.*
The letter *c* represents the words *can, come, copy, credit.*
The letter *d* represents the words *dear, do, due, did, date, would.*
The letter *e* represents the words *he, the.*

2.6 The letter *f* represents the words *for, from, if, find.*
The letter *g* represents the words *go, get, good, glad, give.*
The letter *h* represents the words *her, him, had, here.*
The letter *i* represents the words *I, it, is, time.*

LESSON 2   PS Cardinal Series-1 / 17

The letter *j* represents the words *just, gentlemen (gentleman)*.

2.7 Write the following sentences in PS:

(a) *An arrow and bow sell at about $5.*

(b) *Be certain and buy hardwood.*

(c) *But, by and by, sun and rain grow crops.*

(d) *Repeat the brief words, "been" and "but."*

(e) *Come and file a credit copy.*

(f) *Can people buy and color canvas?*

2.8 Write the following sentences in PS:

(a) *Dear Jim: A credit copy would be due today.*

(b) *Did Bill hear about a date pad?*

(c) *Do Bill and Pete recall Pat's job date?*

(d) *He and I can credit the new copy.*

(e) *I would mail the slip for supplies from the mine.*

(f) *If I can find the credit copy, be certain and buy lumber at about $22.*

2.9 Write the following sentences in PS:

(a) *He would give credit for good copy paper, if I can buy it and just go home and work.*

(b) *He would be glad if I could get home.*

(c) *He wrote her about the test the school had held here.*

(d) *I told him he would type a carbon copy.*

(e) *I heard it is the right time for play.*

(f) *Just come for the copy at 4 p.m. today.*

(g) *The gentlemen signed the credit copy at the place due.*

Personal Shorthand

CARDINAL SERIES

BRIEF FORMS

3.1 The letter *k* represents the words *kind, make, take.*
The letter *l* represents the words *all, also, will, well, letter.*
The letter *m* represents the words *am, me, my, made, man, and men.*
The letter *n* represents the words *when, not, in, no, know, information.*
The letter *o* represents the words *out, of, on, what.*

3.2 The letter *p* represents the words *possible, price, please, put.*
The letter *q* represents the words *enclose, require, quite.*
The letter *r* represents the words *are, or, our, return, order.*
The letter *s* represents the words *sincerely, she, so, see, wish.*
The letter *t* represents the words *that, thank, there, to, too.*

3.3 The letter *u* represents the words *you, up, under, us.*
The letter *v* represents the words *very, ever, every, have, receive.*
The letter *w* represents the words *with, which, we, were, how, now.*
The letter *x* represents the word *check!* (And *only* this one word.)
The letter *y* represents the words *why, your, they.*
The letter *z* represents the words *as, has, his, was.*

3.4 Write the following sentences in PS:

(a) *Make the gentlemen an extra copy, if the credit slip is due.*
(b) *Take food and help the kind gentlemen who make all copies here.*
(c) *I could take the letter well, but I could not make up the credit copies also.*
(d) *All the girls will like some food at about 10 p.m.*

(e) *I am positive 50 men can do more for me and my team.*

(f) *My best hope is to be made captain at the meet.*

(g) *He is the man who made my study hard.*

3.5   Write the following sentences in PS:

(a) *When will the information be mailed in for copy work?*

(b) *I do not know when the information will arrive nor do I know if the date is right.*

(c) *No one man could make a bad credit error on Tuesday.*

(d) *What is the reason for dark copies of new time cards.*

(e) *On what date did the gentlemen from the East find the letter?*

3.6   Write the following sentences in PS:

(a) *Would you please repeat the price listed in the latest catalogue?*

(b) *Is it possible the prices would be out of date?*

(c) *He will require of the firm an enclosed carbon of all letters.*

(d) *It is quite possible the letter is dated and is in the club office.*

(e) *Please return a carbon copy of our order in due course.*

(f) *Is it Jim's plan to return or are the builders on leave?*

3.7   Write the following sentences in PS:

(a) *I sincerely hope she plans a good, happy trip.*

(b) *I wish to apply for the free class, so the gentlemen can see I am serious about my job.*

(c) *I wish to thank all workers for this help in my office.*

(d) *It is too early for this type of credit score, and that is the belief there, too.*

(e) *That letter is of great value, if I had the time to study it.*

(f) *You would be delighted to serve under us in the capacity of team leader?*

(g) *It is up to that office to return the order to us for credit on the due date.*

3.8   Write the following sentences in PS:

(a) *It is very possible that we will receive the credit letter by next week.*

(b) *Did it ever occur to you that every letter would have to be retyped?*

(c) *With which loan firm are we now in debt.*

(d) *How did you know that we were to visit the office?*

(e) *Would you please mail the check to our local office, plus a carbon copy of the letter?*

(f) *Why did they drop the dinner plates at your home?*

(g) *Was it his plan to bill every office for its bit of the cost?*

(h) *Has he donated the new cabinet, as he advised us he would do?*

Personal Shorthand

CARDINAL SERIES

4.1 Remember: Most Brief Forms are represented by the *first* letter of the word. A number, however, are represented by the *last* letter of the word. For example, *would* is represented by *d; he* and *the,* by *e; if,* by *f; all, will,*and *well,* by *l;* and *am,* by *m.*

4.2 Some additional Brief Forms are represented by their *last* letters, rather than *first* letters: *in, information* and *when,* are represented by *n; our* and *or,* represented by *r; you,* by *u; how* and *now,* by *w;* and *why* and *they,* by *y.*

4.3 Although most Brief Forms are represented by the *first* letter of the word, with a few being indicated by the *last* letter. There are a number of Brief Forms that have been assigned for "mathematical" or "arithmetic" reasons; that is, reasons having to do with the "frequency" of words in the English language. For example, *time* is represented by *i, gentlemen,* by *j; take* and *make,* by *k; also,* by *l.*

4.4 Additional Brief Forms that have been assigned for "mathematical" reasons, and not according to first or last letters, are as follows: *n* for *know; o* for *what; q* for *enclose* and *require; r* for *are* and *order;* and *s* for *wish.*

4.5 A final group of Brief Forms assigned for "mathematical" reasons, and not based on first or last letters, includes: *v* for *ever, every, have,* and *receive; x* for *check;* and *z* for *was, his, as,* and *has.*

4.6

> The *past tense, gerund,* and *plural* forms are very easy to handle in PERSONAL SHORTHAND. For example, the word *thanked* simply is written *td,* the word *thanking, tg;* and the word *thanks,* ts. Merely add a *d,* a *g,* or an *s* whenever the derivation calls for it. For example, how would you write these words:
>
> | buying | copying | credited |
> | pleases | priced | enclosing |
> | checks | received | returning |

4.7   Keeping these and other Brief Forms in mind, write the following sentences in PS:

(a) *I am glad to give the information to him, if he can mail the check on the above date.*

(b) *When possible, it is hoped that Baker or Mason will give you credit or that they will enclose the letter, now that we need it.*

(c) *The gentlemen stressed that it also was time to take steps to make a new list.*

(d) *I do not know what they will wish to require or enclose with the order, nor are they specific about this matter.*

(e) *Has it ever occurred to you that every worker does not have to receive the same kind of check, assuming his pay was as high as it has to be at this time?*

(f) *Please accept our thanks for your order, and do let me say how very willing we are to help at any time with that task.*

4.8   Still concentrating on Brief Forms and the six Basic Theory Rules, write the following sentences in PS:

(a) *Is it right for the men to sell all of the fuel?*

(b) *The busy man and the widow did what they could to help with the work.*

(c) *My duty is to work with map and key when the letter is due.*

(d) *It is your duty to name big city firms and assign a firm name.*

(e) *The duty of the man and Al is to name the city and bus.*

(f) *The bus is to go to the city and to the depot for some signs.*

4.9   Now write the following sentences in PS:

(a) *It is Bill's wish to enamel and fix signs for the busy firms.*

(b) *The objective of the town is to pay duty to the six busy men.*

(c) *They wish to fix the signs and enamel every one for the big city.*

(d) *It is Pam's duty to list the pay when they do the work.*

(e) *She is to blame the crew of girls for the old work papers.*

(f) *He pays for the big maps and then signs every page for work.*

4.10 And for extra practice, these sentences:

(a) *The busy men did heavy work and paid for the eight cartoons.*

(b) *Happy but busy men will give silver dollars for the cars.*

(c) *The crude but busy man did his best work on the boat.*

(d) *Real vigor is the key to the busy men of the civic firms.*

(e) *Buz is to go to the city and fix the signs for the mayor.*

(f) *The title to the great field of grain was released by the man.*

Personal Shorthand

CARDINAL SERIES

5.1 Actually, PERSONAL SHORTHAND can be written, quite effectively, *without* applying the phonetic abbreviations to be introduced in this lesson. It is true, however, that the use of these abbreviating principles will facilitate the further *telescoping* or *condensing* of longhand and thus will enable you to write PS at a faster rate. Do *not* expect to learn all of these abbreviating principles at one time. Some will be mastered far sooner than others, primarily because of the frequency with which they are used.

5.2 While not really a phonetic abbreviation in PS, remember that the letter *a*, represents the *sound* of *long a*, regardless of the phonetic unit that represents this sound in the longhand word —for example, *a, ay, aye, eigh, nee, quet*, etc.

5.3 Using the letter *a* to represent the sound of long *a*, write these words:

braid brad	*obey* oba	*prey* pra
suede swad	*sleigh* sla	*steak* stak
array ara	*weigh* wa	*croquet* croka

5.4 In PS, the letter *b* represents its own *basic* sound, plus the sound of *ble*, and, of course, like all consonants, it can carry the sound of *long e* when this sound *follows* the consonant and is so assigned. With these phonetic principles in mind, write the following words:

beat bt	*best* bst	*humble* hmb
bait bat	*crumble* crmb	*believe* blv
beard brd	*beaten* btn	*bramble* brmb

5.5 When writing PERSONAL SHORTHAND, remember that the letter *c* can represent its basic sounds (usually an *s* or a *k* sound); and, in addition, the sounds of *ch, com, con*, and, of course, *c* plus *long e*.

5.6 Applying the above principles, write these words:

deceive *dcv*	card *crd*	reach *rc*
catch *cc*	chamber *cambr*	batch *bc*
chase *cas*	circus *crcs*	church *crc*

5.7 Again working with the phonetic principles introduced in paragraph 5.5, remember that the letter *c* represents its *basic* sounds (usually *s* or *k*), plus the sounds of *ch*, *com*, *con*, and *c* with *long e.*

5.8 Using these principles, write the following words:

comply *c pli*	consider *csdr*	ceiling *clg*
commute *c mut*	control *ctrol*	compendium *cpnd*
ceaseless *cs/s*	cannon *cnn*	touch *tc*

5.9 Although not really a phonetic *abbreviation* in PS, remember that the letter *d* represents its own basic sound, and, of course, the sound of *d* plus *long e.*

5.10 Keeping these principles in mind, write the following words in PS:

debate *dbat*	faded *fadd*	decelerate *dclra*
stated *statd*	deceive *dcv*	deadwood *ddwc*
degrade *dgrad*	deal *dl*	delegated *dlgat*

5.11 In PERSONAL SHORTHAND, the letter *e* usually represents only the sound of *long e* and, therefore, normally need not be written, because the sound of *long e* is assigned to (or carried by) any *preceding* consonant—whenever that consonant is representing its basic sound or sounds.

5.12 Generally, however, it is more prudent to write the letter *e* at the very beginning of a word (Basic Rule No. 3); and, of course, in the case of words with double *ee* combinations, one *e* is retained and the other is dropped. (Basic Rule No. 4).

5.13 For practice purposes, write these words:

eastern *estrn*	seat *st*	repair *rpr*
meet *met*	ease *es*	tame *tm*
beat *bt*	neat *nt*	beehive *beh*

5.14 The letter *f* represents its own basic sound, and, in addition, the sounds of *f*, plus *long e*, *ph*, *for*, *(fore)*, *ful* and *ify.*

5.15 Keeping these phonetic abbreviations in mind, write the following words:

fat *ft*	fever *fvr*	phone *fon*
formal *fml*	before *bf*	reform *rfm*
careful *Crf*	forceful *fcf*	fortify *ftf*

5.16 Reviewing the letter *f* again—remember that *f* can represent its own basic sound and, in addition, the sounds of *f* plus *long e, ph, for, (fore), ful* and *ify*.

5.17 Applying these phonetic abbreviations, write the following words in PS:

fearful *frf*	harmful *hrmf*	phonetic *fntc*
notify *notf*	magnify *mgnf*	forceable *fcb*
forest *fst*	physics *fscs*	formidable *fmdb*

5.18 The letter *g* represents its own basic sounds (primarily those used in the words *gate* and *genus*) and, in addition, the sounds of *g* plus *long e, ng, nge, ing,* and *dge.*

5.19 Applying these phonetic principles, write the following words:

guide *gid*	germ *grm*	geography
gene *gn*	bring *brg*	bridge *brgj*
danger *dagr*	budget *bgt*	willing *wlg*

5.20 Again—the letter *g* represents its own *basic* sounds (primarily those used in the words *gate* and *genus*) and, in addition, the sounds of *g* plus *long e, ng, nge, ing,* and *dge.*

5.21 Using the phonetic principles in paragraph 5.20, write these words in PERSONAL SHORTHAND:

long *lg*	ring *rg*	geologic
ridge *rg*	song *sg*	fudge *fg*
running *rng*	genial *gnl*	singe *sg*

Personal Shorthand

CARDINAL SERIES

6.1 The letter *h* represents its own basic sound, and, in addition, the sound of *h* plus *long e*. In short, *h* does not function as a true phonetic abbreviation and has relatively little work to do in either longhand or PERSONAL SHORTHAND.

6.2 Applying these principles, write the following words in PS:

hop *hp*	hair *hr*	heel *hel*
hide *hid*	heritage *hrtg*	horrible *hrb*
heal *hl*	hibernate *hibrnat*	humidify *humdf*

6.3 Keep in mind that while it is not a true phonetic abbreviation, the letter *i* represents the sound of *long i*, regardless of the phonetic unit that represents this sound in the longhand word —for example, *i, igh,* or *y.* No matter how it is spelled in longhand, if the sound is *long i*, write *i* in PERSONAL SHORT-HAND.

6.4 Now write these words in PS, applying the above principles:

light *lit*	comply *cpli*	dye *di*
ignore *ignr*	nigh *ni*	high *hi*
style *stil*	myopia *miopa*	right *rit*

6.5 In PS, the letter *j* represents its own basic sound and, in addition, the sound of *j* plus *long e*. Like the letter *h*, *j* is not a true "abbreviation" and has comparatively little to do, in either longhand or PERSONAL SHORTHAND.

6.6 Applying the information above, write these words:

jet *jt*	jam *jm*	jaywalk *jawk*
jail *jal*	jeep *jep*	jingle *jgl*
jargon *jrgn*	jungle *jgl*	journey *jrn*

6.7 The letter *k*, while it functions as a rather limited phonetic abbreviation, represents its own basic sound, and in addition, the sounds of *k* plus *long e*, the *ck* (k) component, and *ct*.

6.8 With these phonetic principles in mind, write the following words in PS:

kit *kt*   keystone *kston*   brick *brk*
fact *fk*   keep *kep*   retract *rtrk*
packing *pkg*   contact *ctk*   lacking *lkg*

6.9 In addition to representing its own basic sound, plus the sounds of *l* plus *long e* and *ly*, *l* also represents the phonetic abbreviations *lity* and *lty*.

6.10 With these PS principles in mind, write the following words:

late *lat*   ability *abl*   lull *ll*
pull *pl*   lease *ls*   realty *rl*
leach *lc*   lonely *lonl*   lately *latl*

6.11 Again—the letter *l* represents its own basic sound and, in addition, the sounds of *l* plus *long e* and *ly*, plus the phonetic abbreviations *lity* and *lty*.

6.12 With these principles in mind, write the following words in PERSONAL SHORTHAND:

quickly *qkl*   briefly *brfl*   finality *fnl*
faculty *fcl*   faulty *fl*   really *rl*
facility *fcl*   casualty *csl*   cruelty *crol*

6.13 When writing PERSONAL SHORTHAND, let the letter *m* represent its own basic sound and, in addition, of course the sound of *m* plus *long e*; also, the phonetic abbreviations *m*- (any short vowel) -*m*; *m*- (any short vowel) -*n*; *moun*; and *ment*.

6.14 With these principles in mind, write the following words in PS:

map *mp*   medium *mdm*   minimum *mm*
mimic *mc*   mineral *mrl*   moment *mon*
amount *amt*   manage *mg*   monument *mm*

6.15 Again reviewing the principles relating to the letter *m*: Let the letter *m* represent its own basic sound, plus the sound of *m* plus *long e*; and, in addition, the phonetic abbreviations *m*-(any short vowel) -*m*; *m*- (any short vowel) -*n*; *moun*; and *ment*.

6.16 Now write these words:

comment *cm*   mountain *mtn*   surmount *smmt*
mounting *mtg*   ferment *frm*   monetary *m+r*
cement *cm*   vehement *vm*   manifold *mfold*

6.17 In PS, the letter *n* represents its own basic sound and the sound of *n* plus *long e*; and it also represents the phonetic abbreviations *nc(e)*, *ns(e)*, *ness*, *nt*, and *nd*.

6.18 Now applying these principles, write the following words in PERSONAL SHORTHAND:

net *nt*	den *dn*	neat *nt*
residence *rsdn*	fence *fn*	happiness *hpn*
defense *dfn*	plant *pln*	land *l n*

6.19 Again reviewing PS principles relating to the letter *n*: Remember that the letter *n* represents its own basic sound and, in addition, the sound of *n* plus *long e*; also *nc(e), ns(e), ness, nt,* and *nd.*

6.20 Write the following words:

condensed *cdnd*	fairness *frn*	bent *bt*
trend *trn*	tenderness *tnrn*	kneeling *nelg*
evidence *erdn*	sent *sn*	hand *hn*

Personal Shorthand

CARDINAL SERIES

7.1 In PERSONAL SHORTHAND, the letter *o* (as you will recall) normally represents the sound of *long o*; however, it can also represent the sound of oo, as in the word *fruit*. (When *u* carries the oo sound in a word, feel free to write the *u* if it helps word recognition.) Although it is not a phonetic abbreviation, in the technical sense, it is still well to review such theory points, again and again.

7.2 Applying the above principles, write these words:

rote *rot*	wrote *rot*	crude *crod*
note *not*	rude *rod*	anecdote *ancdo*
float *flot*	devote *dvot*	cruel *crol*

7.3 Again—the letter *o* normally represents the sound of *long o*; however, it also can represent the sound of oo, as in the word *fruit*. (Remember that when you see the letter *o*, in PS, you know that it is representing the sound of *long o, oo,* or a *double vowel* combination.)

7.4 Now write these words in PERSONAL SHORTHAND:

crucible *crub*	loan *lon*	boot *bot*
boon *bon*	boat *bot*	quote *qot*
remote *rmot*	denote *dnot*	cruiser *crusr*

7.5 You will need to remember that the letter *p* represents its own basic sound and, in addition, the sound of *p* plus *long e*; and— as word beginnings only—the phonetic abbreviations *pr; p* -(any *short vowel*) - *r; pro* and *por* (either *long* or *short* o).

7.6 Using these PS principles, write the following words:

pot *pt*	pecan *pcn*	prove *pov*
prevalent *pvln*	party *pt*	porch *pc*
proper *ppr*	preface *pfc*	perilous *pls*

7.7 Again reviewing principles relating to the letter *p: P* represents its own basic sound and, in addition, the sound of *p* plus *long e*; and—as word beginnings only—the phonetic abbreviations *pr; p* - (any *short vowel*) - *r; pro* and *por* (either *long* or *short* o.)

LESSON 7   **PS Cardinal Series-1 / 31**

7.8　Applying these PS principles, write the following words:

pursue *psu*	proper *ppr*	preamble *pemb*
perhaps *phps*	preach *pec*	perishable *psb*
profuse *pfus*	private *pivt*	predict *pdk*

7.9　In the preceding paragraph, the words *preach* and *preamble* are written *pec* and *pemb*. In these words, the *long e* is written because the letter *p* cannot represent the *pr* word beginning and *also long e*. Again—the letter *p* can represent its own basic sound; it can represent *p* plus *long e*; and, *as word beginnings only,* the sounds of *pr, p* - (any *short vowel*) - *r; pro* and *por* (either *long* or *short o*).

7.10　Keeping these points in mind, write the following words in PERSONAL SHORTHAND:

practice *pctc*	predispose *pedspos*	purpose *pps*
primitive *pmtv*	prefix *pefx*	portray *ptra*
prince *pn*	preserve *psrv*	produce *pduc*

7.11　The letter *q* represents the phonetic abbreviation *qu*, which normally is pronounced with a *kw* sound; and, when appropriate to the longhand, it also represents the sound of *k*. Essentially the *q* in PERSONAL SHORTHAND performs the same function it does in longhand.

7.12　Applying the PS principles in paragraph 7.11, write these words:

quench *qnc*	queer *qer*	quote *qot*
quota *qota*	quality *ql*	clique *clq*
queasy *qes*	quickly *qkl*	qualm *qm*

7.13　In PS, the letter *r* represents its own basic sound and, in addition, the sound of *r* plus *long e,* and the phonetic abbreviations *rity,* and *ur(e).*

7.14　With these principles in mind, write the following words in PS:

reference *rfrn*	retail *rtal*	prosperity *pspr*
assure *asr*	red *rd*	rarity *rr*
secure *scr*	during *drg*	temerity *tmr*
measure *msr*	authority *atr*	demurring *dmr*

7.15　The letter *s* represents its own basic sound, the sound of *s* plus *long e,* and the phonetic abbreviations *sh; s* - (any *short vowel*) - *s; c**- (any *short vowel*) - *s;* and *all* of the *shun (chun)* word parts *(sion, tion, cian, shion, cien,* etc.). (* When *c* has an *s* sound.)

7.16 Now write the following words, applying the *s* principles: _t_ | _vs_

sum _sm_	*sequence* _sgn_	*television*
ship _sp_	*confess* _cfs_	*mission* _ms_
push _ps_	*rush* _rs_	*mention* _ms_
suspect _spk_	*perish* _ps_	*pauses* _ps_

7.17 Again reviewing *s* principles and related phonetic abbreviations: The letter *s* represents its own basic sound, the sound of *s* and *long e*; and the phonetic abbreviations *sh; s* - (any short vowel) - *s; c** - (any short vowel) -*s*; and *all* of the *shun (chun)* word parts *(sion, tion, cian, shion, cien, etc.).* (*When *c* has an *s* sound.)

7.18 Applying the *s* principles, write these words:

chances _ans_	*sustain* _stan_	*motion* _mos_
cases _cas_	*careless* _crls_	*punishment* _pnsm_
season _ssn_	*semblance* _smbln_	*efficient* _efst_
occasion _ocas_	*optician* _opts_	*fashion* _fs_

7.19 In PS, the letter *t* represents its own basic sound, the sound of *t* plus *long e*, and, in addition, the important phonetic abbreviation, *th.*

7.20 Based on these principles, write the following words in PERSONAL SHORTHAND:

tag _tg_	*teach* _tc_	*their* _tr_
tease _ts_	*teeth* _tet_	*thought* _tt_
salty _sl_	*taught* _tt_	*thing* _tg_

7.21 Again—the letter *t* represents its own basic sound, the sound of *t* plus *long e*; and the phonetic abbreviation, *th.*

7.22 Applying the above principles, write these words:

through _tro_	*path* _pt_	*theme* _tem_
thesis _tes_	*think* _tnk_	*throw* _tro_
whether _wtr_	*health* _hlt_	*tooth* _tot_

7.23 In the previous paragraph, you may have questioned *why* the words *theme* and *thesis* are written *tem* and *tes.* The reason, of course, has to do with the initial *th* sound. For when the *preceding consonant* is representing some sound *other* than its own *basic* sound (in other words, when it is busy doing something else), it cannot also carry the *long e* sound.

7.24 Keeping this in mind, write these words: *telogn*

thief *tef*	*theory* *ter*	*theologian* *telgc*
theorize *te riz*	*theater* *tetr*	*theological*
theomorphic *temrfc*	*theorem* *term*	*theoretical* *terte*

7.25 In PS, the letter *u* represents the *long u* sound and the word part (as well as brief form) *under*, as in the word *underwater*. Actually, the letter *u* has relatively little to do in either longhand or PERSONAL SHORTHAND.

7.26 With the foregoing principles in mind, write the following words:

museum *musm*	*duplicate* *duplcat*	*virtue* *vrtu*
duress *durs*	*underwrite* *urit*	*view* *vu*
mutilate *mutlat*	*underneath* *unt*	*understanding* *ustng*

Personal Shorthand

CARDINAL SERIES

8.1 In PERSONAL SHORTHAND, the letter *v* represents its own basic sound and, in addition, the sound of *v* plus *long e* —and nothing more. No phonetic abbreviations have been assigned to it. Like the letter *u, v* has relatively little to do, in either longhand or PERSONAL SHORTHAND.

8.2 With the above points in mind, write the following words in PS:

vending *vng*	victory *vctr*	vehicle *vcl*
venus *vns*	vibrate *vibrat*	venial *vnl*
vehement *vm*	veil *val*	Venus *vns*

8.3 The letter *w* represents its own basic sound, the sound of *w* plus *long e*, and the phonetic abbreviations *wh* (as in *where*), *ou* (as in cloud), *ow* (as in cow), and *aw* (as in raw).

8.4 Using these principles, how should the following words be written in PS:

wed *wd*	whether *wtr*	foundry *fwnr*
crowded *crwdd*	lawful *lwf*	weave *wv*
doubt *dwt*	loud *lwd*	shower *swr*

8.5 Let's review the *w* principles again: The letter *w* represents its own basic sound, the sound of *w* plus *long e*, and the phonetic abbreviations *wh* (as in where), *ou* (as in cloud), *ow* (as in cow), and *aw* (as in raw).

8.6 Now write the following words in PS, using the above principles:

weed *wed*	white *wit*	weary *wr*
browse *brws*	lounge *lwg*	gnawing *nwg*
weakling *wklg*	scout *scwt*	shout *swt*

8.7 The letter *x* simply represents its own basic sound plus the sound of *x(z)* and *long e*. No phonetic abbreviations have been assigned to this letter.

8.8   Based on this one principle, write the following words:

flex *f·lx*   flexible *f lxb*   next *nxt*
fix *fx*   relax *r lx*   complex *cplx*
taxable *txb*   annexed *anxd*   perplex *pplx*

8.9   In PS, the letter *y* represents its own basic sound, the sound of *y* plus *long e*, and the phonetic abbreviations *oi* and *oy* (as in *boil* and *toy*).

8.10 Based on the foregoing principles, write these words:

yes *xs*   yeast *yst*   loyal *lyl*
void *vyd*   year *yr*   toil *tyl*
voice *vyc*   noise *nys*   annoy *any*

8.11 Although no phonetic abbreviations have been assigned to it, the letter *z* represents its own basic sound, the sound of *z* plus *long e*, and, on occasion, it carries a kind of *zh* sound, as in the word *azure*.

8.12 With the above points in mind, write these words in PS:

zero *zro*   zephyr *zfr*   zone *zon*
barrage *brg*   zebra *zbra*   zealotry *zltr*
zirconium *zrconm*   zymology *zimlg*   zymolysis *zim ls*

8.13 Now, based on the brief forms and shorthand principles that we have reviewed together, write the following sentence in PERSONAL SHORTHAND:

Some people have the notion that we amaze our readers with big words and long sentences.

8.14 Write the following sentence in PS:

We think the more we say and the more pompously we say it, the better our letters will be.

8.15 Write the PS for this sentence:

Good, plain letters are the kind that readers really like to receive.

8.16 Write the following sentence in PS:

If your letters are complex and wordy, you can make them simple and short.

8.17 Applying the PERSONAL SHORTHAND knowledge that you have aquired in the first eight lessons, see how many of these supplementary practice sentences you can write in the time available to you:

(a) *Their duty is to fix their element, for it is to work right.*

(b) *Buz is to work for the big civic firm and work for the town.*

(c) *Pepe did us a turn when he paid for their title to the land.*

(d) *The key to a profit element for the firm is the eight signs.*

(e) *It is then the wish of the auditor and the man to rush work.*

(f) *The problem of the city and the town is to do their duty.*

(g) *It is their wish to rush to the city and spend their profit.*

(h) *The girl with auburn hair did the work for the six busy men.*

(i) *He is to spend his profit and work for the title to the land.*

(j) *Al is to work for the auditor and fix the usual title forms.*

(k) *Eighty men did their quantity of forms and did them right.*

(l) *The problems of the proficient auditor tend to rush civic meetings.*

(m) *The usual number of committees spent much time with the problems.*

(n) *The panel members and the proficient auditor wish to amend the form.*

(o) *The city is to rush work when the quantity of problems pays.*

(p) *Proficient committee members and an auditor spent much time with the title.*

(q) *Nancy, a proficient girl with auburn hair, is a city chairman.*

(r) *Both the man and the department do social work with proficiency.*

(s) *Their proficient men did considerable work and paid for the eight designs.*

(t) *Proficient and busy men spent much time on the ornament.*

(u) *The proficient and busy lawyer did much work on the ornament.*

(v) *Visible vigor is the key for busy men in the civic sections.*

(w) *Buz is to go to the town and fix the signs for the chairman.*

(x) *Transfer of title to the land is directed by the manager.*

(y) *The social chairman disowns their right to amend the titles.*

(z) *It is their right to fight the department and work for a penalty.*

Personal Shorthand

CARDINAL SERIES

9.1 All word *beginnings* and word *endings* can be written accor- ding to the theory principles already introduced. However, there are a few, high-frequency word *beginnings* that may be *abbreviated* somewhat, but only if it seems natural and conve- nient for you to do so. Certainly, you never are wrong when you write word beginnings according to the abbreviating principles introduced in the preceding lessons.

9.2 The word beginning *em* may be written *m*, except before *vowels.* Using this principle, write:

emblem mblm	*employ* mply	*emotion* emos
embrace mbrac	*emergency* emrgncy	*emulsify* emls
emplacement mplacm	*emolument* emlo	*embarrass* mbrs

9.3 The word beginning *im* may be written *m*, except before another *m*. Applying this short cut, write the following words in PERSONAL SHORTHAND:

imagine mgn	*imbibe* mbib	*impulsive* mplsv
immature imtr	*immediate* imdt	*immoral* imrl
immortal imrtl	*immediately* imdtl	*immovability* imov

9.4 The word beginning *um* may be written simply *m, at any time.* Applying this short cut, write these words:

umber mbr	*umbrella* mbrla	*umpire* mpir
umbrage mbrg	*umbriferous* mbrfrs	*umlaut* mlw
umbilical mblcl	*umbral* mbrl	*umpirage* mpir

9.5 The word beginning *in* may be represented by *n*, except before another *n*. Applying this abbreviating principle, write these words:

inside nsid	*incorrect* ncrk	*inner* inr
innate inat	*innovation* invas	*innumerable* inum
inapplicable nplcb	*incoherence* ncohrn	*innocence* incn

9.6 The word beginning *un* may be represented by *n*, except before another *n*. Applying this abbreviating principle, write these words in PS:

unable nab   *uncertain* ncrtn   *unnoticed* unotcd
unnecessary unsr   *unnamed* unamd   *unaccom-* nemdatg
                                                  modating
unnegotiable ungosb *unnavigable* unvgb   *uncomplimen-* ncplmr
                                                  tary

9.7 The word beginning *en* may be written simply *n*, at any time.
     Applying this short cut, write these words:

enjoy njy   *enable* nab   *enlarge* nlrg
encircle ncrcl   *engross* ngros   *enactment* nkm
encompass ncps   *endorsement* ndrsm   *encroach* ncroc

9.8 The word beginning *ex* may be represented by the letter *x*, at
     any time because the *e*, of course, is *silent.* Write these words
     in PS:

extra xtra   *exciting* xcitg   *exist* xst
exceed xced   *examine* xm   *excommunicate* xcmuncat
execution xcus   *expansible* xpnsb   *expandability* xpnbl

9.9 The common word beginnings *intra, inter,* and even *intro* (in-
     cluding *long o*) may be abbreviated *ntr.* Using this abbrevia-
     tion, write these words:

ntrgat *interrogate* ntr   *introduce* ntrduc   *intramural* ntrmurl
ntrvn *intervene*   *interrupt* ntrpt   *interference* NTRfrN
ntrnsgn *intransigent*   *introversion* ntrvrs *in-* ntrdpnr
                                                    terdependence

9.10 The word beginning *post* contains a *long o* sound; however,
     pst provides a very handy and workable abbreviation. Applying
     this short cut, write these words in PERSONAL SHORTHAND:

pstgrdt *postgraduate*   *postmark* pstmrk   *postmaster* pstmstr
pstscrpt *postscript* pst   *postpone* pstpon   *postoperative* pstprtv
pstd   *postdate*   *posthaste* psthast   *postimpres-* pstmprssm
                                                    sionism

9.11 Though the word beginnings *super* and *supr* frequently include
     half-long or *long u* sounds, it is both convenient and practical
     to represent these beginnings with *spr.* Based on this princi-
     ple, write these words in PERSONAL SHORTHAND

sprmc *supremacy*   *superlative* sprltv   *supersede* sprsd
sprrbtl *supraorbital*   *superstition* sprsts *supraliminal* sprlml
sprhum *superhuman*   *supersonic* sprsnc   *supervision* sprvs

9.12 Now write the following paragraphs in PS:

9.13 *Few young people realize just how important it is to work up to capacity. Even more vexing than this frequent problem is the lack of interest. You, after all, control your knowledge.*

9.14 *In pushing ahead for faster and better typewriting, are your thoughts flexible in line with differing word sequences? In realizing how complex this job of typing can become, you are more in a position to vary speed and rhythm to fit differing letter patterns. Make this your goal as you continue study. This may entail a major effort on your part, but the results will make it worthwhile.*

9.15 *Little did we dream of the excitement that lay ahead as we took off from a lazy ocean inlet near a Pacific Island. Although the pilot had received warnings of heavy winds in and around our destination, he decided not to postpone our take off. Many of us in the plane were superstitious and worried unnecessarily about taking off into an angry Pacific storm. We were not sure whether we might have to make an emergency landing. Quietly, however, a very skillful pilot put our worries at ease and landed home where we found the weather also quite stormy. It looked like we would be needing overcoats and umbrellas for some time.*

10.1 It is important to remember that *all* word *beginnings* can be written phonetically. The short cuts, to which you were introduced, are recommended—not required. If they seem natural, convenient, and easy for you to use—then use them. But it is never wrong to write word *beginnings* phonetically, without use of the short cuts. However, their use will increase your writing speed.

10.2 Now, let's write some special words in PERSONAL SHORTHAND. Remember—*primarily* we are interested in how a word sounds—and only secondarily in how it *looks!* Don't be mislead by the "spelling" of a word. Your objective is to write the word—by sound—as fast as you can. (You may have to refer to a dictionary from time to time.)

10.3 Keeping these thoughts in mind, write these words in P.S:

braid	*brad*	obey	*oba*	play	*pla*
suede	*swad*	sleigh	*sla*	treat	*trt*

10.4
steak	*stak*	conceit	*cct*	inveigh	*nva*
grieve	*grv*	people	*ppl*	negligee	*nglga*

10.5
tea	*te*	referee	*rfre*	risque	*rska*
quay	*ke*	key	*ke*	seismic	*sismc*

10.6
tie	*ti*	reply	*rpli*	proselyte	*pslit*
dye	*di*	high	*hi*	sleight	*slit*

10.7
boat	*bot*	flow	*flo*	chauffeur	*cofr*
plateau	*plto*	shoulder	*soldr*	cue	*cu*

10.8
ewe	*eu*	view	*vu*	amateur	*amtr*
adieu	*adu*	duet	*dut*	beauty	*but*

10.9
island	*iln*	knock	*nk*	feint	*fan*
often	*ofn*	night	*nit*	dilettante	*dltn*

10.10
calm	*cm*	wrong	*rg*	thumb	*tm*
listen	*lsn*	who	*ho*	hymn	*hm*

10.11 guest *get*   abridge *abrg*   succumb *scm*
       sweater *swtr*   honor *onr*   weighed *wad*

10.12 psychology *siclg*   talk *tk*   knickknack *nknk*
       though *to*   tough *tf*   thought *tt*

10.13 thorough *tro*   through *tro*   once *wn*
       bough *bw*   cough *cf*   champagne *cmpar*

10.14 drought *drwt*   hiccough *hcp*   harangue *hrg*
       switch *swc*   laughable *lfb*   bouquet *boka*

10.15 The following sentences provide good review of both *theory* and *brief forms.* See how quickly you can write them.

(a) The new umpire was a little nervous about his first game.

(b) The umpire quickly picked up the umbrella and threw it under the seat.

(c) My recent experience includes executive jobs with aerospace companies.

(d) It is true that most of us should talk less and listen more.

(e) The man is rich who knows how to make his mind work for him.

(f) Please fill in the enclosed forms and return them as soon as possible.

(g) Please place a check beside the items that are of interest to you.

(h) When you think you are perfect, you may be using a poor grading scale.

(i) The personnel manager interviews the few candidates who apply daily.

(j) The best job insurance you can get is work well done.

(k) The hikers emerged from the woods looking rather weary.

(l) The employer was upset about the rate of absenteeism in his company.

(m) I hope to get a job in his firm by the end of the day.

(n) Set for yourself some kind of a goal as you begin every new day.

(o) A little extra effort here and there will pay off.

(p) Aim to do each job with a little more zeal.

(q) Experts tell us that the right surroundings will help greatly in concentrating.

(r)   There are no two whose experience is alike in every respect.

(s)   Should the man lend a hand to those who work hard?

(t)   Why is it important that both men read the entire form carefully?

(u)   The rate charge exceeded what I had expected to pay.

(v)   The new executive is considered an expert in his field.

(w)   Be sure to enclose all the information needed to complete the report.

(x)   It is right to be cautious, but it is foolish to be fearful.

(y)   All of us have the wish to excel in our work.

(z)   Much of what was written in ancient times has meaning even now.

Personal Shorthand

CARDINAL SERIES

11.1 For the purpose of review, remember that *consonants* (letters *other* than *a, e, i, o,* and *u*) may contribute, in addition to their own basic sounds, the sound of long e, making it unnecessary, in most cases, to write the *long e* (Example: *cs* for *cease* and *rpl* for *repeal*). However, the e must be written when the *long e* sound is derived from a double *ee* combination or if the preceding consonant represents a *phonetic abbreviation*—in other words, some sound other than its own *basic* sound or sounds.

11.2 Keeping the above principles in mind, write the following words in PS:

cheat	shield	wheat
theater	phoenix	chief

11.3 Now let's write some sentences in PERSONAL SHORTHAND.

(a) *Do not make a habit of repeating what is said in a letter you answer.*

(b) *Know your subject so well you can discuss it naturally* and confidently.*

(c) *Use short words, short sentences, and short paragraphs.*

(d) *Do not qualify your statements with irrelevant words.*

11.4 *Remember to let the letter *l* represent *any* word ending terminating with an *ly*: (example, ily, ally, etc.)

11.5 See how many of the following sentences you can write in PS—and how long it takes you.

(a) *The city is visible from the high tower at the south end of this lake.*

(b) *The world is full of good intentions that are willing to be applied.*

(c) *Many people find it easier to be critical than to be helpful.*

(d) *The chairman said it was his duty to handle the problem immediately.*

(e) *Please include these two statements in the contract as you write it.*

(f) *Do not be afraid to tackle new and difficult problems.*

(g) *He traded the garage in the city for a house on the crest of the hill.*

(h) *A few members of the team signed the statement when they were in town.*

(i) *They can handle the order more quickly with the use of this system.*

(j) *Nobody can get very far until he has truly learned to make time count.*

(k) *She should sign the form at once and return it to us.*

(l) *No one who receives a business letter expects it to read like a novel, but he does want it to be clear and to the point.*

(m) *All the figures must be posted by tomorrow morning.*

(n) *Many firms require using these four large signs even though the price is quite high.*

(o) *Attempt to achieve a thorough understanding before reaching decisions.*

(p) *Men should be at work today trying to solve the problems of the world.*

(q) *The firm may make some profit if the chairman can handle its problems.*

(r) *You took extra effort to pass the long, major quiz covering your vocabulary textbook.*

(s) *We will not suggest shipping small baggage by express for three weeks.*

(t) *The puzzled football coach called a committee meeting on the matter.*

(u) *Facts do not cease to exist simply because they are ignored.*

(v) *The first step in eliminating your bad habits is to realize that you are not perfect.*

(w) *Thank you for sending us the good comments that you have heard about our new selling plan.*

(x) *The chairman repeatedly emphasized his point.*

(y) *The entire day will be spent practicing for the big game tomorrow.*

(z) *The new employee was able to work with very little supervision.*

Personal Shorthand

12.1 For purposes of practice and review, write the following sentences in PERSONAL SHORTHAND (see how long each group takes you):

(a) *The men are skeptical about the correctness of the formation.*

(b) *It is the duty of the girls to handle the quantity of forms.*

(c) *The committe meeting scheduled for tomorrow has been postponed until Friday.*

(d) *The city authority will handle the amendment.*

(e) *A formal audit may be made of the books of the civic group.*

12.2 (f) *The authority with which you speak depends on what you know.*

(g) *We think the sentences provide excellent alertness training.*

(h) *If you want to succeed, always keep fun and work in the right perspective.*

(i) *The man who knows he is right will usually speak with quiet authority.*

(j) *Some men will learn from experience, but others never recover from it.*

12.3 (k) *Please send me an application form for a charge account with your store.*

(l) *People must remember that having fun is of secondary importance when they have work obligations.*

(m) *The new student did exceptionally well in the school band.*

(n) *There are many problems that need to be thought through to a solution.*

(o) *We try to treat top executives as we always treat our other customers.*

12.4 (p) *The chairman claims that a majority of the members like the amendment.*

(q) *Five or six good ski jumpers whizzed quickly by with superb form.*

(r) *The letter was postmarked three days ago.*

(s) *It is a part of the work of a proficient typist to proofread the work.*

(t) *To be proficient in office work, you must find and correct all errors.*

12.5 (u) *We found that the elements of the problem are difficult to determine.*

(v) *The inventory includes a very large quantity of books.*

(w) *He implied that many of the union men were employed at a minimum rate.*

(x) *Thank you for the booklet enclosed with your check.*

(y) *His extraordinary sales record entitled him to an expense-paid vacation.*

(z) *I would come to the meeting except it is on the same date as our club banquet.*

12.6 Compare your time on these two final groups with the time it took you to write groups 12.1 through 12.5 (Don't hesitate to review theory principles or brief forms whenever necessary):

12.7 (a) *You should go and file a claim immediately for the goods that you did not receive.*

(b) *Just put the note on the table so she can find it easily.*

(c) *I wish they were not out of the kind of fabric I like.*

(d) *The printing bill is also due this Friday.*

(e) *How can we ever thank him sincerely?*

12.8 (f) *I will be glad to take the book to the elderly gentleman.*

(g) *A copy of your credit will be sent today.*

(h) *I am going to buy my dear friend a new watch.*

(i) *Give her a copy of the newsletter, too.*

(j) *Did you anticipate receiving the credit memorandum enclosed with the purchase order?*

13.1 The more you practice *writing* PS, the *faster* you will write PS. Now see how quickly you can convert the following sentences into PERSONAL SHORTHAND:

(a) *Information that can aid the reader is offered freely, even though he/she does not request it.*

(b) *The Administrator spoke to me this morning about your proposal to reduce the clerical cost.*

(c) *Our employees have no reason to be alarmed by the current reduction in force requested by the State.*

(d) *Occasionally we had trouble getting* train reservations, but usually we reached the office in time.*

(e) *When we met, the division chief decided that Baker should act on the case at once.*

13.2

> ***Keep in mind that it never is incorrect to write a word *phonetically*, even though there may be a somewhat shorter way of writing it. For example, the word *getting* could be written *gg*, if, for the sake of speed, we took advantage of the fact that *g* is the Brief Form for *get* and that by adding another *g* the word could be written simply *gg*. Even so, this calls for a greater degree of transcribing skill, and you may wish to write *gtg*.**

13.3 See how many minutes it takes you to write the next two paragraphs in PS:

13.4 *If you keep the staff posted on changes in our sales policy, they will be able to do a much better job of working as one. Only by working as one, will they be able to jump our sales.*

13.5 *He was told to turn a copy of his books over to the firm for an audit. This firm will check on all items that are not up to date. We hope that the audit will assure you that we are trying to keep a good set of books. If this is not what you want, please call me at my home or at my office in the city.*

13.6 Using either lower case (small) or capital letters, here are the most convenient ways to handle letter "salutations" in PERSONAL SHORTHAND (Because "salutations" are in a position to be easily recognized, it is suggested that the letters be joined):

Gentlemen - *j*   Dear Mrs. - *dmrs dmz*

Dear Miss - *dms*   Dear Sir - *ds (dsr)*

Dear Ms. - *dms. (dmz)*   Dear Mr.- *dm (dmr)*

13.7 Again, using either lower case (small) or capital letters, here are the most convenient ways to handle "complimentary closings" in PS (Because "complimentary closings," also, are easy to identify and there is little chance of confusion, it is suggested that the letters be joined):

Cordially - *c*   Very sincerely yours - *vsy*

Cordially yours - *cy*   Very truly yours - *vty*

Respectfully - *r*   Yours sincerely - *ys*

Respectfully yours - *ry*   Yours truly - *yt*

Sincerely - *s*   Yours very sincerely - *yvs*

Sincerely yours - *sy*   Yours very truly - *yvt*

13.8 See how quickly and easily you can write the following letter in PERSONAL SHORTHAND:

Dear Mrs. Martin:
Our firm should be very willing to pay the stores all of the money that is due on the loan. If we fail to pay notes when they are due, we are going to lose a good deal of good will. Since good will is hard to gain and harder to keep, we cannot afford to lose it by not paying our bills as they are due. We must change this policy in the near future. Please send this memo to every person involved in the local office. Sincerely yours,

13.9 See how many minutes it takes you to write the following letter in PS:

Dear Mr. Canfield:

Ms. James was concerned with the many research errors that were made by the company scientists. The errors were not made by the beginners; they were made by her top scientists. In her attempts to eliminate these very costly errors, she arranged a monetary incentive plan. The plan was to reward all those showing a high technical skill. As a result, intense effort was soon being shown by all the company scientists involved. Cordially yours,

Personal Shorthand

14.1 Write the following paragraphs in PS; don't hesitate to review theory principles and/or brief forms, at any time:

14.2 *Most of our daily arrivals are written first for the Morning Star. Because you have an interest in ocean shipments, your first copy can be ready for your home reading pleasure soon.*

14.3 *Should your boy come out some morning and leave the copy, we could have more money ready at once. After writing up stock quotations without a supply of copies of the Star, your note came at just the right moment. We shall be happy to request more copies from month to month, each request coming Monday.*

14.4 *What reason could have prompted Jack to leave a large supply company? You will recall that he first had a position fully as valuable in working with charge accounts. When one takes long, hard months to prepare for a career, it would indicate at first some stability in a young scholar. Despite leaving the supply company, however, our house shall be glad to back him through writing if requested. Please tell Jack to call.*

14.5 *Living prices were affected by the immense oil deposits that were found in off-shore locations in California. These high prices will surely offer problems in California oil centers.*

14.6 *Sam had to make quite a few erasures in his reversing entry. He thought that the corrections should bring all the columns into balance. However, upon rechecking his totals, he found there was still an error in the entries. In desperation, he called upon several members of his department for some help.*

14.7 *In a business letter, a buffer can be the difference between success and failure. The buffer appears with the reader. You will often see buffers used in good collection letters. Business letter writers must accept the buffer opening as a good will builder. Try using the buffer in your next bad-news letter. You will probably find it just as necessary as good grammar.*

14.8 The following letter is comprised of exactly 60 shorthand words. See how quickly you can write it in PS:

Dear Miss McDonald: We are writing to remind you that we are holding a summer dress for you on which a $5 deposit was paid. Please let us know if you still want this dress.

If we do not hear from you within the next week, we shall assume that you no longer want the dress and will place it back in stock at that time. Very truly yours,
(60 words) (s.i. 1.21)

14.9 Here is another 60-word letter. Time yourself as you write this one in PERSONAL SHORTHAND:

Dear Miss Smith: Thank you so much for sending us the good comments you have heard about our new sales plan.

We should like to send you complete details of this plan; but because it has not been in effect long enough for us to test it completely, we cannot do so. When we are certain it will work, we shall be glad to explain it to you. Sincerely,
(60 words) (s.i.1.22)

Personal Shorthand

15.1　Now let's do some reviewing of PS theory, phonetic abbreviations, brief forms, and word beginning short cuts. The more we know, the more "automatic" these principles will become—and that is what builds shorthand speed.

15.2　In learning PS (PERSONAL SHORTHAND), there are no special "symbols" to master, since PS uses nothing but the 26 letters of the longhand alphabet; nor is there any prescribed way that individual letters must be written; no costly "unlearning" of established habit patterns.

15.3　Remember that PS—unlike other so-called ABC, alphabetic, or abbreviated longhand, shorthand, or notetaking systems—uses *only* the 26 letters of the longhand alphabet and does not require that letters of the alphabet be written in some *specific* or *unnatural* manner. In short, write all letters as it is *natural* for you to write them, although you are urged to write as neatly as possible, simply for the sake of readability.

15.4　In PERSONAL SHORTHAND (PS) *capital* letters may be handled in one of two ways: They may be written in the normal manner; or capitalizing may be ignored entirely, since most PS writers have no trouble remembering (when they transcribe) that the initial letter in each sentence should be capitalized and that proper nouns (names of people, cities, organizations, etc.) should be capitalized.

15.5　PS can be *typed* just as easily as it is written with pen or pencil. When typing PERSONAL SHORTHAND, letters can be capitalized in the normal way or (as in longhand) simply ignored. It should be emphasized that PS can be typed without *any* changes or modifications whatsoever. This is possible because—again—PERSONAL SHORTHAND uses nothing but the 26 letters of the alphabet—no strange symbols, dashes, dots, curves, etc.

15.6   In PERSONAL SHORTHAND theory, emphasis is on simplicity, above all else. For this reason, even *punctuation marks* are used exactly as they are in longhand. *Paragraphing* may be indicated by a single diagonal line or, if you prefer, you may indent as you do in longhand.

15.7   *Brief Form Letter No. 1.* This letter is made up entirely of brief forms or brief form derivatives (e.g. *qd* for *enclosed*). While letters or articles of this type could not happen *naturally* (most letters and articles will average 48-50 percent brief forms), they still provide excellent practice in the quick recall of brief forms.

15.8   See how rapidly you can write this letter:

Gentlemen: Thank you for the information enclosed with your check. I did not know that you would buy the copy at[1] our price. We are pleased with your order and will see that you receive a credit. Do you wish to buy on time just now; [2]or, if possible, would you require us to be there on that very date? Sincerely yours,

15.9   Write this 60-word letter in PS:

Dear Mary: I am planning on going to the coast for a week's vacation the first of August. Would it be possible for you to go with me? I would like to explore some of the interesting places I hear are on the coast. Have you ever been to Sea Lion Caves?

Let me know by the end of the week if you can come. Yours truly,
(60 words) (s.i. 1.24)

15.10   Now see how long it takes you to write this 60-word article:

The first day on a new job, be yourself. Don't try to be someone you're not. Don't try to impress people with how much you know or how popular you are. If you really are a great person, your fellow workers will find this out in time. If you let people get to know you in a natural, gradual way, they will probably like you much more.
(60 words) (s.i. 1.25)

15.11   Let's see how quickly you can read (transcribe) this 120-word PS article:

z a mplye n e wrld o wrk, u sd tri t d y
jb z l z u c. u sd alwas (lwas) wrk hrd

a d o u r told. i i mprtn t g z mc
acplsd z p. / y mplyr l aprsat i f u c s
tgs t ned t b dn a c d tm wo bg told.
sn y mplyr i pag u, u o h a g da's wrk,
a u sd alwas (lwas) dlvr. / bsids wrkg
hrd, u l ned t g alg w otrs. smis ts
aspk i mr (mor) mprtn tn hrd wrk a c k e
dfrn btwen losg r kepg a jb. ts abl t g
alg w otrs c k r brak u o e jb.

(120 words) (s.i. 1.32)

Personal Shorthand

16.1 Continuing with our "review" of PS principles, remember that there are six Basic Theory Rules for PERSONAL SHORTHAND; and that once you have learned these well, you will have mastered an important part of the system.

16.2

> **RULE NO. 1 Never write a *silent* vowel. The English language has thousands of silent vowels that actually contribute *no* sound whatsoever. Avoid writing these. For example: The word *kite* would be written *kit;* the word *late, lat,* etc.**

16.3

> **RULE NO. 2. Even *sounding* vowels *within* a word should be omitted, unless they have the *long* sound of *a, e, i, o, u* or *oo*. Normally, the long sound of *e* is assigned *automatically* to *any preceding consonant.***

16.4 Remember — except in the case of a double *ee* combination or when the consonant is representing some phonetic unit *other than its own basic sound* (such as *c* representing *ch*), the sound of long *e* is automatically assigned to any *preceding* consonant.

Note: Treat *half-long* vowels as you would *short* vowels and omit them.

16.5

> **RULE NO. 3. Always write a *sounding* vowel whenever it occurs at the very *beginning* of a word. True, as your skill and confidence increase, there are some short-cuts that will enable you to avoid writing certain initial vowels, but the rule is still a very valid one; and you are never wrong (and always safer) when you write *beginning vowels*. Based on Rule No. 3, then, the word *acre* would be written *acr;* the word *abate, abat; estate, estat.***

16.6

> **RULE NO. 4.** If a word contains a *double* vowel, write only *one* of these. Therefore, in a word like *broom,* we keep one of the two *o's* and discard the other. The word *book* would be written *bok* and the word *deep,* simply *dep.*

16.7

> **RULE NO. 5.** Omit all *silent consonants* (just as we omit silent or non-long vowels); and if a word contains *double consonants*, write only one. There are thousands of silent consonants in the English language, which contribute nothing at all to the sound of a word. Do *not* write these. And remember to handle *double consonants* just as you would handle *double vowels*—keep one and discard one. Examples: The words *right, planner,* and *ball* would be written, *rit, plnr,* and *bl.*

16.8

> **RULE NO. 6.** A *sounding vowel* at the *end* of a word should be *written,* except for the *short i* sound of the letter *y.* which we tend to pronounce like a *long e.* This *short i* sound of the letter *y* therefore should be assigned *automatically* to the preceding consonant. For example: The word *salary* should be written *slr,* with the *short i* sound of the letter *y* being carried by the *r. All other terminal sounding vowels* should be written, including the *long i* sound.

16.9   *Brief Form Letter No. 2.* Except for the word "sir," in the salutation, all of the words in the following letter are brief forms (or brief form derivations; e.g., *lg* for *willing*). See how fast you can write it in PS:

16.10   *Dear Sir: If our check is due, we will find men to return the letter; but what if they are not under my* [1] *orders? I can see the good in it, and I am very willing to come and make it possible for him to give* [2] *his information; but I do not see why every man is here at the time. Cordially,*

16.11   Write this 120-word article in PERSONAL SHORTHAND:

You will save yourself a lot of time if you learn to take notes successfully. In order to do this, you must first choose a notebook which allows you to write easily.

Don't choose a pocket-sized notebook, as it is too hard to keep neat and will fill up too quickly. Don't choose too large a notebook, as it will be too bulky; and, in some classrooms, you will not have a large enough writing surface to hold it easily.

Choose a notebook that will lie flat when you write. It is wise to purchase a loose-leaf notebook, as you can easily remove or insert pages. Finally, choose a notebook with metal or plastic spiral binding, so it can be doubled over on itself without damage.
(120 words) (s.i. 1.3.)

16.12   How quickly can you write this 180-word letter in PER-SONAL SHORTHAND?

Dear Mr. Dailey: The letter we received from you did not contain all the credit information which we need. Please check our letter of July 14 for the information required. We will be glad to send your goods when we receive this credit information.

You will find enclosed a check list of required information. Please take time to go over this enclosure now, so that your goods may be shipped as soon as possible. We are also enclosing a price list from which you can obtain information you will need for this kind of order.

The men here in our order department will be glad to receive your orders at any time. Please call on them for help whenever you wish. They will be glad to come to your aid and will do their best to please you.

If you should wish to return goods to us, please give the date the order was sent out; and I am quite sure you will be pleased with our service. Every man here has been well trained. We make every effort to give you the best possible buy. Thank you for writing us. Very truly yours,
(180 words) (s.i. 1.30)

16.13   See how many minutes it takes you to read (transcribe) this 180-word article:

g wrk c nvr b dn o a rndm bas.   vwn (v-1) neds t plan z wrk; tn, wrk o z pln.   i i e lk o r a stm t pdus e "i m swmpd" stat o min. / a dsrdrl min i bwn t rslt n nfst, amls wrk. n w orgniz r tnkg, w c esl orgniz r akg. e rit mtd o wrkg i t d w o neds t b dn w. fns e jb a hn; tn g o t e nxt jb. / min st dtrms vtg. e es r dfcl o an pc o wrk dpns o w w tnk a i. f w pswad rslvs t e wrk w v bf u i hrd, tn i l b hrd. f, o e otr hn, w strt o a pc o wrk w e tt t w c d i, w l d i. / e basc pncpl o tnkg pstvl i o dtrms scs a stsfcs n l aspks o r livs. n mplyes c apli ts pncpl t tr wrk, y l b dg tr cpn (co.) a tmslvs a rl srvc. (180 words) (s.i. 1.30)

16.14   Important Notetaking Pointers also will be introduced in succeeding lessons. Look for these helpful pointers. Keep in mind that the more you *write* PERSONAL SHORTHAND, the faster your skill will develop. So, careful Notetaking in this and other classes (as well as at special meetings) not only will provide you with better study material but will increase your shorthand skill, at the same time.

16.15

> *Notetaking Pointer:* As soon as possible, start using your PERSONAL SHORTHAND for notetaking—both in class and for outside study. Proper use of PS will give you more time in which to concentrate on the material, select key points, evaluate relationships, organize facts, and record all of the necessary information.

16.16 The following words (Brief Forms) are represented by what letters:

	1		2		3
1	was		just		can
2	enclose		very		of
3	check		be		for
4	with		when		am
5	you		dear		go
6	why		sincerely		I
7	thank		all		take

Personal Shorthand

17

CARDINAL SERIES

17.1   Let's continue our "review" of important PS principles. The better you automatize these principles, the faster you will *write* shorthand—and the easier it will be to read back (transcribe).

17.2   *Review.* There are many words that contain vowel "combinations" which, regardless of how they *look,* provide *long vowel sounds.* For example: The *ia* combination in the word, *dial,* provides a *long i* sound, which we write; but the *short* (non-long) *a* sound, we eliminate. *Dial* is therefore written *dil.*

17.3   *Review.* Though relatively few words in the English language *end* with a *sounding vowel,* any *sounding vowel* at the end of a word should be *written,* except the short *i* sound of the letter *y* (which we tend to pronounce the long e). This vowel sound may be carried by the preceding consonant, automatically. Therefore, as covered in Rule 6, the word, *academy,* would be written *acdm.*

17.4   *Review.* You always are free to use a standard abbreviation with which you are thoroughly acquainted—ave. for avenue, etc.—provided you can read it back with ease.

17.5   *Review.* At all times, treat *half-long vowels* as you would *short vowels:* Omit them!

17.6   *Numbers* in PS are written as they are in *longhand.* There is nothing special about them and no special way in which they must be written (except that they should be written with care).

17.7   Because of the frequency with which they are written, *Days of the Week* are represented by their *initial letters,* with the exception of Sunday and Tuesday, which are expressed by *Sn* and *Tu.* Monday, Wednesday, Thursday, Friday, and Saturday, therefore, are written *M, W, T, F,* and *S.* Of course, lower case letters may be used in place of capitals, if you prefer.

17.8   In PERSONAL SHORTHAND, *Months of the Year* also are represented by their *initial letters*, except for January, *Jn;* March, *Mr;* July, *Jy;* and August, *Ag.* Of course these, too, can be written with small letters only: *jn, mr, jy,* and *ag.* Again, all other months are expressed by *initial letters.*

17.9   *Brief Form Letter No. 3.* Except for the proper noun, *Jim,* all of the words in the following letter are brief forms. How fast can you write this letter in PERSONAL SHORTHAND?

17.10   *Dear Jim: It is quite good that you can also require the information from her and, at the time, see how well[1] she will get the copy to us. As I see it all now, it is up to the gentlemen if they are ever[2] to go out from here and check about that which is as we know it to be. Sincerely,*

17.11   The article and letter in the following paragraphs (17.12 and 17.13) each has exactly 60 shorthand words. See how quickly you can write these in PS.

17.12   *Most people use only a small percent of the ability they actually possess. We should always try to find out how we can get out of ourselves the most that is in us. It is a sad fact that many people today do as little as they can and still get by. If you adopt this attitude and don't wake up, life will pass you by.*
        (60 words) (s.i. 1.27)

17.13   *Dear Miss Blake: Your account in the amount of $50 is now two months past due. Is there some reason why payment is being withheld? Has our merchandise or our service been unsatisfactory?*

        If we are at fault, please let us hear from you; and give us a chance to make things right. If not, please let us have your check by return mail. Yours truly,
        (60 words) (s.i. 1.29)

17.14   Write this letter (120 shorthand words) in PS. If any words cause you to hesitate, find out *why!*

        Dear Mr. Harrington: The sale of the house at 3211 East Park Street is an object of particular concern to me. This house has been empty for two years, with no interested buyer in sight.

        I have come to the conclusion that an all-out effort should be made to sell this house by the end of the month. If we are not successful, then it should be torn down and the land used as a commercial site. This would be subject to zoning laws, of course.

As you may have already concluded, I am turning this pro-
ject over to you and am confident that you will handle it to
the best of your ability. Please contact me if you need any
help. Yours very truly,
(120 words) (s.i.1.33)

17.15   See how many minutes it takes you to read (transcribe) this
180 word article:

e frst (1st) a most mprtn tg t d, w rgrd
t wn's (1's) crer, i t fcs wn's (1's)
ambss. t sctr y nrg ovr a nmbr o tgs
mns t nn o tm i gg t g y bst wrk. alwas
(lwas) v a dfnt mtl pctr o e tg u wn t
bc, a t l ccntrat y eft trd is rlzas. /
u ma dcid latr t ts i n e tg u rl ned,
aftr l, a cag y crs ntirl. b e ccntras
u v xrcisd n e orgnl dsir l stn u n g
std n e nu wn (1); a sn ntg i 1st, a r
mins d n wrk n jmps, aftr l, u l f t e
frst (1st) tg lgcl ld u t e lst. / e trb
w most o u i t w don' s hrd enf t g o a
k r ss c tro. i i e sprm s t mpls t acs.
u l alwas (lwas) oba e strgr dsir. f u
dsir scs w l y hrt a sol a bd a min, ntg
n l e wrld l kep i f u. (180 words) (s.i. 1.32)

17.16

> *Notetaking Pointer:* **You can study more effectively in**
> **an environment that assures freedom from noise,**
> **reasonable privacy, and a minimum of distractions.**

17.17

> *Notetaking Pointer:* When you have found a good place in which to study quietly, use it—regularly! Changing from place to place may offer variety, but it also is distracting in itself and does not encourage good study habits.

17.18

> *Notetaking Pointer:* When you study, make sure that you have adequate light, that the temperature is comfortable (not too hot), and that you have the necessary supplies. Inadequate equipment, lack of supplies, poor light, and the wrong temperature, all tend to distract and dissipate study time.

17.19   The following words (Brief Forms) are represented by what letters:

	1	2	3
1	price	which	not
2	an	under	do
3	her	your	she
4	he	that	also
5	our	gentlemen	come
6	his	ever	out
7	require	by	from

Personal Shorthand

CARDINAL SERIES

18.1 Review of Brief Forms. Some words occur so often in the English language that there is no reason at all for writing them in full, even phonetically. In fact, there are some 100 words that comprise well over 50 per cent of our general vocabulary. PS Brief Forms are probably the most important of the high-frequency (or most-used) words in the English language. These are represented by single letters. For example:

18.2 The letter *a* represents the words *a, an, and, at, about.*
The letter *b* represents the words *be, by, buy, been, but.*
The letter *c* represents the words *can, come, copy, credit.*
The letter *d* represents the words *dear, do, due, did, date, would.*
The letter *e* represents the words *he, the.*

18.3 The letter *f* represents the words *for, from, if, find.*
The letter *g* represents the words *go, get, good, glad, give.*
The letter *h* represents the words *her, him, had, here.*
The letter *i* represents the words *I, it, is, time.*
The letter *j* represents the words *just, gentlemen (gentleman).*

18.4 The letter *k* represents the words *kind, make, take.*
The letter *l* represents the words *all, also, will, well, letter.*
The letter *m* represents the words *am, me, my, made, man, men.*
The letter *n* represents the words *when, not, in, no, know, information.*
The letter *o* represents the words *out, of, on, what.*

18.5 *Brief Form Letter No. 4.* Except for the title, *Mr.*, and the proper noun Kerr, all of the words in the following letter are either brief forms or brief form derivatives. See how quickly you can write this letter in PS.

18.6   *Dear Mr. Kerr: By and by we will receive the order copy; and*
       if it is not too good, we can take what we have[1] made, if and
       when we have the time. The copy has not been dated, but I
       would be glad to do so, if it were to be[1] made an order by
       me or by her, and we had the check to see. He was to receive
       the required information,[3] but at no time was he to receive
       that kind of letter. I know it to be so. All in all, that was[4] to be
       a kind of credit check about which we are very pleased.
       Sincerely,

18.7   The letter and article in the following paragraphs (18.8 and
       18.9) each has exactly 60 shorthand words. How quickly can
       you write 60 words in PS?

18.8   *Dear Mr. Jones: Enclosed in this letter is your new credit*
       card for the coming year. We have enjoyed your business
       this past year and hope that we have been able to please
       you in every way.
       May we take this opportunity to wish you and yours a most
       pleasant New Year. We look forward to serving you in the
       coming year. Yours very truly,
       (60 words) (s.i. 1.29)

18.9   *If your boss is going to be out of the office for more than two*
       days, find out where he can be reached by mail and
       telephone. Before he leaves, find out if he likes to be con-
       tacted by the office or whether he prefers to have everything
       wait until he returns. Also find out if you should answer in-
       coming letters as they arrive.
       (60 words) (s.i. 1.31)

18.10 See how fluently and easily you can write this next letter.
       (120 shorthand words) in PERSONAL SHORTHAND. When
       you have finished, give special attention to (and practice)
       any *troublesome* words.

18.11 *The more you have to be supervised when you go to work,*
       the more you will have to pay for that supervision; or, to put
       it another way, the less you will get for your work. The per-
       son who can do his work with a minimum of supervision is
       the one whose salary advances and who gets promoted to
       higher responsibilities.
       Think about yourself. When you do better work in class, you
       are bettering yourself. The thoughts you think, the words
       you speak, and the work you do each day all make you better
       or worse. In a real sense, you can become what you deter-
       mine to become.

Start studying and practicing the right way today. It is the
way that will benefit you most.
(120 words) (s.i. 1.34)

18.12 Time yourself and see how long it takes you to *read* the
following 180-word article (make a note of those words that
cause you to hesitate unduly):

*smis o a dep blo ski, amg flotg clwds o
wit, u ma dscvr a sml spt o drk gra. i
ma b a v sml spt, b kep y i o t nsgnfcn
lokg ltl clwd. i usul mns mscf. / o e
wtr, i i ofn e frnr o a sdn sgl n o bd
wtr o sm k.   o ln, i usl mns a gst swr,
f ntg wrs. f i i gg t b ugl, ts ltl drk
clwd l gro lrgr a lrgr ntl i swlos u e
wit clwds, a e strm i uo u. i i bst t k
t sltr n u s e drk clwd grog, f sc strms
c u v gkl. / a evnl gra ski ds n nsrl mn
ran. w v my gra das n n ran fls, to smis
e gra ski sns dwn sprnklg swrs. / a ran
clwd i cld a nmbs clwd. e drftg, wit
clwds t clg t a tr tmslvs o e sids o e
mtns r cposd o hv mst, w gnrl l b cdnd
nt ran bf e da i ovr.* (180 words) (s.i. 1.33)

18.13

> *Notetaking Pointer:* Schedule a certain amount of time for studying and stick to your schedule. Don't set aside more time for study than you need but use the time planned—and use it regularly! Studying should be a *habit*; but habits are formed only by following prescribed schedules and procedures. A haphazard study schedule will result in nothing more than haphazard studying. Although some subjects require more time than others, make a point of scheduling your toughest subjects *first*. If you put these off until last, you may rationalize and never get to them.

18.14

> *Notetaking Pointer:* Try to establish a regular time and place for studying; if possible, at the same time each day. But to the extent you can, follow a specific lecture with a study period of your own.

18.15

> *Notetaking Pointer: Learning* is not necessarily *listening* and *listening* is not necessarily *learning.* We can listen casually, with very little learning; *active* learning takes *active* listening. This requires concentration. It means that you must actively *participate*—mentally—in what you are learning and hearing.

18.16 The following words (Brief Forms) are represented by what letters:

	1	2	3
1	me	the	that
2	get	or	every
3	it	as	buy
4	kind	quite	no
5	please	we	due
6	and	up	so
7	him	they	will

Personal Shorthand

19.1 Continuing our review of Brief Forms:

The letter *p* represents the words *possible, price, please, put.*

The letter *q* represents the words *enclose, require, quite.*

The letter *r* represents the words *are, or, our, return, order.*

The letter *s* represents the words *sincerely, she, so, see, wish.*

The letter *t* represents the words *that, thank, there, to, too.*

19.2 The letter *u* represents the words *you, up, under, us.*

The letter *v* represents the words *very, ever, every, have, receive.*

The letter *w* represents the words *with, which, we, were, how, now.*

The letter *x* represents the word *check!* (And *only* this one word.)

The letter *y* represents the words *why, your, they.*

The letter *z* represents the words *as, has, his, was.*

19.3 Now practice writing *Brief Form Letter No. 1* again. See if you can write it without hesitation.

Gentlemen: Thank you for the information enclosed with your check. I did not know that you would buy the copy at[1] our price. We are pleased with your order and will see that you receive a credit. Do you wish to buy on time just now;[2] or, if possible, would you require us to be there on that very date? Sincerely yours,

19.4 How quickly and easily can you write the following letter (paragraph 19.5) and article (paragraph 19.6) in PS? Each has exactly 60 shorthand words. Analyze any words that cause you to hesitate and practice those words until you can write them easily.

19.5　*Dear Mrs. Gray: I showed our bookkeeper your letter about the incorrect bill we sent you for painting your truck. You are right—our bill was indeed an overcharge.*

We have no idea how this mistake was made, but I can promise you that we shall do our very best to see that our bills and statements are correct in the future. Yours truly,
(60 words) (s.i. 1.31)

19.6　*Happiness is where you find it. Those not looking for happiness seldom find it or really want it. They seem content to look on the sour side of life. It is said that a person who is happy will see happiness everywhere and everyone will see happiness in him. We should all strive to make the world a happier place in which to live.*
(60 words) (s.i. 1.31)

19.7　This next letter has 120 shorthand words. How fast can you write it in PERSONAL SHORTHAND—in 4 minutes, 3, 2? Determine which words need extra practice.

19.8　*Dear Mr. Ames: I am sorry to say that we are not at all satisfied with the person you sent to fill the job of credit manager in our store. He has been with us only two weeks, and already he has made many enemies and has disrupted the entire office staff. He also has failed to do his work properly. Much of his work is left completely untouched. We have no choice but to release him.*

Although we have tried repeatedly to make him conform to company policies and have made every effort to furnish all of the help he needs, every measure has met with failure. We regret that we must give him notice at the end of the week. Sincerely yours,
(120 words) (s.i. 1.35

19.9　How fast can you read (transcribe) the following letter?

dms gregson:　e (los Hrs i lokg f sals rprsntvs (reps.), a w tt u mit b ntrstd, sn u wrkd f u n ts lin f svrl yrs. / w r lokg f etr fl-i r pt-i hlp, z e dmd f r clos stils i grog rpdl.　u d b a xcln cndat f r trang pgrm f nu rprsntvs *(reps), w strts n mr. / f u dcid t acpt r ofr, u c xpk t ern z mc z $800 a mt (mo.), t strt, f u cos t wrk fl i. evn f u cos t wrk onl pt i, u l b kg s mc xtra my t son u l wn t rprsn u o a fl-i bas. / w r gg a crd w c b mrkd a rd f u d lik t csdr ts pss frtr. n w v y crd, mr. paul francis, r psnl mgr, l ctk u f a ntrvu. / b crtn t fwrd y crd son, z w d lik t v u jyn r stf z son z p. yvt,*

19.10

Notetaking Pointer: Notetaking during a classroom lecture is a demanding and specialized skill. It calls for active listening and conscientious learning, for you must comprehend what you are hearing and, at the same time, concentrate on essential ideas and concepts.

19.11

Notetaking Pointer: Psychologists tell us that we forget at least 50 per cent of what we hear immediately after hearing it; with loss of another 25 to 40 per cent within two or three months from the date of hearing.

19.12

Notetaking Pointer: Active listening must be practiced. It is a skill and an art (like any other skill or art) and cannot be mastered in a matter of days. If you are to listen effectively: (a) concentrate, (b) screen for essential ideas, (c) stay alert.

19.13   Practice writing these high-frequency phrases in PS:

	1	2	3
1	on the	we are	we have
2	it is	of the	of our
3	in the	to the	for the
4	to you	I am	of your
5	with the	will be	and the
6	and the	about the	to be

19.14   The following words (Brief Forms) are represented by what letters:

	1	2	3
1	copy	possible	there
2	on	at	have
3	if	had	been
4	my	are	know
5	good	has	did
6	is	how	see
7	make	us	well

Personal Shorthand

20.1 Continuing with our review: Remember that most Brief Forms are represented by the *first* letter of the word. A number, however, are represented by the *last* letter of the word. For example, *would* is represented by *d; he* and *the,* by *e; if,* by *f; all, will,* and *well,* by *l;* and *am,* by *m.*

20.2 Some additional Brief Forms are represented by their *last* letters, rather than their *first* letters: *information, in,* and *when,* are represented by *n; our* and *or* are represented by *r; you,* by *u; how* and *now,* by *w;* and *why* and *they,* by *y.*

20.3 Although most Brief Forms are represented by the first letter of the word, with a few being indicated by the *last* letter, there are a number of Brief Forms that have been assigned for "mathematical" or "arithmetic" reasons; that is, reasons having to do with the "frequency" of words in the English language. For example, *time* is represented by *i; gentlemen,* by *j; take* and *make,* by *k; also,* by *l.*

20.4 Additional Brief Forms that have been assigned for "mathematical" reasons, and not according to first or last letters, are as follows: *n* for *know; o* for *what; q* for *enclose* and *require; r* for *are* and *order;* and *s* for *wish.*

20.5 A final group of Brief Forms assigned for "mathematical" reasons, and not based on first or last letters, includes: *v* for *ever, every, have,* and *receive; x* for *check;* and *z* for *was, his, as,* and *has.*

20.6 The past tense, gerund, and plural forms are very easy to handle in PERSONAL SHORTHAND. For example, the word *thanked* simply is written *td,* the word *thanking, tg;* and the word *thanks, ts.* Merely add a *d,* a *g,* or an *s* whenever the derivation calls for it.

20.7 Here is *Brief Form Letter No. 2,* again. See how quickly (and easily) you can write it in PS:

Dear Sir: If our check is due, we will find men to return the letter; but what if they are not under my[1] orders? I can see the good in it, and I am very willing to come and make it possible for him to give[2] his information; but I do not see why every man is here at the time. Cordially,

20.8 The following paragraphs (one, a letter and the other, an article) each contain exactly 60 shorthand words. See how quickly you can write them in PERSONAL SHORTHAND, but make sure you are applying Brief Forms correctly and thoroughly understand your use of each theory principle and phonetic abbreviation.

20.9 *Dear Members: Central Drama Club is planning its annual fall production and needs your help. We are having a planning meeting on July 2 at 2 p.m. and hope you will attend. The meeting will be at Ann Smith's home, 210 Lake Drive.*

Please plan to come with lots of good ideas. Refreshments will be served. We hope to see you there. Yours,
(60 words) (s.i. 1.33)

20.10 *What is the difference between high school and college? There is one major factor in college that usually means the difference between failure and success there. The student will have to be self directed. He will have to set up his own study routines. It will be up to him to see that he reviews for tests and gets reports in on time.*
(60 words) (s.i. 1.33)

20.11 Analyze and practice some of the more difficult words in the following article, before you see how fast you can write it in PS:

Because of the changes that are taking place in the business world today, many people are finding themselves without jobs, even though they may have received a high school diploma or a college degree.

Many of these people are trained in only one line of work and must accept the first job that is offered to them, because they do not have the time to be patient. They need money to live on at once.

If you are an office worker in this situation, you should start out by brushing up on your skills, as they have probably become rusty through lack of use. Once these skills are improved, you will find yourself in a better position to compete for well-paying, satisfying jobs.
(120 words) (s.i. 1.35)

20.12   Read (transcribe) the following 180-word PS article. It is a
        good idea to list—and practice writing—any particularly
        troublesome words.

*u ma n v tt a i, b v bsn, v trad, a v
pfs i j a fiit, a ctst f sprr; a n e en,
i l b fwn t e bst m i sr t wn. / l u v t
d i hg u sm srt o priz, a i ks ltl dfrn
o t piz i, a a twsn m l rn tmslvs o o
brt trig t cptr i. i ned n b antg o
mtrl vlu, f f u lok closl, u l f t most
(mst) ctsts r ft smpl f e onr t sems t b
gand n wng. / i i n e slvr trof r e mdl
t ks a ctst wrtwil, f tos r onl e vsb
mblms o vctr--nic t v, b n a l nsr a n n
wa afkg e rl abl o e ctstn. / e vlu o an
ctst lis n e sprt o rivlr i pdus, e felg
t wn (1) i bg p t a tst a i bg gn a
oprtunt t so o t i n h.* (180 words) (s.i. 1.37)

20.13

Notetaking Pointer: If you are *listening* effectively—and expect to take notes effectively—you must
listen for "ideas" and pay no attention to the "source";
i.e., do not let the speaker's appearance, voice, dress,
or any other mannerisms distract you.

20.14

> *Notetaking Pointer:* We know that the average listener probably can *comprehend* at a rate that is four to six times faster than most speakers talk. This "extra" time should be used for organizing thoughts and actual writing of notes—and not for gazing out the window.

20.15

> *Notetaking Pointer:* Active listening and learning de-mand *self-discipline* in notetaking. This means that you must pay attention at all times—and sustain this state of attention throughout the entire discussion, lecture, or meeting.

20.16 How quickly can you write these high-frequency phrases in PS?

	1	2	3
1	of this	at the	by the
2	to be	you have	to make
3	you can	there is	we can
4	I have	for your	in our
5	is the	to get	you are
6	from the	as your	by it

20.17 The following words (Brief Forms) are represented by what letters:

	1	2	3
1	credit	time	now
2	what	about	to
3	find	here	receive
4	made	return	but
5	glad	were	in
6	just	from	good
7	get	an	require

Personal Shorthand

21.1 Continuing with our review of PERSONAL SHORTHAND theory principles:

21.2 Actually, PERSONAL SHORTHAND can be written, quite effectively, *without* applying the phonetic abbreviations to which you have been introduced. It is true, however, that the use of these abbreviating principles will facilitate the further *telescoping* or *condensing* of longhand and thus will enable you to write PS at a faster rate. Do *not* expect to learn all of these abbreviating principles at one time. Some will be mastered far sooner than others, primarily because of the frequency with which they are used.

21.3 While not really a phonetic abbreviation in PS, remember that the letter *a*, represents the *sound* of *long a*, regardless of the phonetic unit that represents this sound in the longhand word—for example, *a, ay, aye, eigh, (n)ee, (q)uet,* etc.

21.4 In PS, the letter *b* represents its own basic sound, plus the sound of *ble*, and, of course, like all consonants, it can carry the sound of *long e* when this sound *follows* the consonant and is so assigned.

21.5 When writing PERSONAL SHORTHAND, remember that the letter *c* can represent its basic sound (usually an *s* or a *k* sound); and, in addition, the sounds of *ch, com, con,* and of course, *c* plus *long e.*

21.6 Although not really a phonetic *abbreviation* in PS, remember that the letter *d* represents its own basic sound, and, of course, the sound of *d* plus *long e.*

21.7 Here's another opportunity to practice *Brief Form Letter No. 3.* The more you memorize it and automatize it, the easier your Brief Forms will be:

Dear Jim: It is quite good that you can also require the information from her and, at the time, see how well[1] she will get the copy to us. As I see it all now, it is up to the gentlemen if they are ever[2] to go out from here and check about that which is as we know it to be. Sincerely,

21.8   Practice writing the following letters in PS (Each has exactly 60 shorthand words).

21.9   *Dear Mr. Crane: Our new catalog of unusual gifts is just off the press! I am sure that you won't want to miss the wide assortment of gifts in our catalog when you are shopping for those hard-to-please people on your Christmas list.*

To receive your copy of our catalog, just fill in the enclosed card and return it to us. Sincerely,
(60 words) (s.i. 1.33)

21.10   *Dear Friend: For furniture and home furnishings, you get the most for your money at Edison's. The bargains that are listed on the enclosed folder are only a sample of the savings you can make when you shop at Edison's.*

If you do not have a charge account here, you will find it is easy to open one. Sincerely yours,
(60 words) (s.i.1.35)

21.11   Here is another article with 120 shorthand words. See how quickly you can write it in PS. Make a point of analyzing and practicing any troublesome words.

21.12   *Once you have a job, there are going to be mornings when you won't want to go to work, because you don't feel well. No one feels perfect, 100 percent of the time. You should go to work, however, if at all possible.*

If you contract a serious illness, that keeps you away from work for any length of time, companies respect this situation. You will be considered a habitual skipper, however, if you miss a day here and there, for no apparent reason.

It is obvious what a firm will do with you if you are consistently absent. Whenever you are gone, it costs them money; and they will find someone to replace you if you start costing them too much.
(120 words) (s.i.1.37)

21.13   Time yourself and see how long it takes you to read (or transcribe) the following article. It contains 180 shorthand words.

21.14   *f u wn t b a g stngrfr, u mst ccntrat o ritg z acrtl z p, a, a e sam i, mg t kep*

*u w e dctatr. u ned t rit ec wrd z clrl
z u c, evn f e olin p dwn i ncrk. / f u
ccntrat o bg acrt z u k dwn e dctas, ts
l k i mc esr a fstr n u trnscrib y nots.
y objkv sd b t rit srthn t l nab u t
rcl e wrd n u rc i drg trnscrps. / evn f
u d n n e crk srthn f a wrd, k sr u p
smtg dwn f i t l hlp u rcl e wrd n u r
trnscribg. b crclg por r ncrk srthn z u
trnscrib y nots, u c mprov y skl n ritg
crk fms. / u sd l lsn t o i bg sd z u k
dctas. i i mc esr t dtrm e sn o e dctas
z i i bg gn, rtr tn latr, n u r
trnscribg.* (180 words) (s.i. 1.39)

21.15

> *Notetaking Pointer:* In taking notes, when you are presented with a key idea, fact, or other piece of information, actively reflect on and *rephrase* this idea in your own words. Again, this involves *active participation* that *reinforces* your learning.

21.16

> *Notetaking Pointer:* In taking notes, listen for related ideas; that is, ideas that can be related *to* or associated *with* key ideas. These not only support the key idea but through association are easier to remember.

21.17

> *Notetaking Pointer:* The more automatic your PER-
> SONAL SHORTHAND becomes (and the more you use
> it, the more automatic it *will* become), the easier it will
> be for you to concentrate on what is being said and
> organize—mentally—the material to be recorded.

21.18 Practice writing these phrases until they become automatic:

	1	2	3
1	it will	of course	we shall
2	to have	to our	we will
3	on your	to your	in this
4	to us	so that	to see

21.19 The following words (Brief Forms) are represented by which letters of the alphabet?

	1	2	3
1	in	order	enclose
2	date	were	check
3	wish	too	with
4	letter	information	you
5	man	would	why
6	give	men	thank
7	possible	was	just

Personal Shorthand

CARDINAL SERIES

22.1   Reviewing our PERSONAL SHORTHAND theory, remember that the letter *e* usually represents only the sound of *long e* and, therefore, normally need not be written, because the sound of *long e* is assigned to (or carried by) any *preceding* consonant—whenever that consonant is representing its basic sound or sounds.

22.2   Generally, however, it is more prudent to write the letter *e* at the very *beginning* of a word (Basic Rule No. 3); and, of course, in the case of words with double *ee* combinations, one *e* is retained and the other dropped. (Basic Rule No. 4).

22.3   The letter *f* represents its own basic sound, and, in addition, the sounds of *f* plus *long e, ph, for, (fore), ful,* and *ify.*

22.4   The letter *g* represents its own basic sounds (primarily those used in the words *gate* and *genus*) and, in addition, the sounds of *g* plus *long e, ng, ing,* and *dge.*

22.5   The letter *h* represents its own basic sound, and, in addition, the sound of *h* plus *long e.* In short, *h* does not function as a true phonetic abbreviation and has relatively little work to do in *either* longhand or PERSONAL SHORTHAND.

22.6   Keep in mind that while it is not a true phonetic abbreviation, the letter *i* represents the sound of *long i,* regardless of the phonetic unit that represents this sound in the longhand word—for example, *i, igh,* or *y.* No matter how it is spelled in longhand, if the sound is *long i,* write *i* in PERSONAL SHORTHAND.

22.7   In PS, the letter *j* represents its own basic sound, and, in addition, the sound of *j* plus *long e.* Like the letter h, j is not a true "abbreviation" and has comparatively little to do, in *either* longhand or PERSONAL SHORTHAND.

22.8   Now practice writing Brief Form Letter No. 4 again. Write it as many times as your study schedule permits. Be on the alert for any Brief Forms about which you are still uncertain.

22.9   *Dear Mr. Kerr: By and by we will receive the order copy; and if it is not too good, we can take what we have[1] made, if and when we have the time. The copy has not been dated, but I would be glad to do so, if it were to be[2] made an order by me or by her, and we had the check to see. He was to receive the required information,[3] but at no time was he to receive that kind of letter. I know it to be so. All in all, that was[4] to be a kind of credit check about which we are very pleased. Sincerely,*

22.10   Each of the following paragraphs (one, an article, and the other, a letter) has exactly 60 shorthand words. See how quickly (and easily) you can write them both.

22.11   *Visit your local bank and ask one of the bank officers to explain the types of accounts available to you, including the charges. If you open an account, have him show you how to keep your check stubs and how to balance your account when you get your statement at the end of the period, either monthly or every three months.*
(60 words) (s.i. 1.35)

22.12   *Dear Mrs. Holgate: I am sorry that we cannot deliver your Model 4 dishwasher by the middle of August. A bad fire in our warehouse did a good deal of damage, and our stock of Model 4 dishwashers will be a total loss. I hope you will bear with us until we can find you a Model 4 elsewhere. Very truly yours,*
(60 words) (s.i. 1.35)

22.13   Write the following letter (120 shorthand words) in PS. Time yourself. Then practice writing any words that seem difficult.

22.14   *Dear John: I am exceedingly pleased to inform you that you have been elected the top salesman in our territory.*

Our staff considered the sales report of each man in the area and his value to the company. When all the ballots were counted, your name led the list. You have topped all sales in the fifty-six year history of our organization.

You have been with the company only seven months and have attained this record in a very short length of time. We are looking forward to the time when your sales record will top that of any man in the country.

Here's hoping you will be increasingly valuable in the future. Keep up the good work! Yours truly,
(120 words) (s.i. 1.39)

22.15 The following PERSONAL SHORTHAND article contains 180 shorthand words. How fast can you read it?

22.16 *a e psn i, slogns r usd pimrl f e pps o advrtisg. f wn (1) nvns a nu k o brkfst fod, e a wn strts n t pduc a slogn t l ft e crcmstns, k e pnsm ft e crim, z u mit sa. f e cn mfkr a slogn hslf, e pas bg my t anwn (an 1) ho c. / a o ds e d w i, n e gs i? e pans i o sinbrds, w e erks alg e hiwa, ts pvng trsts f gg a glmps o e snr, a tg w pmots mc nhpn o bhf o tos sam trsts. i z pmotd s mc hstl, t lwkrs v trid to fgr o sm wa t rmd i. / i i dwtf t an rmd c b fwn, bcs a slogn i wrt a lt o my, a antg w trns t stp is us i sr t b ft t e lmt n e crts. l e sam, alto e sinbrds k e trsts agr, e slogn pand o tm rmans stmpd n tr mr.*

(180 words) (s.i. 1.40)

22.17

> *Notetaking Pointer:* **The more you can prepare in advance for your notetaking (whether from lectures or other media), the more effective your notetaking will be. If there is material that you can record or scan ahead of time, your listening (or recording) will be just that much more effective when the time comes for notetaking.**

22.18

> *Notetaking Pointer:* When you are taking notes at a lecture, have on hand the supplies you will need; make sure you have a good writing surface and are not balancing your notebook on top of a pile of books; and see to it that you are comfortable and ready to learn.

22.19

> *Notetaking Pointer:* Get in the habit of properly labeling or identifying your notes: the course or subject involved; the particular aspect or element of that subject; etc.

22.20 Practice writing these high-frequency phrases in PS:

	1	2	3
1	they are	with you	for you
2	that is	there are	with us
3	have been	with your	you may
4	should be	as the	that are
5	you will	if the	may be

22.21 The following high-frequency words (Brief Forms) are represented by which letters of the alphabet:

	1	2	3
1	just	can	price
2	very	of	an
3	be	for	her
4	when	am	he
5	dear	go	out
6	sincerely	I	his
7	all	take	require

Personal Shorthand

23.1 Theory Review: The letter *k*, while it functions as a rather limited phonetic abbreviation, represents its own basic sound and, in addition, the sounds of *k* plus *long e*, the *ck* (k) component, and *ct*.

23.2 In addition to representing its own basic sound, plus the sounds of *l* plus *long e* and *ly*, *l* also represents the phonetic abbreviations *lity* and *lty*.

23.3 When writing PERSONAL SHORTHAND, let the letter *m* represent its own basic sound and, in addition, of course, the sound of *m* plus *long e;* also, the phonetic abbreviations *m*, any short vowel, and *m; m*, any short vowel, and *n; moun;* and *ment*.

23.4 In PS, the letter *n* represents its own basic sound and the sound of *n* plus *long e;* it also represents the phonetic abbreviations *nc(e), ns(e), ness, nt,* and *nd*.

23.5 In PERSONAL SHORTHAND, the letter *o* (as you will recall) normally represents the sound of *long o;* however, it also can represent the sound of *oo*, as in the word *fruit*. Although it is not a phonetic abbreviation, in the technical sense, it is still well to review such theory points, again and again.

23.6 Let's practice Brief Form Letter No. 1 again. See how quickly you can write it.

Gentlemen: Thank you for the information enclosed with your check. I did not know that you would buy the copy at[1] our price. We are pleased with your order and will see that you receive a credit. Do you wish to buy on time just now;[2] or, if possible, would you require us to be there on that very date? Sincerely yours,

23.7 Practice writing paragraph 23.8 in PS. Then try paragraph 23.9. Time yourself, whenever possible.

23.8   *A secretary must know how to type, but she must also know the best way to make a correction. There are many work savers on the market to aid the typist in erasing, and she should find the one that helps her the best. Remaining calm is important, because erasing in a bad temper can cause more holes than the eraser does.*
(60 words) (s.i. 1.35)

23.9   *Dear Mrs. Smith: Welcome to the city of Portland. By now, you no doubt have had time to become settled in your new home.*

At your convenience, our Welcome Wagon representative would like to make a call at your home to help you in answering questions about Portland, and to bring you some fine products of our city and state. Yours truly,
(60 words) (s.i. 1.37)

23.10   Now write the following letter in PERSONAL SHORTHAND. Out of 120 words, how many cause you to hesitate? List these and practice them separately.

23.11   *Dear Mr. Lander: I noticed in this morning's paper your ad for a furnished apartment. It mentioned that it had four rooms, a garage, a basement with an oil furnace, and, furthermore, an electric washing machine.*

This is just the kind of apartment my husband and I have been hoping to find. He is in the service but will be home shortly, and we are hoping to get settled at that time.

We have some furniture of our own. Would it be possible for us to bring these pieces with us if we decide to take the apartment? Also, do you furnish the utilities?

May I have an appointment to inspect the apartment on Monday, April 21? Yours truly,
(120 words) (s.i. 1.4)

23.12   The following PERSONAL SHORTHAND article contains 180 words. How fluently can you read it?

23.13   *wtr u r a srthn studn, a stngrfr (steno), r a scrtr (sec.), u sd k dwn y srthn nots w a g pn. e pn u cos sd n smr r skp wrds r ls z u rit y nots. i sd l strt ritg e nstn i tcs e papr. / u sd us*

a pn t c stn u da aftr da u e ritg pnsm
o a crt rprtr. e pn sd l rspn egl l t e
ftr tc r t e hv hn. i sd p bot e ritr
ho liks e drk, bold, hv lin a e ritr ho
liks e tn, nro lin. / w tip o pyn u
dcid t g o y pn dpns o ec ndvdl srthn
ritr, b xprts agre o e us o e mdm pyn f
srthn ritg. e dcidg fctr sd b e lgbl
o e ritg. e mdm pyn sems t g mr lgb
srthn nots bcs e mdm pyn rits a hvr lin
t i esr t rd an i, espsl u artfsl lits.

(180 words) (s.i. 1.42)

23.14

> *Notetaking Pointer:* Some speakers provide an outline which will serve as a "blueprint" for the taking of your notes. Others do not provide such outlines, but are careful in the organization of their material and indicate the various steps and stages of their lecture with certain words or phrases.

23.15

> *Notetaking Pointer:* Many speakers deliver special "cues," as "in summary," or "in addition to the foregoing points," etc.

23.16 Practice writing these high-frequency phrases in PS:

	1	2	3
1	if you	very much	to do
2	and that	one of the	he is
3	one of our	to me	will you
4	of these	can be	would be

23.17 Which letters of the alphabet represent these high-frequency words (Brief Forms)?

	1	2	3
1	which	not	me
2	under	do	get
3	your	she	it
4	that	also	kind
5	gentlemen	come	please
6	ever	out	and
7	by	from	him

Personal Shorthand

CARDINAL SERIES

24.1 Theory Review: You will remember that the letter *p* represents its own basic sound and, in addition, the sound of *p* plus *long e;* and—as word beginnings only—the phonetic abbreviations *pr; p,* any *short vowel, r; pro,* and *por* (either *long* or *short o*).

24.2 In Lesson 7, it was pointed out that the word *preamble* is written *pemb.* In this case, the *long e* is written because the letter *p* cannot represent the *pr* word beginning and *also long e.* Again—the letter *p* can represent its own basic sound; it can represent *p* plus *long e;* and, as word beginnings only, the sounds of *pr, p,* any *short vowel, r; pro* and *por* (either *long* or *short o*).

24.3 The letter *q* represents the phonetic abbreviation *qu,* which normally is pronounced with a *kw* sound; and, when appropriate to the longhand, it also represents the sound of *k.* Essentially, the *q* in PERSONAL SHORTHAND performs the same function it does in longhand.

24.4 In PS, the letter *r* represents its own basic sound, the sound of *r* plus *long e,* and the phonetic abbreviations *rity,* and *ur(e).*

24.5 The letter *s* represents its own basic sound, the sound of *s* plus *long e,* and the phonetic abbreviations *sh; s,* any *short vowel, s; c,* any *short vowel, s;* and *all* of the *shun* word parts *(sion, tion, cian, shion, cien,* etc.).

24.6 Practice Brief Form Letter No. 2 until you can write it in PS without the slightest hesitation:

Dear Sir: If our check is due, we will find men to return the letter; but what if they are not under my[1] orders? I can see the good in it, and I am very willing to come and make it possible for him to give[2] his information; but I do not see why every man is here at the time. Cordially,

24.7 Here are two more practice letters (60 shorthand words in each). See how rapidly you can write them in PS.

24.8   *Dear Miss Taylor: I want to bring your attention to the fact that our company has moved its office from 13 Main Street to Fourth and Jackson Streets. When you sent your June statement, you mailed it to the Main Street address.*

We would appreciate your changing your records so that, in the future, all correspondence is sent to our new address. Yours truly,
(60 words) (s.i. 1.37)

24.9   *Dear Miss Black: We are sorry the statement we sent you last month was incorrect. We found that we credited the wrong account for merchandise you returned last month. Enclosed is a corrected statement. We hope you will excuse our errors.*

We have enjoyed your patronage in the past and hope to serve you again in the future. Yours very truly,
(60 words) (s.i. 1.38)

24.10   The following article has 120 shorthand words. After writing it in PS, review it carefully for troublesome words and then practice these separately.

24.11   *Some businesses, in order to encourage prompt payment of bills from customers, offer bonus discounts if bills are paid within a certain period of time. This bonus is referred to as a cash discount.*

On the invoice, the cash discount rate is shown, as well as the deadline for this payment, in order to receive the discount. For example, the terms might read 2/15, n/25.

This means that the customer may deduct 2 per cent of the net price, if he pays the invoice within 15 days. If it is not paid within that period, he must pay the entire price of the invoice, not more than 25 days after the date located at the top of the invoice.
(120 words) (s.i. 1.41)

24.12   List (and then practice writing) those words that cause you to hesitate when reading this PS letter:

24.13   *dms irving: wn (1) o y flo mplyes, mrs. jane moore, sgstd t w sn u a bx o r asrtd stils o crane. tipg erasrs. tf, w r sng a bx tda, w r cplms. / n u opn y*

pkg o crane tipg erasrs, u l b pd w tr
fin gl. tes erasrs r usd b my o e
finst tipsts n e cntr a rprsn (rep.) e
hist gl n erasrs fwn anwr. / w r sng u a
vrit o erasrs w r usd o vrs tips o papr.
w l r gg a boklt w xplans e ppr us o ec
o r erasrs. aftr u rd ts boklt, p r
smpls t e tst. w r sr u l us r brn o
erasrs f w o , basd o e rslts o y tsts.
/ w d lik t met y ofc neds n v wa p. b
rg e gd crd, w c sn u e nam a adrs o y
locl crane dlr, ho l b hp t srv u. sy,

(180 words) (s.i. 1.42)

24.14

> *Notetaking Pointer:* **When you are making notes, don't be afraid to use special symbols (brackets, underscores, arrows, etc.), in order to emphasize the importance of different points.**

24.15

> *Notetaking Pointer:* **Listen for special instructions during a lecture; and then go over your notes as soon after a lecture as possible. The sooner you can review such notes, the less you will forget; and the more you will reinforce your learning.**

24.16   Write these high-frequency phrases as rapidly as you can in PS:

	1	2	3
1	to this	he was	in his
2	to come	your order	some of the
3	as well	in order	you need
4	of any	if you have	we know
5	they have	do not	fact that

24.17   The following high-frequency words (Brief Forms) are represented by which letters of the alphabet:

	1	2	3
1	the	that	copy
2	or	every	on
3	as	buy	if
4	quite	no	my
5	we	due	good
6	up	so	is
7	they	will	make

Personal Shorthand

25.1 Theory Review: Again reviewing *s* principles and phonetic abbreviations: The letter *s* represents its own basic sound, the sound of *s* plus *long e;* and the phonetic abbreviations *sh; s,* any short vowel, *s; c,* any short vowel, *s;* and *all* of the *shun* word parts *(sion, tion, cian, shion, cien,* etc.).

25.2 In PS, the letter *t* represents its own basic sound, the sound of *t* plus *long e;* and, in addition, the important phonetic abbreviation, *th.*

25.3 In your practice work, from time to time, you may have questioned why the words *theme* and *thesis* are written *tem* and *tes.* The reason, of course, has to do with the initial *th* sound. For when the *preceding consonant* is representing some sound *other* than its own *basic* sound (in other words, when it is busy doing something *else*), it cannot also carry the *long e* sound.

25.4 In PS, the letter *u* represents the *long u* sound and the *word part* (as well as Brief Form) *under,* as in the word, *underwater.* Actually, the letter *u* has relatively little to do in either longhand or PERSONAL SHORTHAND.

25.5 Here's a chance to practice (and automatize) Brief Form Letter No. 3, again:

Dear Jim: It is quite good that you can also require the information from her and, at the time, see how well[1] she will get the copy to us. As I see it all now, it is up to the gentlemen if they are ever[2] to go out from here and check about that which is as we know it to be. Sincerely,

25.6 See how long it takes you to write paragraph 25.7 in PS. After that, time yourself on paragraph 25.8. Try to determine *why* one paragraph takes more time to write than the other—and which words require some extra practice.

25.7 *Dear Miss Ellington: Thank you for your recent order. We are pleased that you find our services satisfactory and hope that we may continue to serve you in the future.*

Your order should arrive by May 20. May we take this opportunity to remind you of our June sale, an event you will not want to miss. Yours very truly,
(60 words) (s.i. 1.40)

25.8　*Fellow Citizens: Please come to the rescue of our local Little Theater group. These friends and neighbors of yours have worked long and hard to bring good plays to our community. Now they are in need of funds to continue their work.*

Send your donations to the treasurer, Miss Jean Smith; and come to play productions whenever you can. Sincerely,
(60 words) (s.i. 1.40)

25.9　Now see how quickly you can write the letter to Miss Clark in PERSONAL SHORTHAND. It has exactly 120 shorthand words.

Dear Miss Clark: Have you heard about the new program our beauty salons are offering? In June, our customers may use health spa facilities for the small fee of $10.

This fee includes the use of all our exercising equipment, steam baths, electric contour tables, and effective diets. All of this is yours for only $10.

Can you imagine what a course of this type will do for your self-esteem. You will have that self-satisfied feeling that comes from knowing that you look your very best.

If you are interested in this program, return the stamped, self-addressed envelope that is enclosed; and we shall forward one of our brochures at once. Yours very truly, (70)
(120 words) (s.i. 1.42)

25.10　See how many minutes it takes you to *read* the following PS letter:

dmrs ellington:　e spkrs' clb hld tr mtl metg a elcs o ofcrs o s 12. / a ts metg, i spn sm i cvrg e nu spkr trang crs t w v 6 lokg nt f e pst 3 mts.　e mos z m a scnd t w adpt ts pgrm; b, o crs, my mbrs *d n fel e pgrm z wrt e pcs p o $125. aftr csdrb dbat, e mos z finl psd. / i i g t n t sc a wrtwil crs l son b avalb t r mbrs. sn a mjr o e mbrs r n favr o e pln, w l b ab t p i nt us z son z e crs arivs. / i sgst t u csdr e gd lst o nams z p tcrs f e crs. f a l p, w sd f smwn t tc e crs wn e nxt 2 weks. w sd tri t g tgtr wn e nxt cpl o das, t wrk o e finl dtals o ts crs.   yt,* (180 words)

25.11

Notetaking Pointer: **When you are studying on your own, active participation is just as vital as it is in notetaking during a lecture. Recite to yourself—out loud, if possible. Make yourself rephrase what you have just read. Only by so doing can you "participate" to the extent necessary. Here are some steps for studying effectively:**

25.12

Notetaking Pointer: Scan the material you are about to study. Leaf through all of the pages involved, with a quick glance at sections, topics, and paragraph headings. This will give you an idea of the "whole" picture and make your later studying more effective.

25.13

Notetaking Pointer: Understand what you need to know. Even while you are going through the preliminary scanning, stop from time to time, and ask yourself what it is you will need to know in order to fully understand the material involved.

Notetaking Pointer: Pitch in! Now go back through the material carefully, in detail. Slug it out! Read carefully and ask yourself questions. Make an *active* (not passive) thing out of studying.

25.15

> *Notetaking Pointer:* **Express yourself verbally on what you have read. Step by step, topic by topic, state your ideas and reactions to the information you have received.**

25.16

> *Notetaking Pointer:* **Review. The more you can review this material and the more actively you participate in the reviewing of it, the more you will *retain* for testing purposes. If you can only review once, then once will have to do. But if time permits, a half dozen rapid reviews can provide tremendous reinforcement.**

25.17 Write these phrases in PS, several times:

	1	2	3
1	you know	of its	of his
2	at least	over the	from your
3	we want	if you are	on this
4	as you	we have been	we hope that
5	hear from you	does not	into the

25.18 Which letters of the alphabet represent the following high-frequency words (Brief Forms)?

	1	2	3
1	possible	what	have
2	at	been	find
3	had	know	made
4	are	did	glad
5	how	see	time
6	us	well	about
7	there	credit	here

Personal Shorthand

26.1 Theory Review: In PERSONAL SHORTHAND, the letter *v* represents its own basic sound and, in addition, the sound of *v* plus *long e*—and nothing more. No phonetic abbreviations have been assigned to it. Like the letter *u, v* has relatively little to do, in either longhand or PERSONAL SHORTHAND.

26.2 The letter *w* represents its own basic sound, the sound of *w* plus *long e*, and the phonetic abbreviations *wh* (as in *where*), *ou,* (as in *cloud*), *ow* (as in *cow),* and *aw* (as in *raw*).

26.3 The letter *x* represents its own basic sound and the sound of *x(z)* plus *long e.* No phonetic abbreviations have been assigned to this letter.

26.4 In PS, the letter *y* represents its own basic sound, the sound of *y* plus *long e,* and the phonetic abbreviations *oi* and *oy* (as in *boil* and *toy*).

26.5 Although no phonetic abbreviations have been assigned to it, the letter *z* represents its own basic sound, the sound of *z* plus *long e,* and, on occasion, it carries a kind of *zh* sound, as in the word *azure.*

26.6 Now let's practice Brief Form Letter No. 4. Write it in PS several times.

Dear Mr. Kerr: By and by we will receive the order copy; and if it is not too good, we can take what we have made,[1] if and when we have the time. The copy has not been dated, but I would be glad to do so, if it were to be[2] made an order by me or her, and we had the check to see. He was to receive the required information,[3] but at no time was he to receive that kind of letter. I know it to be so. All in all, that was[4] to be a kind of credit check about which we are very pleased. Sincerely,

26.7 Write this letter in PS; then practice any troublesome words several times:

Dear Mr. Scott: I believe that you must have overlooked something at the end of last month. We have not yet received your payment on your automobile. This obligation is now fifteen days past due.

We are confident that you will place your check in the amount of $90 in the mail today. Don't delay--pay today. Sincerely yours,
(60 words) (s.i. 1.42)

26.8   Now write this paragraph in PS:

Just a few words make all the difference between the courteous person and the person who lacks good manners. Some people are rude because they have never learned small courtesies that are so important in a good relationship between friends, with older people, and with parents. A few friendly words can make all the difference in the world.
(60 words) (s.i. 1.42)

26.9   See how many minutes it takes you to write the following 120-word article in paragraph 26.10. Lesson by lesson, it is a good idea to make a list of the words that cause you to hesitate when writing PS—and then practice those words several times.

26.10   *When you transcribe letters from machines, you probably will run into one big problem--the dictator. Many times he has not listened to how his voice sounds on the machine; therefore, he does not speak clearly. He mumbles or speaks with an accent, which makes it hard to understand what is being said.*

Dictating with a cigar or cigarette in one's mouth also makes it difficult for typists. It is also easier for typists if dictators spell out technical words and tricky names.

The dictator should indicate changes as he goes along, rather than at the end of the tape or belt. The latter procedure may cause the typist to have to retype the entire letter.
(120 words) (s.i. 1.44)

26.11   How fast can you read the following PS article (180 shorthand words)?

t r crtn trats w mrk e g wrkr. frst (1st), e wrks ttfl. e keps z min o o e

i dg. e i alwas tnkg a y e i dg ts wrk
a w i rlats t e bsn z a hol. / scn (2n),
e g wrkr i acrt. n wn (1) i brn w ts gl.
i mst b dvlpd t e pyn wr i bcs hbt. e wa
t acgir an hbt i b rpts, w atns, ntl e
rit wa bcs scn natr. / trd (3rd), e g
wrkr wrks cstnl a ctnusl. fr t my ppl
wrk b fts a strts. y bgn smtg, b alw
tmslvs t b dstrkd f o y r dg. t r plnt
o ppl ho r g nf (enf) strtrs, b mit fu
ho kep o wrkg ctnusl, ntl y v cpltd e jb.
/ n ads t tes trats, e g wrkr i l cratv.
e brgs nt bg ids f gg tgs dn. e c s o
ot t b dn a tn tnk u was o gg i dn.

(180 words) (s.i. 1.42)

26.12

Notetaking Pointer: **Let's review the important study steps again: 1) Scan the material; 2) Understand what you need to know; 3) Pitch in!; 4) Express yourself verbally on that which you have read; 5) Review. To keep these five steps in mind, think of the key word - SUPER!**

26.13

Notetaking Pointer: **When making notes from printed material, find the author's central idea. Usually there is only one key idea per paragraph, although occasionally there may be two or three.**

26.14

> *Notetaking Pointer:* In studying from textbooks or other printed materials, there often is a tendency to copy verbatim. Where a direct quotation is required, this is justifiable; but usually you will be screening and scanning for *key points* and *concepts*. It is far better to make such notes in your own words.

26.15

> *Notetaking Pointer:* In the first place, the making of notes in your own words requires that you think for yourself, that you select, that you analyze, interpret, and relate. It is this active participation that reinforces your learning. If you merely *copy,* there is little participation—and therefore little *learning*—that can take place.

26.16   Practice writing these phrases in PS:

	1	2	3
1	we cannot	I should like	we are sure
2	of it	send us	of their
3	to keep	send you	thank you
4	from our	it has	we feel
5	after the	he will	that it is

26.17   Which letters of the alphabet represent the following high-frequency words (Brief Forms)?

	1	2	3
1	return	wish	information
2	now	letter	would
3	to	man	men
4	receive	give	was
5	but	order	enclose
6	in	were	check
7	date	every	with

Personal Shorthand

CARDINAL SERIES

27.1 Theory Review: All word *beginnings* and word *endings* can be written according to the theory principles introduced in Lessons 1-8. However, there are a few, high-frequency word beginnings that may be *abbreviated* somewhat, but only if it seems natural and convenient for you to do so. Certainly, you never are wrong when you write *word beginnings* according to the abbreviating principles introduced in the first 8 lessons.

27.2 For the sake of convenience, however, the word beginning *em* may be written *m, except before vowels.*

27.3 *The word beginning im* may be written *m,* except before another *m.*

27.4 The word beginning *um* may be written simply *m,* at any time.

27.5 Now see how smoothly and rapidly you can write Brief Form Letter No. 1 in PS. Perhaps you have it memorized by now. If so, you'll write it that much faster.

27.6 *Gentlemen: Thank you for the information enclosed with your check. I did not know that you would buy the copy at[1] our price. We are pleased with your order and will see that you receive a credit. Do you wish to buy on time just now;[2] or, if possible, would you require us to be there on that very date? Sincerely yours,*

27.7 Write this letter in PS. Time yourself:

Dear Paul: A number of important subjects were brought up at the last meeting. I wish you had been there.

The question of purchasing more property was again mentioned. I know your opinion in this matter is that we definitely should not go further into debt. In general, I believe most of the members take that view. Yours truly,
(60 words) (s.i. 1.42)

27.8　This article has the same number of shorthand words as the preceding letter. Write it in PS and compare your "time" with paragraph 27.7

We must try to understand what we listen to in the classroom, so we can remember the main ideas. We seldom rehear the same lecture. Because we forget, it is essential for us to take good notes while we are listening. Good listening and good notetaking go hand in hand. Active listening is the essence of good notetaking.
(60 words) (s.i. 1.42)

27.9　How quickly can you write the following letter (120 shorthand words) in PERSONAL SHORTHAND?

27.10　*Dear Mr. Crandall: The Save More Drug Company is sending you, with our compliments, the enclosed sample of Imperial Shave Cream.*

This is a new product on the market; one we believe you should have an opportunity to try. You are probably already familiar with the outstanding qualities of this shave cream, due to the extensive advertising campaign launched on all local radio and television stations.

If you find you are pleased with this new type of shave cream and want to purchase more, Save More Drug Company will be keeping a good supply in stock.

Please use this sample with our compliments. We hope you will come in and visit our store soon. Yours truly,
(120 words) (s.i. 1.45)

27.11　Now read (or *transcribe*) the following letter:

ddr hilton: v u v sen a yg by wkg homwrd aftr scol, tro wn (1) o e ls dsirb pts o twn? z e trgs alg, z stps bc slor. e i n anxss t g hom bcs t i n plac f h t pla n z nabrhod, n plac t us z pn-u nrg, n plac t cltvat z cratv ntrsts. / f e ctzns o ts cmunt hop t v yg ppl gro t mhod a wmhod w a hlty olok o lif, tn tr cildhod mst b m scr f e

dagrs o t mc idl i a t frgnl idl hns. /
e fmas o a yg ppl's clb d d mc t hlp tes
bys a grls st tr gols hi a t pmt tm t
lok fwrd t a stsfig a rwrdg adlt lif.
won' u p csdr hlpg ts wrtwil eft b sng a
sbstnsl donas t e yg ppl's clb w i bg
orgnizd n y nabrhod? / t u f an astn u c
w g u. sy,   (180 words) (s.i. 1.42)

27.12

> *Notetaking Pointer:* In making notes, write down as many of the *essentials* as possible—and as few of the *unessentials*.

27.13

> *Notetaking Pointer:* That does not mean that you can do completely away with all of the short words (to, of, at, etc.); but to the extent possible, stick to the *important* words—and ideas—and eliminate the *unimportant*.

27.14

> *Notetaking Pointer:* There is a danger of being *too* brief. Notes that are too brief sometimes are unintelligible. Make sure that you can effectively review what you are laboriously writing.

27.15   Practice writing these phrases in PERSONAL SHORTHAND:

	1	2	3
1	why not	you have been	I can
2	in fact	on you	and are
3	how much	was not	for me
4	and will	if there is	about it
5	have you	I received	any time

27.16   The following high-frequency words (Brief Forms) are represented by which letters of the alphabet?

	1	2	3
1	now	wish	information
2	to	letter	would
3	receive	man	men
4	but	give	was
5	about	order	enclose
6	in	were	check
7	date	too	now

Personal Shorthand

CARDINAL SERIES

28.1 Theory Review: The word beginning *in* may be represented by *n*, except before another *n*.

28.2 The word beginning *un* may be represented by *n*, except before another *n*.

28.3 The word beginning *en* may be written simply *n*, *at any time*.

28.4 The word beginning *ex* may be represented by the letter *x*, at any time, because the *e*, of course, is *silent*.

28.5 Practice writing Brief Form Letter No. 2 until you can write it automaticallty:

Dear Sir: If our check is due, we will find men to return the letter; but what if they are not under my[1] *orders? I can see the good in it, and I am very willing to come and make it possible for him to give*[2] *his information; but I do not see why every man is here at the time. Cordially,*

28.6 Write the following letter (60 shorthand words) in PS:

Dear Miss Smith: We are happy to welcome you to our family of credit card members. We received all of the necessary forms and are glad to issue you the enclosed card.

We hope you can use your new credit card during our January clearance sale. Members will receive advance notice of all our special sales.
(60 words) (s.i. 1.42)

28.7 This article contains the same number of shorthand words as the letter in paragraph 28.6. See if you can improve your speed as you write it in PS:

When you take dictation, the dictator often gives you the original letter. Place a figure at the top of this letter that matches the figure at the beginning of your shorthand notes. Then place the letter beside you, face down. This saves writing in your shorthand notes the entire address of the person to whom the letter is going. (60 words) (s.i. 1.42)

28.8   In how many minutes (or seconds) can you write the follow-
       ing letter in PERSONAL SHORTHAND?

28.9   *Dear Mr. Johnson: When you have finished reading the
       enclosed contract, I am sure you will want to confer with Mr.
       Parnell about the details.*

       *I hope you will compare notes and make any comments or
       suggestions you feel will accomplish your goal, and then
       return it to me. I hope you will find no room for complaint
       and will complete the contract as soon as possible.*

       *You will notice that each clause contains ample space for
       complete descriptive analysis and consists of detailed
       outlines to insure thorough understanding on the part of all
       the contract members.*

       *We shall continue to work on this contract until you are
       completely satisfied with it. Very truly yours,*
       (120 words) (s.i. 1.46)

28.10 Time yourself and see how long it takes you to read (or
       transcribe) the following letter:

*dm packwood: ystrda i tkd w mr. paul
bart o y vg dprtm.   e nfmd m t y lst
spm f u z n a cplt wn (1).   w asrd h t
r spg dprtm d trac e spm t dscvr e 10
(tn) msg pkgs. / w r crtn t w sl b ab
t f tes msg itms.   v mt w sn hndrds
(100's) o pcls t locass n e wstrn
stats, a w v onl lst 13 spms n e lst
30 yrs.   w fel ts z b a g rcrd o dlvrs.
/ w l k v eft t locat y msg pkgs wn e
nxt 24 hrs.   f r src ks lgr, w l notf u
o r efts dal.   z son z r spg dprtm i
ab t dtrm o hpnd t e 10 (tn) msg pkgs,
w l cl u a wn. / w sl k v eft t stl ts
mtr gkl a t y cplt stsfcs.   w hop u l*

ctnu t d bsn w u n e futr. cy,

(180 words) (s.i. 1.44)

28.11

> *Notetaking Pointer:* When taking notes, don't forget to use standard longhand abbreviations. For example: UN (United nations); TVA (Tennessee Valley Authority); CPA (Certified Public Accountant); i.e. (that is), etc.

28.12

> *Notetaking Pointer:* Abbreviations are fine—and are in wider and wider use today—but make sure that you use abbreviations with which you are familiar—and which you can read back!

28.13

> *Notetaking Pointer:* When taking notes in a lecture class, at a meeting, a discussion, or in the library, don't be afraid to take *more* notes than you might need. There is never any real danger of your having *too many* notes; but it is very easy to have *too few;* and having too few notes can be far more wasteful (from a time and learning standpoint) than having too many.

28.14   Write these phrases in PS until you can write them automatically:

	1	2	3
1	I have been	he is	thank you for
2	we shall be	this letter	on the market
3	let us know	of time	to him
4	at all times	are not	to find
5	years ago	and our	it has been
6	we should like	of them	as possible
7	send me	I shall be	give you

28.15 Which letters of the alphabet represent these high-frequency words (Brief Forms)?

	1	2	3
1	with	when	an
2	you	dear	go
3	why	sincerely	I
4	thank	all	take
5	just	can	price
6	very	of	an
7	be	for	her

Personal Shorthand

CARDINAL SERIES

29.1 Theory Review: The common word beginnings *intr*, *inter*, and even *intro* (including *long o*) may be abbreviated *ntr*.

29.2 The word beginning *post* contains a *long o* sound; however, *pst* provides a very handy and workable abbreviation.

29.3 Though the word beginnings *super* and *supr* frequently include half-long or *long u* sounds, it is both convenient and practical to represent these beginnings with *spr*.

29.4 See how quickly you can write Brief Form Letter No. 3 in PS:

Dear Jim: It is quite good that you can also require the information from her and, at the time, see how well[1] she will get the copy to us. As I see it all now, it is up to the gentlemen if they are ever[2] to go out from here and check about that which is as we know it to be. Sincerely,

29.5 Can you write the following letter in PS (60 words) without hesitating on any word or phrase?

Gentlemen: Yesterday my daughter and I visited your department store. When I purchased some articles of clothing, I must have put my coat on the counter. After we were several miles from Long Beach, I discovered my coat was missing. Could you please let me know if anyone has turned in the coat to your office. Very truly yours,
(60 words) (s.i. 1.42)

29.6 As you write this letter in PERSONAL SHORTHAND, compare your speed with the letter in paragraph 29.5. Always practice writing any word or phrase that causes you to hesitate.

29.7 *Dear Doctor Sampson: We wish to express our sincere appreciation for your choice of the Hotel Washington on your recent trip to Dallas, Texas. It was a privilege to have been of service to you, and we look forward to the pleasure of your again being our guest the next time you are in the area. Very truly yours,* *(60 words) (s.i. 1.42)*

29.8　The next letter has twice as many words as those in paragraphs 29.5 and 29.7. How fast can you write it? Analyze the reason for any hesitation.

29.9　*Dear Mr. Hanson: I hope it will not embarrass you if I ask you to sign the enclosed contract and return it to us.*

It has often happened before that an applicant has omitted his signature from the employment contract; therefore, we hope you will not get the impression or feeling that we are implying you are the first. This situation has occurred many times before. Perhaps more emphasis needs to be placed on this part of the contract.

It is important that a large company like ours makes a good impression on people; therefore, anything you say that will help us to improve our image will be greatly appreciated. Yours very truly,
(120 words) (s.i. 1.47)

29.10　How long will it take you to transcribe (or read) the following PERSONAL SHORTHAND letter?

dm garrett: d u b ntrstd n rdg sm mtrls t l k y min awa f y bsn a vda hpngs? f u r, tn u l b ntrstd n r brosr, <u>favrt vacass</u>. n ts brosr, u l rd artcls a plas a sns t r a jy t tnk a. / <u>favrt vacass</u> c b usd f rfrn e ntir yr. u l njy rdg a e wrm ars o sprt a rlxas t apl t tos lokg f a wrm climt drg e wntr mts. t r l my nfmtv artcls a vacas spts wr u c "bt e ht" drg e smr mts. / ts brosr l b rd son, a w l sn i t u fre o crg. l u ned d i fl o a mal e gd rsrvas crd f u d lik a c. w rqst t u sn n ts crd pmptl, s w ma b sr t v nf brosrs t fl l rqsts n e brosr i rd f malg. sy, (180 words) (s.i. 1.45)

29.11

> *Notetaking Pointer:* Use 5x3 cards when making research notes, or when digesting (condensing) more voluminous notes, for ready review. 5x3 cards lend themselves to effective organization of notes and to quick and easy review.

29.12

> *Notetaking Pointer:* When taking notes from printed materials, be particularly careful to indicate your sources. The source may be of no help to you from the standpoint of preparing for an examination, but it is vital that you have such information when preparing a research paper; and, all in all, you will find it a helpful habit for the future.

29.13

> *Notetaking Pointer:* When using 5x3 cards for notetaking, use some kind of identification or "catch line" in the upper left corner. This will make the organization and reorganization of your notes much easier and will facilitate the quick review of notes, prior to an examination.

29.14 See how quickly and easily you can write these important phrases in PS:

	1	2	3
1	if you can	and is	we hope
2	as soon as possible	which will	I should
3	I wish	what is	at this
4	before the	if your	at this time
5	up to date	for it	in addition
6	I could	out of the	has not
7	with which	there was	very glad

29.15 Which letters of the alphabet represent these high-frequency words (or Brief Forms)?

	1	2	3
1	her	under	do
2	he	your	she
3	our	that	also
4	his	gentlemen	come
5	enclose	ever	out
6	require	by	was
7	which	not	from

Personal Shorthand

30.1   *Theory Review:* It is important to remember that *all* word *beginnings* can be written phonetically. The short cuts to which you were introduced, are *not* required—they are *optional.* If they seem natural, convenient, and easy for you to use—then use them. But it is never wrong to write word beginnings phonetically, without use of the short cuts. However, it may cost you precious time.

30.2   Remember—*primarily* we are interested in how a word sounds—and only secondarily, in how it *looks!* Don't be mislead by the "spelling" of a word. Your objective is to write the word—by *sound*—as fast as you can.

30.3   Here is Brief Form Letter No. 4 again. See if you can write it without the slightest hesitation.

30.4   *Dear Mr. Kerr: By and by we will receive the order copy; and if it is not too good, we can take what we have[1] made, if and when we have the time. The copy has not been dated, but I would be glad to do so, if it were to be[2] made an order by me or her, and we had the check to see. He was glad to receive the required information,[3] but at no time was he to receive that kind of letter. I know it to be so. All in all, that was[4] to be a kind of credit check about which we are very pleased. Sincerely,*

30.5   Write this letter in PERSONAL SHORTHAND:

Gentlemen: Please send me a copy of your booklet entitled, How to Get a Well-Paying Job in Ten Days. Enclosed is 25 cents. I understand you will refund double this amount to me if I cannot get a well-paying job within ten days after I receive the booklet and have read it thoroughly. Very sincerely yours, (60 words) (s.i. 1.45)

30.6   This next article has the same number of words as the letter in paragraph 30.5. Can you write it just as fast? Faster?

30.7   *Footnotes have two basic purposes. One is to give credit to the source of a fact or a theory used in a research paper. To use someone else's ideas without giving him credit is plagiarizing or stealing. Footnotes are also used to tell the reader where the information can be found, if he wants to find more details.*
(s.i. 1.45)

30.8   This letter is twice as long as the article in paragraph 30.7. Will it take you twice as long to write it in PS?

Dear Miss Drake: Your letter of June 5, regarding a position with our company, reached me today. I would appreciate it if you could come in and see me concerning the possibility of your joining our staff as a secretary.

Your uncle, Tom Field, spoke to me about you two months ago. He spoke highly of you and said that you would be available upon graduation from high school.

Until I talk with our personnel department, I cannot say whether there is an opening in our company where we can take advantage of your training.

Please call me at your convenience and arrange for a visit to discuss your letter. Yours very truly,
(s.i. 1.49)

30.9   See how fast you can read the following letter. If you have the opportunity to do so, transribe it in pen or pencil or (better still) at the typewriter.

30.10   *dmrs roy: sn u wrk n dwntwn dnvr, i d b xtrml cvnn f u t opn a savgs acwn (acct.) a e lncn savgs bnk n e dwntwn ara. ts brnc i locatd o e crnr o 23d stret (st.) a stat avnu (ave.). / sn ts ofc i alwas (lwas) opn m tro f, f 9 am to 7 pm, u c esl c n drg cfe braks, lnc, r aftr wrk, t trnsk an bsn. f u r n n e dwntwn ara a s t us wn (1) o r bnks, t r 5 otr brncs locatd troo dnvr. u l b lcd (wlcd) a an* *o tes ofs. / u c alwas (lwas) xpk a "g dl" a an lncn savgs bnk. r latst dvdn i 5 % pad (pd.) f e da o dpst o blns o $10 r mr (mor). u psn lws, ts i e bst dvdn w c g. / c n a lt u opn a acwn (acct.) f u. w d lc (wlc) e oprtunt o dg bsn w u. vty,* (s.i. 1.46)

30.11

Notetaking Pointer: When preparing for an examination: 1) review lecture notes as soon after the lecture as
possible; 2) do not be content with a single review of
notes but review them as many times as possible; 3)
last-minute review prior to an exam, usually increases
frustration; 4) in reviewing your notes before an examination, remember to review "actively," rather than
"passively." Recite to yourself. Ask yourself questions.
When in doubt, make yourself go back and find the proper answer.

30.12

Notetaking Pointer: If your notes for a particular subject are especially voluminous and detailed, it is extremely helpful to make a digest or condensation of
these notes, reducing the new set of notes to only the
key ideas and concepts.

30.13   Here are more important phrases to automatize in PS:

	1	2	3
1	to change	we hope you will	we may have
2	we may be	in it	to be able
3	and was	of you	you must
4	to serve you	to consider	next time
5	send them	this means	I suggest
6	you will not	this information	we could not
7	to fit	we shall be able	send them

30.14   Which letters of the alphabet represent these extremely im-
         portant and high-frequency words (Brief Forms)?

	1	2	3
1	me	him	we
2	get	the	up
3	it	or	they
4	kind	his	that
5	price	require	every
6	please	as	buy
7	and	quite	by

Personal Shorthand

31.1   *Theory Review:*

31.2

> **Rule 1. Never write a silent vowel.**
>   **EXAMPLES:** kite · kit   boat · bot

31.3

> **Rule 2. Even a sounding vowel *within* a word should be omitted unless it has the long sound of *a, e, i, o, u*, or *oo*. Normally, the long sound of *e* may be assigned to any preceding consonant.**
>   **EXAMPLES:** bet · bt   cat · ct
> *Note:* Treat a half-long vowel as a short vowel and omit it.
>   **EXAMPLE:** more · mr

31.4

> **Rule 3. Always write a sounding vowel whenever it occurs at the very *beginning* of a word.**
>   **EXAMPLES:** acre · acr   abate · abat

31.5

> *Transcription Pointers:* **The Comma.**
>   The comma is the most frequently used mark of punctuation. It denotes a mild break in thought, and it is the weakest mark of punctuation. However, since the clarity of a sentence depends upon its placement, the comma is one of the most important marks of punctuation.

31.6

Use the comma:

1. To separate words, phrases, or clauses in a series.

Friends, employees, and executives attended the meeting.

A thorough study of words is essential for the businessman, for teachers, and for students.

If one desires to understand business, if one wants to teach business subjects, or if one wishes to acquire a broader education, one should study economics.

2. To set off introductory words, phrases, or clauses.

On the contrary, it is better that the orginal plan be adopted.

When you are in the city, please call my office.

Meanwhile, I shall keep you informed about our progress.

3. To separate adjectives equal in rank and modifying the same noun.

A large, black, foreign car was demonstrated by the salesman.

4. To separate co-ordinate clauses joined by simple conjunctions.

Use a comma to separate clauses joined by the conjunctions *and, but, for, or, nor,* or *either.*

For the present, we plan to maintain production at the same level, and we hope that this action will have your approval.

We do not assume responsibility for any changes in the specifications, but we shall be pleased to give you the benefit of our advice.

31.7   See how easily and quickly you can write the following article in PERSONAL SHORTHAND:

A poor school attendance record could keep you from getting the job you want. Some businesses ask to see attendance records of young people who are being considered for employment. They feel that if a student has developed a pattern of poor attendance in school, he may follow this pattern on the job and will not be dependable.
(60 words) (s.i. 1.45)

31.8   Can you improve your speed in writing the following 60-word letter in PS?

Dear Mr. Barnes: Thank you for your letter of May 9, in which you inform us of a difference of $65 between your records and ours.

In order to find the reason for this difference, will you please return your statement and canceled checks for the period in which the discrepancy exists. Thank you for your help. Sincerely,
(60 words) (s.i. 1.45)

31.9   This letter contains 120 words. How fast can you write it in PERSONAL SHORTHAND?

Dear Mrs. Nelson: Thank you for your letter of January 27, in which you requested the prices of brief form charts and other materials that could be displayed in your beginning shorthand class. Our company makes various types of charts and other materials that could be used in your classroom. Rather than listing them all here, we have chosen to send you our latest catalog of these materials. If you would like to receive any of the items in this catalog, simply fill out and return the enclosed order blank. We shall be happy to fill your order at that time. Thank you for your interest in our material. Cordially,
(120 words) (s.i. 1.50)

31.10 Now see how quickly (and accurately) you can transcribe the following article. Check your punctuation, as well as your spelling. Transcription requires a good command of punctuation and spelling—as well as the ability to read shorthand fluently.

31.11 *ec gnras o amrcn ut z is on ida o advntr. n a yg m h a dsir t s e wrld, my yrs ag, e jynd e nav r bcam a arlin pilt. 2 cntrs ag, wv, my yg m fwn xcitm a ncdnl agird tr bsn educas b crg a pdlr's pk a trvlg f stlm t stlm troo e wldrn. / most o tes pdlrs cam f nu egln, bcs t z wr my sml mfctrg ntrpris w crd o. y h t b rkls a srod yg flos, ho cd k cr o tmslvs o wild a rf trals, etg a slepg n e opn a facg my dagrs. / wil y ld a lonsm lif o e tral, y w asrd o a hrt wlc (lc) f e stlrs n y cam u t tr dors. cldrn d stp plag, e wm d lv tr hwshold crs, a e m d k i f tr wrk t gtr arwn e pdlr t hr z tals a t xm z wrs.* (180 words) (s.i. 1.47)

31.12　Practice writing the following phrases in PS. You should be able to write them (and transcribe them) without hesitation.

	1	2	3
1	will be glad	it is worthwhile	as long
2	which you	gave me	has made
3	for your letter	from his	to give us
4	who can	help you	from which
5	this month	any information	he would
6	as a result	how many	will be glad
7	we find	in a position	gave me

31.13　Practice speedbuilding on Brief Form letters No. 1 and No. 2:

31.14　*No.1*

Gentlemen: Thank you for the information enclosed with your check. I did not know that you would buy the copy at[1] our price. We are pleased with your order and will see that you receive a credit. Do you wish to buy on time just now;[2] or, if possible, would you require us to be there on that very date? Sincerely yours,

No.2

Dear Sir: If our check is due, we will find men to return the letter; but what if they are not under my[1] orders? I can see the good in it, and I am very willing to come and make it possible for him to give[2] his information; but I do not see why every man is here at the time. Cordially,

31.15   Practice calling the Brief Forms for these high-frequency
        words:

	1	2	3	4
1	an	he	her	have
2	buy	for	can	up
3	due	with	all	out
4	find	time	the	there
5	about	thank	his	my
6	what	and	require	is
7	return	please	be	well
8	but	when	had	now
9	under	put	order	that

Personal Shorthand

32.1   *Theory Review:*

32.2

> **Rule. 4. If a word contains a double vowel, write only
> *one*.**
>   **EXAMPLES: broom · brom   book · bok   feed · fed**

32.3

> **Rule 5. Omit silent consonants within a word; and if a
> word contains a double consonant, write only *one*.**
>   **EXAMPLES: right · rit   planner · plnr**

32.4

> **Rule 6. A sounding vowel at the end of a word should
> be written.**
> *Exception:* **The letter *y* at the end of a word is carried by
> the preceding consonant, unless it has a long *i* sound.**
>   **EXAMPLES: idea · ida   berry · br   cry · cri**

32.5

> *Transcription Pointers:* **The Comma (continued).**
>   **Use the comma:**
>
> **1. To set off nonrestrictive clauses. A nonrestrictive
> clause adds an additional thought to the sentence and
> may be omitted without destroying its meaning.**
>   *Your company, which has an outstanding record, is
> invited to take part in the conference.*
>   *Your company_____is invited
> to take part in the conference.*
> **However, a restrictive clause defines the topic; thus
> the comma is not used in this case.**

Any item that does not measure up to standard must be discarded.

2. In direct address.

I believe, Mr. Morrow, that you will find our prices satisfactory.
Miss Smith, will you please read the minutes.

3. To set off parenthetical expressions.

You should, of course, consider all offers.
Mr. Schaffer, I believe that is his name, said he would call you later this afternoon.

4. In pointing off quotations, figures, reference lists, names and titles, dates, etc.

He said, "I shall be at the office on Monday," but he did not appear.

Note: An indirect quotation does not require a comma

He said he would read the paper.

$3,500	*11,000 shares*
150,000 miles	*2,350,000 population*

Note exceptions:

Insurance Policy No. 786432	*Page 1096*
373-7600	*1300 Second Avenue*

Abbot, Paul D.
Anderson, Carl S.

Robert Sheldon Reynolds, A.B., M.A., Ph.D.

July 4, 1776

5. After namely, viz., that is, etc. introducing an illustration.

The income statement will show approximately the same amount for sales; namely, $400,000 for the first quarter.

32.6   Write this short article in PS:

Have you ever stopped and thought about your future career? Sometimes it is difficult for a person still in high school to think seriously about a vocation, but the serious student should give consideration to his future now.

The school counselor is the ideal person to look to for guidance. She is well trained in this field.
(60 words) (s.i. 1.48)

32.7   Now see if you can write this short letter (with the same number of words) even faster:

Dear Miss Jones: Yes, we do have a vacancy for a business teacher in the areas of typing and shorthand, and we would be glad to see your credentials.

I am enclosing an application form that you should fill out and return to us. We will arrange an interview when your credentials and application have arrived. Sincerely,
(60 words) (s.i. 1.48)

32.8   Time yourself (or have someone time you) as you write the following 120-word article in PERSONAL SHORTHAND:

Whenever you make a telephone call, always have all of the necessary information at hand. In this way, you are ready to talk when the individual called is on the line. When you place long-distance calls through an operator, you should also have any information ready that the operator may require.

If you are making a long-distance call for your boss, reach an understanding with her that she should stay in her office until the call is either completed or a report has been received that the individual cannot be reached at that time.

In any telephone conversation, remember to use tact, courtesy, and a friendly manner.
(120 words) (s.i.. 1.54)

32.9   What is your best "time" for reading (or transcribing) 180-word PS letters like the following?

32.10   *d mary: v u hrd o e wndrf trp t sally a i r kg ts smr? z u n, sl tcs hstr a strn orgn clg a z alwas (lwas) wnd t vst sm o e hstrcl lnmrks n ts cntr a abrd. / ts yr sl vd e baker awrd, w l pmt u t trvl n e unitd stats (u.s.) a egln (eng.), xpn fre. i sems almost (lmost) t g t b tro. r frst (1st) stp, o crs, l b wsgtn, wr w pln t vst cgrs;*

tn o t lxgtn a jamestwn. / o ag 27, w
sal o e u.s.s. amrca, f grat brtn, wr
w l sta 3 weks a oxfd. tn w sl vst
bckghm plc bf rg t e unitd stats (u.s.).
/ i sd b a trlg xprn, a i m lokg fwrd t
i. nxt yr w r hopg t vst cnda (can.) a
hwie (hi), a tn r trvlg l b dn. i sl
sn u svrl pst crds t kep u nfmd o r
trvls. yvt, (180 words) (s.i. 1.47)

32.11 Practice these phrases until you can react to them (in writing PS or reading it) without the slightest hesitation.

	1	2	3
1	of those	in the market	it would
2	you see	by this	I have had
3	among the	if you do not	that they are
4	as much	was the	as yet
5	that have	more and more	in order that
6	from us	we must	inform you
7	do it	we do	for yourself

32.12 Now see how fast (and automatcially) you can write Brief Form Letters No. 3 and No.4.

32.13 *No. 3*
Dear Jim: It is quite good that you can also require the information from her and at the time, see how well she will get the copy to us. As I see it all now, it is up to the gentlemen if they are ever to go out from here and check about that which is as we know it to be. Sincerely.

32.14 *No. 4*
Dear Mr. Kerr: By and by we will receive the order copy; and if it is not too good, we can take what we have made, if and

when we have the time. The copy has not been dated, but I would be glad to do so, if it were to be made an order by me or by her, and we had the check to see. He was to receive the required information, but at no time was he to receive that kind of letter. I know it to be so. All in all, that was to be a kind of credit check about which we are very pleased. Sincerely,

32.15   How many seconds will it take you to call (or write) the Brief Forms for these high-frequency words?

	1	2	3	4
1	him	very	come	make
2	at	check	information	too
3	price	if	men	get
4	copy	credit	were	no
5	also	quite	am	dear
6	go	been	know	made
7	why	so	enclose	us
8	which	ever	how	we
9	by	just	date	in

Personal Shorthand

33.1　*Theory Review:*

33.2　Phonetic Abbreviations. In addition to representing their own basic sounds, carrying a long *e* sound, and carrying the final *y* (unless it has a long *i* sound), a number of consonants also are used to represent certain phonetic units or word parts:

33.3　*Phonetic Abbreviations:*　　　　　　　　　　*Word Examples:*

　　　b = -ble　　　　　　　　　　*trou**ble** · **trb***

　　　c = ch-, -ch, com-,　　　*church ·crc; compel · cpl*
　　　　　con-　　　　　　　　　*continue ·ctnu*
　　　　　(k), (s)

　　　f = ph-, -ph, for-, -for,　*phone · **fon**; form · **fm**; helpful ·*
　　　　　-ful,　　　　　　　　　***hlpf**;*
　　　　　-ify　　　　　　　　　　*magnify ·**mgnf**;*
　　　　　　　　　　　　　　　　*magnified ·**mgnfd***

　　　g = -ng, -ing, -dge　　　*sing · **sg**; singing ·**sgg**; fudge ·*
　　　　　-nge　　　　　　　　　***fg**; singe ·**sg**; danger ·**dagr***

　　　k = -ct　　　　　　　　　　*act · **ak**; conduct ·**cdk***

33.4

Transcription Pointers: **The Period.**

　Use the period:

1. After a complete declarative or imperative sentence.

　The bank closes at three o' clock.
　Please send us your remittance before the first of the month.

2. After an abbreviation.

　William A. Beck, M.D., has an office in Boston, MA.

3. For miscellaneous uses.

　As a decimal:

　The pavement was 22.5 feet wide.

> Between dollars and cents:
>
> *The price was $12.95*
>
> To show an omission of words or sentences (ellipses):
>
> *The wide use of tests...indicates their importance for measuring performance.*
>
> *Note:* Do not use the period after percent or a Roman numeral in a sentence.
>
> *In Book III, there are a number of one-hundred percent tests.*

33.5   See how quickly you can write this next article (60 shorthand words) in PS; practice any troublesome words several times.

33.6   *There are many clubs available for high school membership. One of these clubs is called FBLA, which stands for Future Business Leaders of America. This hard-working club is tailor-made for students with a desire to know more about the business world. Many worthwhile projects are planned every year, and working on the projects is fun.*
(60 words) (s.i.) (s.i. 1.48)

33.7   The following article is comprised of 60 shorthand words. Can you improve your speed on this one? (How do you plan to write the words *corporation, ownership, outstanding, permanent?*)

33.8   *When you buy stock in a corporation, you are buying a share in the ownership. The extent of that ownership depends on the number of shares you own in relation to the number of shares outstanding. The money paid into a corporation for common stock becomes the permanent capital of the firm. It is not paid back.*
(60 words) (s.i. 1.48)

33.9   The next article contains 120 shorthand words. Can you write it in two minutes or less? "Preview" the more difficult words before you start!

33.10   *In order to write about any subject effectively, the writer must have something to say and be able to say it in words that are commonly used when talking about the subject. When writing in business, the writer should use words and phrases that have business connotations. When writing about medical situations, the physician should use medical terms and phrases.*

When material is written that conveys the thought clearly and accurately, it is good writing. We need to use short, simple, and sincere words, so that people will understand what we are saying. The trouble is that some people write primarily to impress others, rather than to inform.
(120 words) (s.i. 1.55)

33.11   The following PERSONAL SHORTHAND article is comprised of 180 shorthand words. See how long it takes you to *read* it—or to *transcribe* it with pen, pencil, or at the typewriter.

33.12   *t i mr n lif tn e mr kg o dlrs r e bg o fnc gs, sc z atmobls a tlvs sts. lif csts n grat pt n e stsfcss u ma g f y wrk, pla, hom, a cpnns. i i e hop o pctcl edcas t l l lrn sm o tes tgs bf y lv tr bsn trang crs n hi scol r clg. / t r my scsf bsn ppl. e wns (1's) t r trol scsf, wv, r n nrl v cas tos ho v smtg abv e mr tcncl skl n tr trad r ocpas. a bsn mplye wo psnl i n e k t gs t e tp n a cosn crer. tos lkg n g egls, g pnmsp, a g gnrl nlg o e bkgrwns o r dmcrtc lif r likl t fal n tr cosn ocpas l. / l bsn stodns sd brnc o nt cvc a cltrl stds, s y l b dbl pprd f scs n tr cosn lin o wrk.* (180 words) (s.i. 1.48)*

33.13   Practice writing these phrases in PS:

	1	2	3
1	you will have	past due	to do this
2	for some time	please accept	to that
3	in spite	we have not	to his
4	I hope that	you could	to try
5	must have	if you would	you would be
6	if it	that these	every one
7	we make	and that the	I hope that

33.14   Again practice writing Brief Form Letters No. 1 and 2.

33.15   *No. 1*

Gentlemen: Thank you for the information enclosed with your check. I did not know that you would buy the copy at our price. We are pleased with your order and will see that you receive a credit. Do you wish to buy on time just now; or if possible, would you require us to be there on that very date? Sincerely yours,

33.16   *No. 2*

Dear Sir: If our check is due, we will find men to return the letter; but what if they are not under my orders? I can see the good in it, and I am very willing to come and make it possible for him to give his information; but I do not see why every man is here at the time. Cordially,

33.17   See how fast you can call (or write) the Brief Forms for these much-used words:

	1	2	3	4
1	has	kind	me	our
2	it	as	not	give
3	your	would	of	wish
4	or	was	I	man
5	every	here	will	to
6	gentlemen	on	good	a
7	take	from	are	receive
8	did	she	they	see
9	possible	you	do	letter
10	glad	sincerely	put	know

Personal Shorthand

CARDINAL SERIES

34.1 *Theory Review:*

34.2 *Phonetic Abbreviations*   *Word Examples:*

l	= -lity, -lty	*utility - utl; faulty - fl*
m	= m-(any nonlong vowel)-m.	*member - mbr*
	m-(any nonlong vowel)-n,	*minister - mstr*
	moun-, -moun,	*mound - md; amount - amt*
	-ment	*torment - trm*
n	= -nc(e), -ns(e), -ness, -nt, -nd	*fence - fn; sense - sn; fairness - frn; bent - bn; send - sn; sending - sng*
p	= (as word beginnings only) pr-,	*pretty - pt*
	p-(any nonlong vowel)-r	*permit - pmt*
	pro- and por- (either long or nonlong o)	*prod - pd; port - pt*
		program - pgrm
q	= qu- (kw)	*quick - qk; queen - qen*

34.3

> ***Transcription Pointers: The Semicolon.***
>
> **The semicolon indicates a longer break in thought than the comma. It is often called an "intermediate stop" in a sentence. The semicolon indicates more of a pause than the comma, but not the final break of the period.**
>
> **Use the semicolon:**
>
> **1. To separate a compound sentence when a conjunction is expressed and the parts are subdivided by commas.**

It is necessary for all requisitions to be typed on the standard form; and if there are any questions about the correct procedure, please refer to the office manual.

2. Between coordinate clauses joined by conjunctive adverbs, such as *however, nevertheless, otherwise,* etc.

We hope that our terms are satisfactory to you; however, should you have any questions, we should be glad to give you further information.

3. Before *however, consequently, therefore, yet, whereas,* etc. when introducing an independent clause or when an abrupt change in thought takes place.

Our engineers have made a thorough study of the plans; therefore, will you please write to Mr. James for full information concerning arrangements.

4. To separate a compound sentence (two independent clauses) when a conjunction has been omitted.

The first two investments are grade A; the latter two are considered grade B securities.

5. To separate members of a series, if the series contains commas.

The company established branch offices in Pittsburgh, Pennsylvania; Chicago, Illinois; Denver, Colorado; and San Francisco, California.

6. Before such words as *for example, namely,* etc.

The Acme Company manufactures a number of related products; for example, desks, file cabinets, tables, chairs, duplicators, and office supplies.

34.4   Write the following letter in PS. Compare your speed with a similar paragraph in Lesson 33. Prepare ahead for any difficult words.

34.5   *Dear Mr. Davidson: Payment of your account, amounting to $45, should have been made by the tenth of this month. This is, no doubt, an oversight on your part. We realize that it is easy to put papers aside and forget about them. If payment already has been made, please ignore this reminder. Yours very truly,   (60 words) (s.i. 1.50)*

34.6   Now write this article in PERSONAL SHORTHAND:

What business do you think is the most difficult one? Every person actually is in a very trying business--the business of

*life. Each individual must question himself as to the direc-
tion he wants to go and the particular level that he wishes to
attain. During his lifetime, his task is to progress toward
that goal. (60 words) (s.i. 1.50)*

34.7   Here is another 120-word article. What is your best speed on
writing an article or letter of this length. If your schedule
permits, practice writing it in PS several times. Carefully
analyze any words that cause you to hesitate.

34.8   *Good grooming is an important part of any job; however, in
almost every company there is an employee whose appearance is wrong for his or her job. Often times other
employees would like to tell this person about the importance of good grooming, but most people find that this subject is a hard one to tackle.*

*Many companies have found a way to handle this matter im-
personally, rather than through a personal discussion.
They let employees know about company grooming stan-
dards by way of group meetings or through the distribution
of free literature. In this way, no one feels singled out for
criticism; yet everyone gets the point.
(120 words) (s.i. 1.56)*

34.9   This PERSONAL SHORTHAND letter contains 180 words.
How fast can you *read* it or *transcribe* it?

34.10   *dmrs carson: e d f e nxt mdcl scrtrs'
cvns, w l b hld n sn frncsco (SF), i o
27. sn i m n crg o e cfrn cmte, i v
strtd gg sm tt t o sd b mfsizd a ts tnt
(10t) anl evn. i d lik t v vtg orgnizd
a lst tn (10) mts n advn o ts cfrn d. /
r plng cmte l met e frst (1st) o nxt mt
(mo.); a, z a mbr o ts cmte, i hop u l b
t. e metg l b hld a e hltn hotl a a i a
d t b anwnd latr. / p brg t ts metg sm
ids a a aproprt tem f e cvns. w r l n
ned o e nams o spkrs ho c ctrbut ntrstg*

a vitl n t r grop. / u l hr f m agn nxt wek ccrng aragms f r frst (1st) plng ss. n e mni, kep n min sgsss ccrng e tem a ctn o ts cvns. sy, (180 words) (s.i. 1.48)

34.11 As you write these phrases in PS, give special attention to any that cause you to hesitate:

	1	2	3
1	upon the	in its	few days
2	let us know	on it	for my
3	if you want	one of the most	we did
4	for them	to these	more or less
5	we enclose	he said	at the time
6	you will see	in this matter	for these
7	to it	and his	between the

34.12 Here are Brief Form Letters No. 3 and 4 again. See how fast (and automatically) you can write them in PS.

34.13 *No. 3*

Dear Jim: It is quite good that you can also require the information from her and, at the time, see how well she will get the copy to us. As I see it all now, it is up to the gentlemen if they are ever to go out from here and check about that which is as we know it to be. Sincerely,

34.14 *No. 4*

Dear Mr. Kerr: By and by we will receive the order copy; and if it is not too good, we can take what we have made, if and when we have the time. The copy has not been dated, but I would be glad to do so, if it were to be made an order by me or by her, and we had the check to see. He was to receive the required information, but at no time was he to receive that kind of letter. I know it to be so. All in all, that was to be a kind of credit check about which we are very pleased. Sincerely,

34.15 How quickly can you call (or write) the Brief Forms for these
       high-frequency words:

	1	2	3	4
1	an	he	her	have
2	buy	for	can	up
3	due	with	all	out
4	find	time	the	there
5	about	thank	his	my
6	what	and	require	is
7	return	please	be	well
8	but	when	had	now
9	under	put	order	that

Personal Shorthand

CARDINAL SERIES

35.1   *Theory Review:*

35.2   *Phonetic Abbreviations*   *Word Examples:*

r	= -rity, -ure	*rarity - **rr**; mature - **mtr***
s	= sh-, -sh	*ship - **sp**; dish - **ds***
	s- (any nonlong vowel) -s	*sister - **str**; basis - **bas***
	c- (any nonlong vowel) -s (when *c* has an *s* sound)	*races - **ras**; cistern - **strn***
	-sion, -tion, -cian	*mission - **ms**; mention -**ms**; physician - **fss**; division - **dvs**; question - **qss**; fashion -*
	-shion, cien -tien	***fs**; efficient - **efst**; patient - **past**; efficiency - **efsc***
t	= th-, -th	*thought - **tt**; north - **nt***
w	= wh- (as in where)	*where - **wr**; whether - **wtr***
	-ou (as in cloud)	*cloud - **clwd**; proud - **pwd***
	-ow (as in cow)	*cow - **cw**; plow - **plw***
	-aw (as in raw)	*raw - **rw**; straw - **strw***
y	= oi-, -oi, oy-, -oy (as boil and toy)	*boil - **byl**; toy - **ty**; oil - **yl** oyster - **ystr***

Note: If a consonant is representing a phonetic unit, it cannot also carry the long *e* sound; so we must write this long *e* sound. Example: cheat - cet

35.3

> *Transcription Pointers:* The colon.
>
> The colon is used to emphasize and focus attention on the material to follow. The colon is often called the "mark of anticipation." This means that the material following the colon explains the topic that precedes this mark of punctuation.

Use the colon:

1. To introduce enumeration of articles or particulars.

We would like for you to send us the following papers: 1. Certifictae of Ownership, 2. Tax Waiver, 3. Affidavit signed before a Notary Public.

2. Before specific illustrations of a general statement.

We have offered them two choices: to give up their claim of ownership, or to pay the full amount due us.

This is our suggestion: A thorough study should be made by an experienced analyst.

3. After the salutation of a business letter.

Dear Mr. Carlson: *Gentlemen:*

4. To separate figures that signify time and in bibliographical references.

3:30 p.m.   *10:00 a.m.*
Portland: National Book Company, 1980

35.4   Quickly scan paragraph 35.5; practice writing any words that might cause you to hesitate in taking dictation; and then see how fast you can write this paragraph in PS.

35.5   *Dear Mr. Blue: We regret to inform you that the reserved seats in the section that you requested for the special summer concert have been sold out. We are, however, holding seats for you in the adjoining section, Row 15, on the center aisle.*

If this meets with your approval, please notify us immediately. Sincerely yours,
(60 words) (s.i. 1.50)

35.6   Now practice writing the following article in PERSONAL SHORTHAND:

When you write order letters, you should check them several times to make sure they are definite and complete. Unlike placing orders over the telephone, the employees who receive your letters cannot ask questions to make sure the orders are clearly understood. Therefore, when you write an order letter, make sure it tells the complete story.
(60 words) (s.i. 1.50)

35.7   The next letter has twice as many words as paragraphs 35.5 and 35.6. How quickly can you write it?

35.8   *Dear Miss Place: According to our calculations, the circulation of our newspaper has now reached over a million peo-*

ple. *This is the result of an accumulation of many years of service to the public.*

This large circulation provides us with added stimulation to do an even better job in the future. Our tabulations show that with the seemingly difficult regulations on advertising, we shall have to limit our advertising space to four pages.

Since you have been a steady customer of ours for years, we are giving you first chance to renew your subscription. May we hear from you as soon as possible. Thank you. Sincerely yours,

(120 words) (s.i. 1.57)

35.9 Here is another 180-word PERSONAL SHORTHAND letter. How fast can you *read* it or (better still) transcribe it with pen, pencil, or typewriter?

35.10 *dmr fry: wn (1) o e most cplcatd bls v t apr n cgrs i w n cmte. w fel t wn (1) o r most mprtn tsks i t k sr t e basc pncpls o ts bl r trl ustod b e gnrl pblc. onl b vg e sprt o edcatd votrs c w hop t g ts lgslas psd. / w ustn t u r e crm o e ctzns' cmte n y cmunt. i i r hop t w ma v e oprtunt t xplan e dtals o ts bl t u, s t u, n trn, ma psn e tru pps o ts lgslas t e pblc. i m sr t u c esl ustn e mprtn o r tsk. / d i b p f u t met w u son t dscs ts mtr frtr? i i ustod, o crs, t t i n oblgas o y pt. u ma cl u an i a 663-3664 f a apynm a y cvnn. vty,*

(180 words) (s.i. 1.49)

35.11 Here are more important phrases that you will need to automatize for dictation purposes. Remember that dictation speed is largely determined by shaving off "fractions" of seconds in the writing of words and phrases.

35.12

	1	2	3
1	and will be	we could	you do not
2	by your	to which	when they
3	for their	as much	for example
4	with his	I cannot	we feel sure
5	hope that	has not been	with him
6	we shall have	so many	I shall be glad
7	for his	and will he	we could

35.13   See if you can write Brief Form Letters No.1 and 2 without the slightest hesitation. Should you hesitate at all, make a note of that Brief Form and give it special attention.

35.14   *No. 1*

Gentlemen: Thank you for the information enclosed with your check. I did not know that you would buy the copy at our price. We are pleased with your order and will see that you receive a credit. Do you wish to buy on time just now; or, if possible, would you require us to be there on that very date? Sincerely yours,

35.15   *No. 2*

Dear Sir: If our check is due, we will find men to return the letter; but what if they are not under my orders? I can see the good in it, and I am very willing to come and make it possible for him to give his information; but I do not see why every man is here at the time. Cordially,

35.16   See how quickly you can call (or write) the Brief Forms for these most-used words:

	1	2	3	4
1	him	very	come	make
2	at	check	information	too
3	price	if	men	get
4	copy	credit	were	no
5	also	quite	am	dear
6	go	been	know	made
7	why	so	enclose	us
8	which	ever	how	we
9	by	just	date	in

BRIEF FORM REVIEW

an	he	her	have
buy	for	can	up
due	with	all	out
find	time	the	there
about	thank	his	my
what	and	require	is
return	please	be	well
but	when	had	now
under	put	order	that
him	very	come	make
at	check	information	too
price	if	men	get
copy	credit	were	no
also	quite	am	dear
go	been	know	made
why	so	enclose	us
which	ever	how	we
by	just	date	in
has	kind	me	our
it	as	not	give
your	would	of	wish
or	was	I	man
every	here	will	to
gentlemen	on	good	a
take	from	are	receive
did	she	they	see
possible	you	do	letter
glad	sincerely	wish	require

Personal Shorthand

CARDINAL SERIES

36.1 *Theory Review:*

36.2 *Word beginnings (Shortcuts)*

For *em* -- Write *m*, unless a vowel follows the *m*.
   EXAMPLES: embrace - *mbrac*   emit - *emt*

For *im* -- Write *m*, unless the *m* is followed by another *m*.
   EXAMPLES: imagine - *mgn*   immature - *imtr*

For *um* -- Write *m*
   EXAMPLE: umbrella - *mbrla*

For *in* -- Write *n*, unless the *n* is followed by another *n*.
   EXAMPLES: inability - *nbl*   innocent - *incn*

For *un* -- Write *n*, unless the *n* is followed by another *n*.
   EXAMPLES: unable - *nab*   unnecessary - *unsr*

36.3

> *Transcription Pointers:* **Question Mark and Exclamation Mark.**
>
> **QUESTION MARK.** Use the question mark after a direct question.
>   *When is the train due? Will he arrive today?*
> Do *not* use the question mark after an indirect question.
>   *The personnel director asked the employee what he had to say.*
> Do *not* use the question mark after a request courteously worded in interrogative form.
>   *Will you please turn in the report before 11 a.m. tomorrow.*
> **EXCLAMATION MARK.** An exclamation point is used to express strong feeling and to intensify or emphasize words, phrases, and sentences.
>   *I have just learned of your latest promotion!*
>   *Congratulations!*
>   *What a beautiful scene this is!*

> *Oh! I believe this is the place.*
> *Yes, sir!*

36.4   Review the following paragraphs carefully (practicing any words that might cause you to hesitate) before writing both paragraphs as quickly as you can.

36.5   *Dear Mr. Morris: As requested, we are sending you a copy of our mail order catalog. You will find camping equipment on pages 5 through 15. Order forms and envelopes for your use in ordering have been inserted inside the front cover of the catalog. It will be a pleasure to serve you. Very truly yours, (60 words) (s.i. 1.50)*

36.6   *Any form of shorthand, once mastered, can be used in many different ways. It can be used to take notes, perhaps in a classroom situation. A stenographer or secretary might use it to take dictation. A housewife could make out her grocery list. The course can be put to use by almost anyone, for countless purposes.*
(60 words) (s.i. 1.50)

36.7   The next paragraph is comprised of 120 shorthand words. How fast can you write it in PS?

36.8   *Dear Mr. Bradford: Yesterday I received your letter requesting that your students be allowed to visit our insurance offices. Would Tuesday, November 12, at 2 p.m. be a convenient time for the visit?*

We hope you can come to our offices before the day of the student visit to become familiar with our operations and to talk with your guide, Miss Mason. Together, we can help plan a more meaningful trip for your students. Please call Miss Mason at 255-3638 to arrange for this visit.

Thank you for your interest in our company. I hope this visit will be a worthwhile experience for your students. Sincerely yours,
(120 words) (s.i. 1.57)

36.9   See how fluently (and easily) you can read (or transcribe) the following 180-word PERSONAL SHORTHAND letter.

36.10   *d subscriber: r cpn (co.) z a sbstnsl my savg ofr t k t u. sn u v b a sb- scribr o r mgzn, fnnsl dal, f 10 yrs*

a v alwas (lwas) pad (pd.) y sbscrps
o i, w sd lik u t v e flog gft. / t
ec tn-yr (10yr) sbscribr, w r psng a
cplmr isu o r mgzn. ts isu ncluds
almost (lmost) v sbstnsl mns o ncrsg
y erng pwr a psnl ftn (fcn). e artcls
w rtn b nsl non atrts ho l frns a
pfsl pyn o vu o w t k a sav mr o y
my. / f u d lik t v a c o ts isu, p
nfold e atcd fm, nsrt y nam a adrs,
a r i t u. sn u lv n e cntr, i l k
a 2 weks bf y c arivs. / f u v an
sgsss u d lik t sbmt t hlp u mprov r
mgzn, w sl b hp t v tm. yvt,

(180 words) (s.i. 1.50)

36.11   Practice writing these phrases in PS until they are completely automatic:

	1	2	3
1	you will be able	they will	when you
2	under the	no doubt	there will be
3	they can	on his	it is not
4	to do so	can you	if you wish
5	and return	cannot be	any one
6	whether or not	under the	they will
7	for which	I understand	you may have

36.12   Strive for automatic control in the writing of Brief Forms letters No. 3 and No. 4, in paragraphs 36.13 and 36.14.

36.13   *No. 3*
Dear Jim: It is quite good that you can also require the infor-
mation from her and, at the time, see how well she will get
the copy to us. As I see it all now, it is up to the gentlemen if

they are ever to go out from here and check about that
which is as we know it to be. Sincerely,

36.14   *No. 4*
Dear Mr. Kerr: By and by we will receive the order copy; and
if it is not too good, we can take what we have made, if and
when we have the time. The copy has not been dated, but I
would be glad to do so, if it were to be made an order by me
or by her, and we had the check to see. He was to receive
the required information, but at no time was he to receive
that kind of letter. I know it to be so. All in all, that was to be
a kind of check about which we are very pleased.
Sincerely,

36.15   Call or write the Brief Forms for these much-used words:

	1	2	3	4
1	has	kind	me	our
2	it	as	not	give
3	your	would	of	wish
4	or	was	I	man
5	every	here	will	do
6	gentlemen	on	good	a
7	take	from	are	receive
8	did	she	they	see
9	possible	you	do	letter
10	glad	sincerely	has	kind

Personal Shorthand

CARDINAL SERIES

37.1 *Theory Review:*

37.2 *Word Beginnings (Shortcuts,* continued*)*

For *en* -- Write *n*
  EXAMPLE: entail - *ntal*

For *intro* - *intr* -- Write *ntr* (whether *o* is short or long)
  EXAMPLE: introduction - *ntrdcs*   intricate - *ntrct*

For *post* -- Write *pst*
  EXAMPLE: postage - *pstg*

For *super, supr* -- Write *spr* (regardless of how the *u* is pronounced)
  EXAMPLES: supercilious - *sprcls*   supreme - *sprm*

37.3

> ***Transcription Pointers:* Dash.**
> **Use the dash:**
> **1. To indicate an abrupt change of thought.**
>
> *The financial experts consider this a good investment--but is it?*
>
> **2. To state a summation of the preceding material.**
>
> *An understanding of administrative problems, initiative, and ability to make decisions--these are the requirements for a good executive.*
>
> **3. To set off interpolations.**
>
> *It was a regular or special charge account--I can't remember which one--that he had with us.*

37.4 Preview (and practice) the more difficult words in paragraph 37.5 and then paragraph 37.6. When you have done this, see how quickly you can write each paragraph in PERSONAL SHORTHAND. On which one do you have the best "time"?

37.5 *Dear Miss Underwood: Have you overlooked something? In reviewing our December accounts, we find that your bill has not been paid.*

We know it is easy to forget about a bill, especially during the Christmas holidays. Won't you please bring your account up to date by sending your check in the amount of $95. Sincerely yours,
(60 words) (s.i. 1.52)

37.6   *It is of value for every business teacher to have had some actual experience. This practical experience enables him to recognize some of the problems which his students may someday face. He then has a better idea of what the business world is going to expect from his pupils when they are on the job.*
(60 words) (s.i. 1.52)

37.7   The following article consists of 120 shorthand words. How fast can you write it in PS?

37.8   *Whenever you address a letter to a business firm or any other organization, you probably will want to use an attention line to make sure your letter is directed to the proper person in that organization.*

By using the attention line, you will help speed up routing of the letter after it has been received by the organization named in the inside address. It also will insure that the letter is directed to the person or department that can best take the required action on your letter.

The attention line may be typed in many acceptable styles, but is always placed immediately after the inside address.
(120 words) (s.i. 1.58)

37.9   See how long it takes you to *read* or *transcribe* this PERSONAL SHORTHAND letter:

37.10   *dmrs emerson: t u f y l o ag 28 n w u pas e pfmn o e bl wsg msen u bt 14 yrs ag. / mfkrrs (mfctrrs) aprsat statms f cstmrs w atst t e stsfcs a ptclr pdk z gn e usr. i i n ofn t ppl k e i t st dwn a rit a l o ts natr; tf, w d n csdr tes ls smpl bsn rotn. / w r pd u tok e trb t rit u sc a frnl l, z ts i e onl wa w c lrn f r pdks r gg a lifi o stsfctr srvc t tr onrs. w r alwas (lwas) srcg f was t mprov e wrkmsp, gl, a dsin o r msens, a i i g t n w r scedg. / w hop y msen l ctnu t pfm stsfctrl a rn smotl. i m sr u c lok fwrd t my mr yrs o srvc f y bl wsg msen. vty,* (180 words) (s.i. 1.51)

37.11 Write these phrases in PS--several times, if possible.

	1	2	3
1	this will	from this	are you
2	in that	has the	on us
3	has had	did not	of that
4	in time	you may be	you cannot
5	that they	this is the	if it is
6	we wish	he can	about this
7	to ship	of such	in that

37.12 *Let's* practice again on Brief Form Letters No. 1 and No. 2. Can you write them now without hesitation?

37.13 *No. 1*

Gentlemen: Thank you for the information enclosed with your check. I did not know that you would buy the copy at our price. We are pleased with your order and will see that you receive a credit. Do you wish to buy on time just now; or if possible, would you require us to be there on that very date? Sincerely yours,

37.14 *No. 2*

Dear Sir: If our check is due, we will find men to return the letter; but what if they are not under my orders? I can see the good in it, and I am very willing to come and make it possible for him to give his information; but I do not see why every man is here at the time. Cordially,

37.15   Call or write the Brief Forms for these important words:

	1	2	3	4
1	an	he	her	have
2	buy	for	can	up
3	due	with	all	out
4	find	time	the	there
5	about	thank	his	my
6	what	and	require	is
7	return	please	be	well
8	but	when	had	now
9	under	put	order	that

Personal Shorthand

38.1 *Theory Review:* Phonetic Abbreviations

38.2 USE OF EACH LETTER OF THE ALPHABET. (When final *y* has the long *i* sound, write *i*.)

Letter	Sounds According to Basic Theory	Phonetic Abbreviations
a	long a (regardless of spelling)	·································
b	b, be·, ·by	·ble
c	c (either s or k sound), ce·, ·cy	ch·, ·ch, com·, con·
d	d, de·, ·dy	·································
e	long e when the preceding consonant represents more than itself; one of two e's occuring together; short or long e at beginning of word or ending of word	·································
f	f, fe·, ·fy	ph·, ·ph, for·, ·for, ·ful, ·ify

38.3

> *Transcription Pointers:* **Hyphen.**
>
> **Use the hyphen:**
>
> **1. To divide words at the end of a line.**
>   *Before dividing words at the end of a line, consult the dictionary for proper syllabication.*
>
> **2. In certain compound words.**
>   *The treasurer gave an up-to-date report.*
>   *It is a well-known concern.*

LESSON 38   PS Cardinal Series-1 / **149**

> *There was a carry-over of $2,300.*
> *He applied for a short-term loan.*
> *He made a matter-of-fact statement.*
> *Send the coupon in a self-addressed envelope.*
> *The officer was a brother-in-law of the president.*
> *The above-mentioned letter is on file.*
>
>   *a six-figure amount*
>   *the over-all gain*
>   *in the not-so-distant future*
>
> 3. In expressing certain numbers.
>
> *The applicant was thirty-eight years old.*
> *The census included the years 1940-1950.*
> *Reference was made to pages 10-15.*
> *Fifty-five accounts were opened this month.*
> *The building includes six 4-room apartments.*
> *Two-thirds of the material was not usable.*

38.4   Preview and practice "key" words in this paragraph and then see how fast you can write it in PS:

Receptionists should never leave their desks unattended. If they are called away for some reason, or it is time to go to lunch, arrangements need to be made for someone to relieve them. Someone is needed at this position, at all times, to guarantee the immediate greeting of a company's client upon arrival.
(60 words) (s.i. 1.53)

38.5   Now follow the same procedure on this article--and then compare your "time" with that on paragraph 38.4.

When you think of what an office would be like without women today, it's hard to believe that until the typewriter was invented, women had no place in the business office. As the typewriter gained acceptance in American business, women attained a means of entering a field that had always been closed to them previously.
(60 words) (s.i. 1.53)

38.6   The following letter contains twice as many words as the preceding paragraphs. How fast can you write it?

38.7   *Dear John: Thank you for your invitation to the clam bake on Friday evening, May 20. My wife and I shall be delighted to attend.*

Let me assure you that I understand and appreciate the purpose of this social event. More and more employers and employees are sharing leisure hours in social activities.

Because of this, many labor and management problems are becoming more thoroughly understood. Personal relationships of this type ease many conflicts and make for more pleasant working conditions in the office. I do not understand why employers have not thought of this before. We are looking forward to this occasion. Sincerely yours,
(120 words) (s.i. 1.60)

38.8   How rapidly can you *read* or *transcribe* the following PERSONAL SHORTHAND letter? Make a note of any words or phrases that puzzle you unduly and then practice writing these several times.

38.9   *v u rn nt an o e flog tips o dctatrs n tipg f a trnscrps msen? frst (1st), e dctatr u c't ustn bcs e i cog gm r smokg a cgr. tn t's e dctatr t tks s fst u cdn't pl flo h. / t r, n dwt, my tips o pblm dctatrs n v ofc. i i hrd t tl tes ppl tctfl (tkfl) t mprovm neds t b m drg tr dctas sss. / ts pblm mit b slvd, wv, f v cpn (co.) ofrg a edcasl pln gav a crs n pblc spkg. y cd g v dctatr t nrol. hopfl, ts d hlp elmat mc o e por spkg w plags tipsts ho v t trnscrib f msens. / bsids por spkg, dctatrs k i dfclt f e tipst n otr was. smis y fal t mrk e dctas slp crkl a fal t spl o nfmlr trms a nams. phps e sam pblc spkg crs cd l b usd t strs tes itms.* (180 words) (s.i. 1.53)

38.10   Practice writing these phrases in PS:

	1	2	3
1	in the future	so much	be sure

2	will you	we do not	at that time
3	good enough	which is	I will
4	that are	is that	with this
5	within the	throughout the	to give you
6	as you know	for that	who is

38.11 Now see if you have completely mastered Brief Form Letters No. 3 and No. 4.

38.12 *No. 3*
Dear Jim: It is quite good that you can also require the information from her and, at the time, see how well she will get the copy to us. As I see it all now, it is up to the gentlemen if they are ever to go out from here and check about that which is as we know it to be. Sincerely,

38.13 *No. 4*
Dear Mr. Kerr: By and by we will receive the order copy; and if it is not too good, we can take what we have made, if and when we have the time. The copy has not been dated, but I would be glad to do so, if it were to be made an order by me or by her, and we had the check to see. He was to receive the required information, but at no time was he to receive that kind of letter. I know it to be so. All in all, that was to be a kind of credit check about which we are very pleased. Sincerely,

38.14 *Call* or *write* (preferably from dictation) these very high-frequency words:

	1	2	3	4
1	him	very	come	make
2	at	check	information	too
3	price	if	men	get
4	copy	credit	were	no
5	also	quite	am	dear
6	go	been	know	made
7	why	so	enclose	us
8	which	ever	how	we
9	by	just	date	in

 *Personal Shorthand*

39.1 *Theory Review:*

39.2 USE OF EACH LETTER OF THE ALPHABET. (cont.). (When final *y* has the long *i* sound, write *i*.)

Letter	Sound According to Basic Theory	Phonetic Abbreviations
g	g (hard or soft zh sound), gē-, -gy	-ng, -ing, -dge, -nge
h	h, hē-	....
i	long i (regardless of spelling)	....
j	j, jē-	....
k	k, kē-, -ky	-ct
l	l, lē-, -ly	-lity, -lty
m	m, mē-, -my	m- (any nonlong vowel)-m; -ment; m- (any nonlong vowel) -n; moun-, -moun,
n	n, nē-, -ny	-nc(e), -ns(e), -ness, -nt, -nd
o	long o and oo	....
p	p, pē-, -py	(as word beginnings only) pr-; p-(any nonlong vowel)-r; pro- and -por (either long or nonlong o)
q	q(k)	qu- (kw)
r	r, rē-, -ry	-rity, -ure

s	s (s or z or zh sound),	sh-, -sh; s- (any nonlong vowel)-s; c-(any nonlong vowel)-s
	sē-, -sy (when c has s sound)	-sion, -tion, -cian, -shion, -cien, -tien

39.3

Transcription Pointers: Parentheses and Brackets.

PARENTHESES. Parentheses are used to enclose a word, phrase, or sentence which is inserted as an explanatory statement. These marks of punctuation usually enclose incidental expressions that are independent of the main thought matter.

Use the parentheses:

1. To enclose incidental remarks that do not affect the structure of the sentence.

We have been waiting (six months as a matter of fact) for your reply to our offer.

2. To enclose explanatory material.

From these data (Table VI), we may conclude that the results of our investigation have revealed important information.

3. To enclose figures that indicate separate parts of a series.

We believe that the company will prosper because (1) the management is sound, (2) its financial position is good, and (3) it possesses an excellent location.

BRACKETS: Brackets are used to set off inserted matter that is foreign to the sentence itself. This matter may be extraneous to the content of the material, such as editorial comment and other comments not by the author of the text.

Use the brackets:

1. To set off inserted matter.

"We have come to dedicate a portion of that field [Gettysburg] as a final resting place for those [combatants] who gave their lives that that nation might live."

"I should like to leave the conclusion of this story to your imagination." [Laughter]

2. For parentheses within parentheses.

> *In support of his claim, the volume he cited (Smith's Business Law [First Edition]) contains some outstanding cases.*

39.4   Preview, practice, and then test your speed on this 60-word letter:

Gentlemen: I am writing this letter in regard to your notice of January 23, asking me to send you $110 to bring my account at your store up to date.

If you will recheck your accounts receivable records, you will find that my check was mailed to you on January 15. Very truly yours,
(60 words) (s.i. 1.56)

39.5   Compare your writing speed on this article with your speed on paragraph 39.4.

With the advent of the supermarket, methods in the retailing of food have changed a great deal. The retail salesperson is spending more time in developing methods of attractive display of merchandise and less in personal contact with the customer. More and more of the retail food stores are employing this method of selling.
(60 words) (s.i. 1.56)

39.6   Scan the following paragraph for difficult words, practice writing any on which you might hesitate, and then see if you can set a new "speed record" on this 120-word letter.

39.7   *Dear Student: We are enclosing a copy of our latest catalog on adult programs of study. You should consult this catalog if you are interested in taking any of these courses.*

In our courses, we have tried to include a broad program to meet the interests of almost everyone. If you would like to take up a hobby, there are classes in art, sewing, tailoring, woodworking, story writing, and painting.

All of our courses will bring results and will provide many happy hours of recreation. Registration for these classes begins on September 15. Very truly yours,
(120 words) (s.i. 1.60)

39.8   See how long it takes you to read (or *transcribe* with pen, pencil, or typewriter) this 180-word PERSONAL SHORT-HAND article. *Writing* shorthand quickly and easily is important but of little or no value if you can't *read* it fluently.

39.9   *n u ned t rit sm tip o bsn cmuncas, cos*

e fm t suts e stas. f u ned t sn a srt notc r rqst, us a pst crd. f u ned t sn a lrg malg, ppr a fm l. f u wn t sn a mr psnl cmuncas, ppr a ndvdl tipd l. / w c u dcid w fm t us? frst (1st), csdr e pps o e l. scn (2n), csdr e rcs u wn t g f y rdr. i i obvs t ndvdl tipd ls r n sutb f sng nots t hnrds (100's) o cstmrs. n ctrst, e psnl, tipd l i e onl crk wa t rqst xtns o c f a splir. / ov fm u us, u mst alwas (lwas) flo crk ritg pcdrs. u mst nclud l nsr fks, g rit t e pyn, a us crk a ntrl lgg. abv l els, k crtn e l i acrt n v dtal bf u sn i. (180 words) (s.i. 1.55)

39.10   Here are more good phrases to practice in PS:

	1	2	3
1	of which	than the	could be
2	in regard	to bring	and have
3	one of these	on which	in case
4	do you	will not	or more
5	that will be	that would	we have had
6	will have	to be sure	had been

39.11   See how fast (and easily) you can write Brief Form Letters No. 1, 2, and 3.

39.12   *No. 1*

Gentlemen: Thank you for the information enclosed with your check. I did not know that you would buy the copy at our price. We are pleased with your order and will see that you receive a credit. Do you wish to buy on time just now; or, if possible, would you require us to be there on that very date? Sincerely yours,

39.13 *No 2*

Dear Sir: If our check is due, we will find men to return the letter; but what if they are not under my orders? I can see the good in it, and I am very willing to come and make it possible for him to give his information; but I do not see why every man is here at the time. Cordially,

39.14 *No. 3*

Dear Jim: It is quite good that you can also require the information from her and, at the time, see how well she will get the copy to us. As I see it all now, it is up to the gentlemen if they are ever to go out from here and check about that which is as we know it to be. Sincerely,

39.15 How fast can you *call* or *write* the Brief Forms for these much-used words?

	1	2	3	4
1	has	kind	me	our
2	it	as	not	give
3	your	would	of	wish
4	or	was	I	man
5	every	here	will	do
6	gentlemen	on	good	a
7	take	from	are	receive
8	did	she	they	see
9	possible	you	do	letter
10	glad	sincerely	he	make

Personal Shorthand

40.1 *Theory Review:*

40.2 USE OF EACH LETTER OF THE ALPHABET (cont.). (Remember - when final *y* has the long *i* sound, write *i!*)

Letter	Sounds According to Basic Theory	Phonetic Abbreviations
t	t, tē·, ·ty	th·, ·th
u	long u (also oo, if spelled with u)	....
v	v, vē·, ·vy	....
w	w, wē·,	wh·, ou (as in cloud), ·ow (as in cow), ·aw (as in raw)
x	x, ·xy	....
y	y, yē·, (ending y when no conso-nant available to carry it)	oi·, ·oi, oy·, ·oy (as in boil, toy, and oyster)
z	z (z or zh sound), zē·, ·zy	....

40.3

Transcription Pointers:

UNDERSCORE: Use the underscore:

1. For titles of books, periodicals, and sub-headings in a manuscript.

The book he had read was <u>The Great Treasure</u>. Later, he noticed a digest of it in the magazine, <u>Author's Digest</u>.

2. To emphasize words and phrases.

Divide words that are hyphenated only at the hyphen.

Note--Material underscored on typewritten manuscript will be set in italic by a printer.

ITALICS: Material to be set in italics is so indicated by underscoring in a manuscript.

Use italics:

1. In writing the titles of books, magazines, newspapers, and manuscripts.

> *Gone With The Wind*
> *Office Management*
> *New York Times*

2. In writing foreign words not yet included in the English language.

> *de facto*
> *noblesse oblige*
> *a priori*

3. In writing a word spoken of as a word.

> The pronoun *he*
> Avoid using *don't* in the third person singular.

40.4   What's your best speed on a 60-word letter? See if you can set a new record on this one:

Dear Mr. Jefferson: Your letter of June 19 requesting more information about domesticating lions has been referred to Mr. John Teal. He has been in charge of this project for more than fifteen years and is probably the foremost authority on lions. I believe he can best answer your questions. Sincerely,
(60 words) (s.i. 1.60)

40.5   Now see if you can write this paragraph even faster:

Most business firms have their company's name printed on letter paper. The size of this heading varies, but often occupies about two inches of space. This heading usually contains the company's name, the type of business, and the business address. The size of this letterhead paper is mostly 8½ by 11 inches.
(60 words) (s.i. 1.63)

40.6   Here is another 120-word paragraph. How fast can you write this one in PS?

Under the Fair Credit Reporting Act, consumers are guaranteed certain rights when credit information is given out about them.

Information in one's credit file and the sources of this information are available for inspection by the consumer. You can also find out who has received employment reports about you during the past two years. The names of those receiving your credit reports within the past six months also may be obtained.

If you want to review your credit record, stop at your local credit bureau and furnish proper identification. If you cannot visit the local bureau, write in and request a telephone interview.

(120 words) (s.i. 1.64)

40.7 Read this PS letter as quickly as you can. If possible, transcribe it at the typewriter.

40.8 *dm harrington: a lrg frm locatd n ls agls z askd u t hlp tm f a hil skld psn t fl e pss o xctv scrtr t tr cpn's (co's) psdn. ts frm mfkrs (mfctrs) wm's clotg, w i sold t hi-fs botgs troo e wrld. / e psn slkd mst v e abl t sprvis e ntir ofc stf, k jgms o mprtn mtrs n e psdn i o o e ofc, a tip a k dctas a hi rats o sped. / ts i a grat oprtunt f e rit psn. e pss l pa $1,000 a mt t strt, w gnrs ras tftr. t i evn a bons a e en o e yr, f e cpn (co.) sos a sbstnsl pft. / f u n o smwn (sm1) ho z e glfcass t fl ts pss a i ntrstd n e jb, v h g n tc w u. w l arag f a ntrvu a z erlst cvnn. yt,*

(180 words) (s.i. 1.57)

40.9   Practice these important phrases until you can write them automatically.

	1	2	3
1	you will be able	if you wish	when you
2	under the	no doubt	there will be
3	they can	on his	it is not
4	to do so	can you	if you wish
5	and return	cannot be	anyone
6	whether or not	under the	they will

40.10   Now see if you can write all four Brief Form Letters without the slightest hesitation.

40.11   *No. 1*

Gentlemen: Thank you for the information enclosed with your check. I did not know that you would buy the copy at our price. We are pleased with your order and will see that you receive a credit. Do you wish to buy on time just now; or, if possible, would you require us to be there on that very date? Sincerely yours,

40.12   *No. 2*

Dear Sir: If our check is due, we will find men to return the letter; but what if they are not under my orders? I can see the good in it, and I am very willing to come and make it possible for him to give his information; but I do not see why every man is here at the time. Cordially,

40.13   *No. 3*

Dear Jim: It is quite good that you can also require the information from her and, at the time, see how well she will get the copy to us. As I see it all now, it is up to the gentlemen if they are ever to go out from here and check about that which is as we know it to be. Sincerely,

40.14   *No. 4*

Dear Mr. Kerr: By and by we will receive the order copy; and if it is not too good, we can take what we have made, if and when we have the time. The copy has not been dated, but I would be glad to do so, if it were to be made an order by me or by her, and we had the check to see. He was to receive

the required information, but at no time was he to receive
that kind of letter. I know it to be so. All in all, that was to be
a kind of credit check about which we are very pleased.
Sincerely,

40.15   See if you can write the PS Brief Forms for all of these high-
frequency words:

	1	2	3	4
1	an	he	her	have
2	buy	for	can	up
3	due	with	all	out
4	find	time	the	there
5	about	thank	his	my
6	what	and	require	is
7	return	please	be	well
8	but	when	had	now
9	under	put	order	that
10	him	very	come	make
11	at	check	information	too
12	price	if	men	get
13	copy	credit	were	put
14	also	quite	am	dear
15	go	been	know	made
16	why	so	enclose	us
17	which	ever	how	we
18	by	just	date	in
19	has	kind	me	our
20	it	as	not	give
21	your	would	of	wish
22	or	was	I	man
23	every	here	will	to
24	gentlemen	on	good	a
25	take	from	are	receive
26	did	she	they	see
27	possible	you	do	letter
28	glad	sincerely	every	quite

SUPPLEMENTARY SECTIONS

DICTATION

1. *Dear Mr. Jones: Enclosed is a check for the price of the pen and pencil set which you returned. We regret that the[1] merchandise did not meet with your approval. / We hope we have an opportunity to serve you again. Yours truly,[2] (40)*

2. *Dear Mr. Paine: It is a pleasure to enclose our record book; we hope you will find it very useful. / At this[1] time, we have no new materials; but if some are issued later, we will send you a copy. Cordially yours,[2] (40)*

3. *Dear Madam: Our Credit Manager recently left a note on my desk, indicating that you had opened an[1] account. / This note is to welcome you and to express our hope that you will use your account frequently. Yours truly,[2] (40)*

4. *Dear Customer: The attached papers explain the charges and balances due us. Please mail payment to the address[1] below, or pay at any of our retail stores. If you prefer, pay this bill with your next mail order. Sincerely,[2] (40)*

5. *Dear Fred: As soon as I can sell my present home, my family and I will be moving to Albany. If possible,[1] would you send me a list of the real estate agencies in Albany? See you in the fall! Sincerely,[2] (40)*

6. *Dear Mr. Anderson: Thank you for your letter, concerning our product and services. It has been our policy[1] to offer the finest products. We impress on our employees the impor- tance of good service. Yours truly,[2] (40)*

7. *Dear Mr. Jones: We notice that you have not paid your re- cent account. Will you please send us your check right away. When[1] accounts are not paid promptly, it results in great expense for us. We would appreciate prompt action. Yours truly,[2] (40)*

8. *Dear Mr. Adams: Your Banker's Life Insurance salesman will call at your home on the evening of August 19,[1] at 9 p.m., to discuss insurance needs with you. / Please mark this date on your calendar. Sincerely yours,[2] (40)*

9. *Dear Sam: I believe that I have just about completed the audit of your records for the past fiscal period.[1] / If you will notify me when you can stop in to see me about them, I shall set up an appointment. James Brown[2] (40)*

10. *Gentlemen: Will you please have your finance committee investigate my credit standing with a view to extending[1] a loan. I am glad to send you information that is necessary to do the job. Yours very sincerely,[2] (40)*

CREDIT BUYING

11. *That first salary does not buy as much as you wish, and it is easy to get the habit of installment buying.[1] Use your credit with care; resist the temptation to buy more than you need, just because it does not require cash. (40)*

CHOOSING A SUBJECT

12. *The first step in getting ready to prepare a research paper is the selection of a subject. Avoid the[1] pitfall of choosing a subject that is too broad. / It is better to choose a subject of personal interest.[2] (40)*

VOCABULARY BUILDING

13. *Look to your vocabulary. A wide vocabulary is the mark of an executive. Let it be a[1] vital part of your equipment as a secretary. Learn right now how to use the dictionary correctly.[2] (40)*

IMPORTANT MEN

14. *If you were asked to name the ten most important men who ever lived, could you quickly name ten? This can be an excellent[1] and challenging question for table conversation; it is an espcially good one for a group discussion. (40)*

THE BUZZER

15. *When the buzzer calls for the secretary to go to her employer's desk to take dictation, she should take the[1] following things with her: A shorthand notebook with an elastic band around it, pen, and two well-sharpened pencils.[2] (40)*

16. *Dear Miss Smith: At the present time, we do not have any vacant apartments in the Flagstaff; however, by the time[1] summer school begins, there is a possibility that we might have just what you desire. / In the meantime, we[2] have placed your request with the agency. Very truly yours, (50)*

17. *Dear Madam: During the next two months, I shall be living in Beaverton while attending summer school. For this reason,[1] I should like to rent a small, furnished apartment, within walking distance of the campus. / Do you know anyone[2] who might have such an apartment to rent? Sincerely yours, (50)*

18. *Gentlemen: We ordered 100 reams of typing paper from you, which was on sale. We requested that the paper[1] be of medium weight. However, it is so light we will be unable to use it. / May we return the[2] 100 reams for credit? Sincerely yours, (50)*

19. *Gentlemen: I purchased a steam iron from you, a week ago. The iron is rough and sticks to the cloth,[1] making it impossible to do my ironing. / I am very dissatisfied with the iron and would like a new[2] one today or my money returned. Yours very truly, (50)*

20. *Gentlemen: Will you please reserve a single room, with a bath, for two nights. I expect to arrive in your city[1] during the evening of March 21 and leave in the afternoon of the 23rd./ Please confirm the reservation[2] at your earliest convenience. Yours very truly, (50)*

21. *Dear Mr. Davidson: Payment of your account, amounting to $45, should have been made by January[1] 10. This is no doubt an oversight, as it is easy to put papers aside and forget about them.[2] / If payment has been made, please ignore this letter. Yours truly, (50)*

22. *Dear Mr. Siles: Please accept, with our compliments, the catalogue we are sending you today. It is a service[1] we offer our customers. / We suggest you show this catalogue to your friends and neighbors, to let them see the numerous[2] articles our catalogue contains. Sincerely, (50)*

23. *Gentlemen: We are running a large advertisement, in*

many national magazines, during the summer months.[1] / We are certain of a large increase in the sale of our products. Reprints of this ad will be available to[2] you, for your local advertising. Yours very truly, (50)

24. *Dear Mr. James: Enclosed is the list of homes you requested. I will be happy to show you the homes on June 1.[1] I have noted such information as location in relation to the campus, location of schools, and things[2] that I thought might be of help in finding a home. Bill Case (50)*

25. *Dear Mr. Case: Thank you for the list. It was interesting, but since I am a research botanist, I would like[1] to find a home with at least three acres, so that I may do some experimenting with plants. If possible, I[2] would like to have a place very close to the campus. James (50)*

26. *To the Editor: Your June 25 editorial, on the development of the city park system,[1] was an excellent example of civic responsibility. It was a pleasure to learn that your newspaper[2] is so wholeheartedly supporting this project. Yours truly, (50)*

27. *Dear Customer: Thank you for your inquiry. The Natural Gas Company is proud to offer its customers[1] free inspection and adjustment service, on all gas appliances. Our Service Department will welcome a call[2] from you if they can be of assistance. Very truly yours, (50)*

28. *Dear Mr. Adams: Thank you for your letter of May 6 and for your check of $50. We have credited[1] the check to your account. / Your request for payment of the balance on July 1 is perfectly satisfactory.[2] We desire to be of service at all times. Sincerely, (50)*

29. *Dear Mrs. Jones: We were pleased to receive your request to open an account with us. / Enclosed is an application[1] form, to be completed and returned to us. As soon as you send us this form, we can process your application[2] and have your credit card in the mail. Yours sincerely, (50)*

30. *Dear Sir: In reply to your request of March 5, several of our sales catalogues are being shipped to you under[1] separate cover. / Thank you for your interest in our organiza-*

tion. We appreciate your help. If we can be of further service, let us know. Sincerely, (50)

31. Dear Miss Hyde: At the last meeting of the stockholders,
Mr. Tyler neglected to jot down the date of our next[1]
meeting. I am making his itinerary for July, and I would appreciate your giving me this information.[2] / It is a pleasure to
correspond with you, as you are so very generous with your
assistance. Cordially,[3] (60)

32. Dear Mrs. Green: This is to confirm the telephone conversation with you regrading accomodations at our hotel. / We
have reserved, for you and your husband, a room with bath,
for February 6 and 7. / A dining[2] room is located on the first
floor, for your convenience. / We look forward to seeing you
soon. Sincerely,[3] (60)

33. Dear Mr. Jones: Today I received your letter, reminding
me of the convention on January 4, 5[1], and 6. / I regret that
it will not be possible for me to attend the first day of the
convention. / You have[2] put in hours of work, and I know it
will be the most successful convention in the company's
history. Yours truly,[3] (60)

34. Dear Jim: Enclosed is a map with directions to Camp
Keen. It is only about an hour's drive from Boston on the[1]
freeway. / I failed to mention in my last letter that facilities
are available, if you wish to spend the[2] night with the kids,
the mosquitoes, and possibly a good selection of bugs in
your sleeping bag. Sincerely, (60)[3]

35. Dear Jim: I am delighted to hear that you were able to
rearrange your schedule, so that you could be with us[1] the
entire length of the camp. / I am doubly pleased, because I
would like to ask that you lead the campfire sing, Tuesday[2]
evening. We have printed song sheets if you would like to
use them. You will find one enclosed for your use.
Sincerely,[3] (60)

36. Dear Mr. Scott: I believe that you must have overlooked
something at the end of last month. We have not yet
received[1] the payment on your automobile. This obligation
is now fifteen days past due. / We are confident that you[2]
will place your check (in the amount of $90) in the mail to-

day. Don't delay—pay today! Sincerely yours, (60)

37. *Dear Mr. Blue: We regret to inform you that the reserved seats, in the section that you requested for the special[1] summer concert, have been sold out. We are, however, holding seats for you in the adjoining section, Row 5, on[2] the inside center aisle. / If this meets with your approval, please notify us immediately. Sincerely yours,[3] (60)*

38. *Gentlemen: On Friday, May 10, Mr. Baker and Mr. Jones will arrive in Seattle. I would like to make[1] reservations for these two individuals. Please reserve separate rooms with private baths. / They will stay for three[2] nights. If possible, will you reserve a large conference room for Friday and Saturday. Please confirm. Yours truly,[3] (60)*

39. *Dear Mr. Ward: Thank you for your recent payment. It has been credited to your account, and your balance has been[1] reduced accordingly./ We have this date written to our Seattle office, and they will contact you shortly. We[2] regret you were not satisfied with volume 10 of our Encyclopedia International. Yours truly,[3] (60)*

40. *Dear Mr. James: At the moment, we have only one home that might fit your needs. This home is located six miles west[1] of Jefferson, near the little town of Hillsboro. There is a nice three-bedroom house, totaling 1500[2] sq. ft. There are 15 acres, with one planted in filbert trees. They are asking $75,000. Bill Case[3] (60)*

41. *Dear Sir: Please send me the latest edition of the book entitled, I'M NEVER TOO SURE, by John Raymond Randolph.[1] I believe it is published by Hanson, Blain, Roy and Company. / Please find enclosed a check for $10.50,[2] to cover the cost of the book, handling, and mailing. Please send it to my summer address, which is 125[3] North Lake Shore Drive, Belmont, California. Yours truly, (70)*

42. *Dear Sir: I would like to call your attention to the sale that our store will be having August 6 to August 10.[1] The ads concerning the sale will be out Thursday, August 3. I am sure you are interested in the big savings[2] that will be available to you. Many satisfied customers have purchased*

our home appliances. Come³ in and enjoy a big saving during this sale. Yours truly, (70)

43. Dear Mr. Wood: We are indeed happy that our restaurant again has been chosen for the annual banquet¹ of the Knitting Club. / We are reserving the banquet room on Tuesday, June 10, from 7 p.m. to 10 p.m.² We understand that there will be an attendance of approximately sixty ladies. / At a later date, we³ shall be pleased to discuss further details with you. Sincerely, (70)

44. Dear Mr. Lee: This morning I received your statement covering my purchases from March 12 to April 12. I¹ note that I was not given credit for the pair of shoes which I returned on March 28. / I am sending my² check for $87.50. You will note that I have deducted $15, the³ price of the returned shoes. Is this all right? Yours very truly, (70)

45. Gentlemen: Please send me your latest price list, quoting the prices of various makes of fishing gear. I am¹ particularly interested in gear suitable for trout fishing. My son will be fourteen next month, and I² would like to give him a suitable rod and reel for his birthday. / I shall appreciate any recommendations³ you can give me before I make my order. Sincerely yours, (70)

46. Dear Sir: I have just received my monthly telephone bill, which I believe is in error. I have been charged for a¹ long-distance telephone call to Kansas City, Missouri, on the day of May 19. I know no one in Kansas² City, so I am certain that I should not have been charged for this call. / Please check your records, to see if they are³ in error, and notify me soon. Very truly yours, (70)

47. Dear Mr. Case: The property you showed us last week seems to be exactly what we want. Although the price seems to¹ be a little high, I will purchase it for the second price you quoted. / Will you please check the county court house for² the record of the deed. Also, I would like to know if I would have first water rights. The water rights are especially³ important to me for my experimentation. Sincerely, (70)

48. *Dear Mr. James: I have checked on the things you requested. I am sorry to say that the deed is not in order.[1] It seems that the actual owner of the house is the six-year-old son of the man you met several weeks ago.[2] / It seems that the last owner, a Mrs. McIntire, placed the land in second trust for her grandson. The property[3] cannot be sold until he becomes of age. Sincerely, (70)*

49. *Dear Sir: Thank you for your order. It received our careful attention. Any changes necessary in filling[1] your order are explained by invoice. / Please do not destroy these papers until you are satisfied that your order[2] is all right in every respect. If you write us about this order, please be sure to return all of these papers.[3] It will help us to give you prompt service. Yours very truly, (70)*

50. *Dear Sir: You have just been appointed an officer of this Court. Your duties and legal responsibilities[1] are many and varied. Therefore, seek and follow the advice of your attorney in all matters pertaining to[2] the administration of the estate. / Your compliance with the law and your attention to directions from the[3] Court will be appreciated. Respectfully yours, (70)*

51. *Dear Patron: "Time waits for no one" is a well-known proverb. Sometimes, I am sure, all of us wonder where we are going[1] and why we are going there so hurriedly. / Your frequent calls to our investment office in New York have ceased,[2] and we are concerned about you. / We take pride in the fact that you are one of our most valued clients. / If our service[3] has been unsatisfactory, we would consider it a real favor if you would let us know. Yours truly,[4] (80)*

52. *Dear Mr. Gray: We are very glad to send the road maps necessary for the trip you are planning. / On these maps,[1] we have marked what we believe to be the most scenic route for you to follow. / If you wish to make any variation[2] in the suggested route, the legends on the map provide helpful information. / Everywhere in the area[3] covered by our maps, you will find the men at our filling stations ready to serve you. / Have a good trip. Sincerely,[4] (80)*

53. *Dear Mr. Bell: As you know, your telephone bill is now considerably overdue. We recently called your[1] attention to this fact by mail, but we have received no reply from you as to when you will pay this bill. / If there[2] is some reason why you cannot pay this bill, please let us know. We want to cooperate with you in arranging[3] for payment of your account. / We have enjoyed serving you and hope this relationship may continue. Sincerely yours,[4] (80)*

54. *Dear Jim: By all means, come the night before camp actually begins. I need help! Enclosed is an hour-by-hour camp[1] schedule showing classes, special activities, and recreational periods. You will notice that I have [2] scheduled your classes for 10 a.m. to 12 noon and 1:30 to 3:30 p.m. This should allow you plenty[3] of time to take your classes on field trips for the purpose of collecting and identifying insects. Sincerely,[4] (80)*

55. *Dear Mr. Smith: I am very sorry that I cannot furnish you with the information you requested. Our[1] supply of pamphlets on vacationing along the coast is temporarily exhausted. We expect to receive[2] a new supply from our publisher within the next week or so. We shall be happy to send you the information[3] at that time. / We welcome the opportunity to serve you in the very near future. Sincerely yours,[4] (80)*

56. *Dear Sir: The speaker that we had originally scheduled for our spring conference had to cancel his appointment[1] with us, because of the pressure of business at his own office. Do you know of an individual who[2] might be able to direct our workshop from April 15 through 18? The subject of our conference is "Job[3] Opportunities in Data Processing." / We welcome any suggestions you may have. Yours very truly,[4] (80)*

PS TRANSCRIPTION

1.
j: smi ag i pcsd f u e 17-jol lifi wc, y
ctlg no. 79. e stanls stel wcbn lnks r cg
aprt n 2 dfrn plas. e bn l v t b rplacd. p
advis m o y crgs d b f a nu bn. / i l aprsat
a erl rpli. yt, (60)

2.
j: ts l cfrm m cvrsas ystrda w e cmsr. i v
a l n m pss, atrizg m t k o grvl f e ara wr e
cwnt (co.) rod cro i hlg grvl. m l i rtn b e
onr o e pt. / i l coprat w u n kepg e gat
lkd. vty, (60)

3.
dmrs woods: ma w s u a v mr crsms a a most
hp nu yr. / atcd t ts gretg u l f y c plat.
i xprs r aprsas o y bsn. p us i frel n dg y
crsms spg. / p c n son, s w ma gret u psnl.
hp hldas! cy, (60)

4.
dms jones: d u lik t k a ltl xtra my f w ntl
e crsms hldas? w l ned adsl wrkrs drg e nxt

2 mts (mos.). / u w a pt o r orgnzas lst yr,
a w hop u l jyn u agn. s mr. bates f n. e i
o e frst (1st) flor o e bldg. sy, (60)

5.
d homkr: u r n dwt nwr o a nu srvc t homkrs
w rdl avalb n y cmunt. strtg j 1, w l v a
stf o xprnd rg clnrs t l b rd t ast u n clng
a rstrg e lif o y rgs. / j dil 226-3546 f
pmpt a crts 24-hr. srvc. yt, (60)

6.
j. i rcnl arivd n houston a m lokg f mplym w
y cpn (co.). m pst xprn z 6 z a sals rprsntv
(rep.) w wst cost lif nsrn (ins.) cpn (co.)
a z e sals trane f pcfc cost lif nsrn cpn
(co.). / e gd aplcas fm gs m ag, rfrns, pevs
mplym a psss hld pevsl. yt, (70)

7.
j: sm fsg n e pcfc nrtwst i a sprt t i rl a
clg t e odorsm. e pcfc nrtwst i e gratst sm
fsg ara n e wrld. / w r kg ts oprtunt t nvit
an mbrs o y lg r orgnzass t vst e sm fsg ara
ts smr. l eqpm i avalb f rn a a mdst cst.
yvt, (70)

8.
d frns: tda, z u rd ts l, 151 amrcns l b
told "u v t. b." / pt o e jb o y tubrclos

asosas (assn.) i t dscvr tes erl nfcss tro
cst x-ra a tubrcln tstg. / ov amt u ctrbut l
b efkvl usd. / t u f y gnrs sprt n e pst a v
a jys hlda ssn.　sy,

9.
dm ross:　drg e pst 8 r 10 yrs, w v isud a
anl rprt.　w fwn t plcholdrs pfr a brf rprt
t a lgr wn (1).　gd, u l f ts yr's rprt. / w
v h a g yr.　e rprt ndcats t w r n btr cds tn
v bf. / w plcholdrs lik u; nxt yr sd b a evn
gratr wn (1) f u.　s, (70)

10.
dm ball:　w w v mc ntrstd n y dsir t k ts
butf ara o orgn (ore.) y hom. / u l f n a
ptln n e foldrs t w r sng u tda.　f u v gsss,
p rit t m psnl. / w r cfdn t u l njy r butf
ct a srwng vacasln f ppl o l ags.　ys, (70)

11.
j: y frm askd t w sn a c rfrn f mr. jake
smythe.　drg e 14 yrs w d bsn w h, w fwn h t
b v pmpt a crts n l dlgs e h w u. / e hist
amt e v h crgd t z acwn (acct.) z $575.　n l
t i, e z nvr lat w z pams.　w blv u l njy dg
bsn w mr. smit.　sy, (80)

12.
dm case: a frn o min ho i tcg a e unvrst sd t

e h sen sm pprt wst o utica, o old crek rd, t
mit b o ntrst t m.   e onr a bldr i a yg m
namd bill williams.   d u p x f m t s wtr r n
e pprt i f sal?   f u ned mr n, p ctk m frn,
dave benson.   z xtns nmbr o cmps i 508.   s,
(80)

13.
dm case: i m sr t hr t e pprt cn b pt u f
sal.   m wif a i r bot v dspynd. / w l b spng
e nxt 2 weks (wks.) motrg tro e wstrn stats.
aftr t w l b movg t atlanta. f a mt (mo.) r
2, w c rn a aprtm (apt.)   f p, cd u f u a 2 r
3 bdrom aprtm w rn n hir tn $325 a mt.   sy,
(80)

14.
n gtrg mtrl f a srt papr, u v t cslt onl 2 r
3 srs.   f mr sclrl paprs, wv, u l pbbl v t
cslt my srs. / most xprts agre t e frst (1st)
stp n locatg y srs i t cslt a g nciclpda.   t
u l pbbl f a atrtatv, cdnd dscs o y tpc r sm
mprtn fas o i. a e en o e dscs ma b a lst o
boks. (80)

15.
smr vacas i e i f trvlg, a trvlr's xs r e
snsb wa t cr y my o y trp.   e cst i v ltl, a
e xs c b csd a an bnk a n my hotls.   e
trvlr's xs r nsrd, s f y r lst, a clam c b

fild t b rpad n cs. kep a rcrd o e nmbrs (nos.) o y xs, n a saf plac a hom, t us n filg f lst r stoln xs. (80)

16.

dm adams: t r 2 sids t v str. t w l rliz. / r sid i t w sn u wn (1) gros o r no. 10 pncls o m 10. e statm cvrg ts spm z mald t u o m 20. sn tn, w v mald u svrl nots t y pam z ovrd. s fr, w v h n wrd f u. / t i r sid o e str. d u min trng ts l ovr a, o e rvrs sid, tlg u y sid. tn i m sr w c g tgtr. yt, (90)

17.

dm case: e hws sems v ntrstg. i sems t b a e rit dstn f twn, a i v alwas (lwas) b ntrstd n e dsin o e a-fram. f e acrg, p, a hws spac r rit, a f e onr ss t sl, w ma b n bsn. i m most anxss t hr wtr r n e onr i lg t sl. i d l lik t k sr t i c g a clr ded. i m l ntrstd n e hiwa. p sn m e n z son z p. s, (90)

18.

dm james: i ctkd dr. benson a e tok m o t e williams' pprt. i lis 5 mils f twn. a e psn i, a 2 mils o e rod i grvl, b e hiwa dprtm (dept.) i bldg a hiwa t l b pavd b nxt yr smi. / w w nab t ctk e onr b d lok arwn e pprt. t i a sml crek t rns nr e hws. e hws,

islf, i a 3-str a-fram. e hws i n fnsd. t r
wndos cpltl arwn e frst (1st) flor. i l tri
t cc e onr ts wek. s, (90)

19.
j: a tipritr i vitl mprtn t jt-ag lvg. i ks
e dg o scol wrk s mc esr, a i's a mst f my
crs. / w e wid ara o tipritrs t cas f, i i
dfclt t n j w wn (1) t b. e cyc i a ndvdl wn
(1), dpng o y tast, bgt, a neds. r rprsntv
(rep) l b n y ara nxt wek, a e l b g t
dmstrat r nust mdl t u. / won' u lt u st u a
apynm? yt, (90)

20.
d rdr: i m v hp t sn u ts spsl anwnm o a
wndrf nu rdg clb f ten-ag grls. i i r wa o
drmtizg a bok clb dsind espsl f grls ho wn t
g e v bst o grls' nvls, a grat savgs n p. /
u n w njyb g boks c b, n y r a e tgs t ntrst
u most. rd crfl e atcd lflt dscribg r ofr.
y rwrd l b e plsr tes fin boks c brg. cy,
(90)

21.
dm james: i v g nus f u! i v ctkd e onr o e
a-fram. / aftr sg e hws, i n t ts i j e hws f
u. e hws z 3 bdroms a 2 btroms, a lrg lvg-
ding rom, w 16 fet (ft.) o gls dors t opn ot
a pto. t i a sgr grnt firplac n e lvg rom a

a swds opn firplac o e pto.　e kcn a utl rom
r fl egpd. / f i i cvnn, cd u a y wif c dwn t
jonesboro t lok ovr e pprt?　s, (100)

22.

dm case:　u w rit n u sd t ts z e pprt f u.
bot m wif a i wn t t u f y hlp. / p drw u e
paprs a sn tm t m f m sgntr.　w d lik t mov
nt e hws b ag 25.　i tkd t mr. williams b fon
ts mrng, a e ss t e tnks e hws l b fnsd b tn.
m wif wnd a fu cags m n e hws.　i v tkd t mr.
wlms a tes cags, a e z agred.　i v lstd tm a
l g tm w ts l.　cd u k sr y r dn?　s, (100)

23.

j:　w s t xtn a nvtas t etr r bot o u t atn r
nxt ss o e advisr cwncl, t sr w u ov n u ma v
o e fml crt stm, ptclrl z i ma afk benton
cwnt. / r nxt metg l b hld a 7:30 p.m., m 7,
n e jovnl ofc o e crt hws.　p advis r jovnl
ofcr, r smwn n z ofc, z t wtr r n i l b p f u
t atn n r t w ma pln.　tu, (100)

24.

d cstmr:　w r v hp t u v slkd mdrn gs egpm a
fel sr t u l b dlitd w is cln, crfre pfmn. /
f y cvnn, w r gg a pam bok, w pvids a smpl
rcrd o y pams a a rmtn slp t b nclodd w ec
mtl nstlm.　u l n b mald a mtl statm o ts

acwn, z e bok ctans wn (1) rmtn slp f ec pam
d. / w r cfdn t u l g my yrs o njym o o y nu
gs egpm. s, (100)

25.
ds: w r sr t r str z n b ab t g e tab a crs
u rd n m. / e cpn (co.) w usl (uzl) obtan tm
f z b o strik f e pst 2 weks. i s blv y l fl
e r z son z e strik i ovr a y r bk n pdcs. f
u s t cncl t r a rr a a latr d, p lt u n. w
d v sm otr v nic tabs a crs t u mit lik j z l.
w c k u a g p o tm. / w l v sm butf nu swds
mdrn dvno a cr sts t u ma b ntrstd n. yt,
(100)

SUPPLEMENTARY   SECTION III

P.S. THEORY REFERENCE

BASIC THEORY RULES

RULE 1   Never write a silent vowel.

        EXAMPLES: kite · kit   boat · bot

RULE 2   Even a sounding vowel *within* a word should be omitted unless it has the long sound of *a, i, o, u,* or *oo.* Normally, the long sound of *e* may be assigned to any preceding consonant.

        EXAMPLES: bet · bt   cat · ct

        Note: Treat a half long vowel as a short vowel and omit it.

        EXAMPLE: more · mr

RULE 3   Always write a sounding vowel whenever it occurs at the very *beginning* of a word.

        EXAMPLES: acre · acr   abate · abat

RULE 4   If a word contains a double vowel, write only *one.*

        EXAMPLES: broom · brom   book · bok   feed · fed

RULE 5   Omit silent consonants within a word; and if a word contains a double consonant, write only *one.*

        EXAMPLES: right · rit   planner · plnr

RULE 6   A sounding vowel at the end of a word should be written.

        Exception: The letter *y* at the end of a word is carried by the preceding consonant *unless* it has a long *i* sound.

        EXAMPLES: idea · ida   berry · br   cry · cri

Brief Forms

a   -- *a, an, and, at, about*
b   -- *be, by, buy, been, but*
c   -- *can, come, copy, credit*
d   -- *dear, do, due, did, date, would*
e   -- *he, the*
f   -- *for, from, if, find*
g   -- *go, get, good, glad, give*
h   -- *her, him, had, here*
i   -- *I, it, is, time*
j   -- *just, gentlemen (gentleman)*
k   -- *kind, make, take*
l   -- *all, also, will, well, letter*
m   -- *am, me, my, made, man, men*
n   -- *when, not, in, no, know, information*
o   -- *out, of, on, what*
p   -- *possible, price, please, put*
q   -- *enclose, require, quiet*
r   -- *are, or, our, return, order*
s   -- *sincerely, she, so, see, wish*
t   -- *that, thank, there, to, too*
u   -- *you, up, under, us*
v   -- *very, ever, every, have, receive.*
w   -- *with, which, we, were, how, now*
x   -- *check*
y   -- *why, your, they*
z   -- *as, has, his, was*

DAYS OF THE WEEK

sn -- *Sunday*
m -- *Monday*
tu -- *Tuesday*
w -- *Wednesday*
t -- *Thursday*
f -- *Friday*
s -- *Saturday*

MONTHS OF THE YEAR

jn -- *January*
f -- *February*
mr -- *March*
a -- *April*
m -- *May*
j -- *June*
jy -- *July*
ag -- *August*
s -- *September*
o -- *October*
n -- *November*
d -- *December*

PHONETIC ABBBREVIATIONS

In addition to representing their own basic sounds, carrying a long
e sound, and carrying the final y (unless it has a long i sound), a
number of consonants also are used to represent certain phonetic
units or word parts:

Phonetic Abbreviations: *Word Examples:*

b =	-ble	*trouble* - **trb**
c =	ch-, -ch, com-,	*church* - **crc**; *compel* - **cpl**;
	con-, (k), (s),	*continue* - **ctnu**
f =	ph-, -ph, for-, -for, -ful,	*phone* - **fon**; *form* - **fm**; *helpful* -
	-ify	**hlpf**; *magnify* - **mgnf**; *magnified* - **mgnfd**
g =	-ng, -ing, -dge	*sing* - **sg**; *singing* - **sgg**; *fudge* -
	-nge	**fg**; *singe* - **sg**; *danger* - **dagr**
k =	-ct	*act* - **ak**; *conduct* - **cdk**
l =	-lity, -lty	*utility* - **utl**; *faulty* - **fl**
m =	m- (any nonlong vowel) -m	*member* - **mbr**;
	m- (any nonlong vowel) -n	*minister* - **mstr**;
	moun-, -moun, -ment	*mound* - **md**; *torment* - **trm**
n =	-nc(e), -ns(e), -ness	*fence* - **fn**; *sense* - **sn**; *fairness* -
	-nt, -nd	**frn**; *bent* - **bn**; *send* - **sn**; *sending* - **sng**
p =	(as word beginnings only)	*pretty* - **pt**;
	pr-, p- (any nonlong vowel)	
	-r	*permit* - **pmt**;
	pro- and por- (either long	
	or nonlong o)	*prod* - **pd**; *port* - **pt**; *program* - **pgrm**
q =	qu- (kw)	*quick* - **qk**; *queen* - **qen**
r =	-rity, -ure	*rarity* - **rr**; *mature* - **mtr**
s =	sh-, -sh	*ship* - **sp**; *dish* - **ds**
	s- (any nonlong vowel) -s	*sister* - **str**; *basis* - **bas**
	c- (any nonlong vowel) -s	*races* - **ras**; *cistern* - **strn**
	(when c has an s sound),	
	-sion, -tion, -cian	*mission* - **ms**; *mention* - **ms**; *physician* - **fss**; *division* - **dvs**; *question* - **qss**
	-shion, cien	*fashion* - **fs**; *efficient* - **efst**;
	-tien	*patient* - **past**
t =	th-, -th	*thought* - **tt**; *north* - **nrt**
w =	wh- (as in where), ou (as	*whether* - **wtr**; *cloud* - **clwd**;
	in cloud), -ow (as in cow),	*cow* - **cw**;
	-aw (as n raw)	*straw* - **strw**

y =   oi-, -oi, oy- (as in boil   *boil* - ***byl;*** *toy* - ***ty;*** *oil* - ***yl***
      and toy)   *oyster* - ***yster***

Note: If a consonant is representing a phonetic unit, it cannot also carry the long *e* sound; so we must write the long *e* sound.
    EXAMPLE: cheat - cet

WORD BEGINNINGS SHORTCUTS

For *em* -- Write *m.* unless a vowel follows the *m.*
    EXAMPLES: embrace - *mbrac*   emit - *emt*

For *im* -- Write *m,* unless the *m* is followed by another *m.*
    EXAMPLES: imagine - *mgn*   immature - *imtr*

For *um* -- Write *m*
    EXAMPLE: umbrella - *mbrla*

For *in* -- Write *n,* unless the *n* is followed by another *n.*
    EXAMPLES: inability - *nbl*   innocent - *incn*

For *un* -- Write *n,* unless the *n* is followed by another *n.*
    EXAMPLES: unable - *nab*   unnecessary - *unsr*

For *en* -- Write *n*
    EXAMPLE: entail - *ntal*

For *intro*, *intr* -- Write *ntr* (whether *o* is short or long)
    EXAMPLES: introduction - *ntrdcs*   intricate - *ntrct*

For *post* -- Write *pst*
    EXAMPLE: postage - *pstg*

For *super*, *supr* -- Write *spr* (regardless of how the *u* is pronounced)
    EXAMPLES: supercilious - *sprcls*   supreme - *sprm*

USE OF EACH LETTER OF THE ALPHABET

(When final *y* has the long *i* sound, write *i.*)

LETTER	SOUNDS ACCORDING TO BASIC THEORY	PHONETIC ABBREVIATIONS
a	long a (regardless of spelling)	....
b	b, be-, -by	-ble
c	c (either s or k sound), ce-, -cy	ch-, -ch, com-, con-
d	d, de-, -dy	....
e	long e when the preceding consonant represents more than itself; one of two e's oc-	....

	curing together; short or long e at beginning of word or ending of word	
f	f, fe-, -fy	ph-, -ph, for-, -for, -ful, -ify
g	g (hard or soft or zh sound),ge-, -gy	-ng, -ing, -dge, -nge
h	h, he-	--
1	long i (regardless of spelling)	--
j	j, je-	--
k	k, ke-, -ky	-ct
l	l, le-, -ly	-lity, -lty
m	m, me-, -my	m- (any nonlong vowel) -m; -ment; m- (any nonlong vowel) -n; moun-, -moun,
n	n, ne-, -ny	-nc(e), -ns(e), -ness, -nt, -nd
o	long o and oo	--
p	p, pe-, -py	(as word beginnings only) pr-; p- (any nonlong vowel) -r; pro-and por- (either long or nonlong o)
q	q(k)	qu-(kw)
r	r, re-, -ry	-rity, -ure
s	s (s or z or zh sound),	sh-, -sh; s- (any nonlong vowel) -s;
	se-, -sy	c- (any nonlong vowel) -s; (when c has s sound) -sion, -tion, -cian, -shion, -cien, -tien
t	t, te-, -ty	th-, -th
u	long u (also oo if spell-ed with u)	--
v	v, ve-, -vy	--
w	w, we-	wh-, ou (as in cloud), -ow (as in cow), -aw (as in raw)
x	x, -xy	--
y	y, ye-, (the ending y when no	oi-, -oi, oy-, -oy (as in boil, toy,

```
     consonant is available
     to carry it)                    and oyster

 z    z (z or zh sound), ze-, -zy    ...................................
```

BRIEF FORM TEST WITH KEY

an	a	he	e	her	h	have	v
buy	b	for	f	can	c	up	u
due	d	with	w	all	l	out	o
find	f	time	i	the	e	there	t
about	a	thank	t	his	z	my	m
what	o	and	a/&	require	q	is	i
return	r	please	p	be	b	well	l
but	b	when	n	had	h	now	w
under	u	put	p	order	r	that	t
him	h	very	v	come	c	make	k
at	a	check	x	information	n	too	t
price	p	if	f	men	m	get	g
copy	c	credit	c	were	w	no	n
also	l	quite	q	am	m	dear	d
go	g	been	b	know	n	made	m
why	y	so	s	enclose	q	us	u
which	w	ever	v	how	w	we	w
by	b	just	j	date	d	in	n
has	z	kind	k	me	m	our	r
it	i	as	z	not	n	give	g
your	y	would	d	of	o	wish	s
or	r	was	z	I	i	man	m
every	v	here	h	will	l	to	t
gentlemen	j	on	o	good	g	a	a
take	k	from	f	are	r	receive	v
did	d	she	s	they	y	see	s
possible	p	you	u	do	d	letter	l
glad	g	sincerely	s	wish	s	require	q

Personal Shorthand

CARDINAL SERIES

BOOK 2

CARL W. SALSER
C. THEO. YERIAN

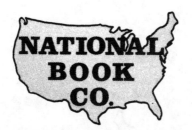

NATIONAL BOOK COMPANY
A Division of
Educational Research Associates
A Nonprofit Educational Research Corporation
333 SW Park Avenue
Portland, Oregon 97205

Personal Shorthand

CARDINAL SERIES

BOOK 2

ISBN 0-89420-107-7

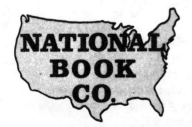

Graphics/Production   John Kimmel
Typesetting   Archetype

PREFACE

TO THE STUDENT:

PS 1 provided you first with the basic theory of this completely alphabetic shorthand. The personal-use and introductory transcription objectives, also, were made integral goals of that text.

The very fact that you have chosen to continue your study of Personal Shorthand indicates that you are interested in developing vocational competency in your notetaking skill. Certainly you can be sure that Personal Shorthand is just as much "at home" in the work-a-day world as it is in its use as a personal-use notetaking skill. Now it becomes increasingly necessary, however, for you to strive for specific "words-a-minute" goals, in order to prepare yourself for the job market. Through diligent effort on your part, you should be able to develop a writing skill that will enable you to handle satisfactorily the dictation in a very high percentage of the American business offices. You may want to discuss with your instructor the manner in which dictation is given in the average office.

In PS 2, then, you will be exposed to more and more speed-building and transcription exercises. After all, most business-style dictation is of practical value *only* when it has been transcribed. Yes, it is important to be able to write your PS notes correctly and rapidly, and major emphasis will be placed on the development of your notetaking skill; but the "finished product," the transcript, will be given equal emphasis.

You are encouraged to pay particular attention to the format of the lessons in PS 2:

1. In the early lessons, you are given a thorough review of the PS theory. Be diligent in your review application.

2. Helpful suggestions are made, from time to time, in the lessons that are based on the author's years of teaching experience. For instance, in Lesson 6, and specifically in 6.3, you will find a suggestion that, if followed, will prove to be very helpful throughout your study of Personal Shorthand.

3. Further, frequently you are urged to practice reading, writing, or transcribing (repetitiously) specific PS notes. Diligent attention to such instructions will pay real dividends in your skill development.

4. Useful transcription pointers are given throughout the text. They are very important in the transcription process and should be given very close attention. You may want to discuss some of them at greater length with your instructor and fellow students.

5. Practical and pertinent vocational pointers provide you with job-like information that will make you a more competent and effective worker.

6. Special phrase/brief form drills provide you with valuable extra skill-building practice ... don't neglect them.

7. Special vocabularies will help broaden your ability to take dictation in varying fields. Here, too, diligent practice will enable you to become a more versatile secretarial worker.

General comments: Remember that it is perfectly all right for you to continue adding meaningful abbreviations to your shorthand vocabulary. For instance, you may find it very natural to use "doe" for "Department of Education"; so, "Oregon Department of Education" becomes "OR (or) doe"; "Future Business Leaders of America" becomes "fbla"; "United Airlines" becomes "UA (ua)," etc. You may find it helpful to accumulate in a notebook a list of abbreviations you find practical to use. On a job, of course, these abbreviations become all the more meaningful because of their frequency of use ... so get into the habit, but don't go overboard.

"A word to the wise" concerning the need and desirability of starting early and maintaining your study momentum will be *agreed to* by everyone, but it is not always adhered to by everyone. Just remember that the student who does not try to make a "weekend of study" take the place of conscientious, day-by-day effort Is the one who progresses satisfactorily. This type of endeavor, too, is a great habit developer for on-the-job experiences ... for the steady and conscientious worker earns and gets the promotions.

Personal Shorthand will serve you well in a job-type situation, so get yourself ready! The authors wish you much success as you continue your study and get ready to join the many other PS writers in the world of work.

TABLE OF CONTENTS

STUDY SUGGESTIONS

1. Remember, you need not change your normal manner of writing. You should strive, however, for *neatness* and *clarity* of writing.

2. Select a quiet place in which to study and practice. Use the same time and place if possible. Do not be tempted to "break into" your study routines for other purposes. Work diligently and as rapidly as you can learn. One hour of concentrated effort is worth more than three hours of "lackadaisical" practice.

3. Your reading rate should increase gradually as you gain confidence in your understanding of PS. Soon you will approach your longhand reading rate. This is to be expected. Strive to recognize words more and more rapidly.

4. Although theory principles are important and make writing and reading easier, you need not be a "slave" to them. It is better to achieve a steady, flowing type method of writing, instead of "hesitating" while groping for specific rule interpretation and application. It is recommended that notes be reviewed for rule violation and **incorrectly** written or omitted PS characters. Practice writing these until they can be written smoothly and correctly. It is the reduction of time *between* PS words that really contributes to the increase in writing speed.

5. It is recommended that you do not write longhand or PS "interpretations" in your textbook, even if it is your property. Use a straight edge to place alongside or underneath words or sentences to be translated into longhand or PS. Develop and maintain the habit of moving along as rapidly as possible in the interpretative process. If a PS word is not readily readable in a sentence, look ahead until another word is recognized. This may assist you to identify the word you had to pass by.

6. Begin early to build "word-carrying" power. For instance, read a longhand sentence completely before beginning to translate it into PS; then write your notes as quickly as you can. You will find that your "word-carrying" ability will increase steadily. This ability is desirable, especially when taking oral dictation.

7. Develop early the habit of *thinking* PS for new and little-known words. PS will open to you a new world of opportunities for recording information in abbreviated form. This will assist you to develop "vocabulary power," as well as correct pronunciation. This is the logical place to recommend that you consult a well-known dictionary when in doubt concerning the proper pronunciation of a word. Learn how to read vowel markings, recognize the "schwa," develop pride in pronouncing words correctly, etc. Remember: YOU CAN WRITE ANYTHING IN PS THAT YOU CAN PRONOUNCE!

8. It is recommended that you keep a record of the types of mistakes you make frequently, not for the purpose of dwelling on them, but for the purpose of eliminating them as quickly as possible. Begin each study period with a review of frequent errors, and you'll be surprised how quickly they become a thing of the past. Design an easily located symbol to identify your errors; a colored pen is helpful.

9. You don't have to wait for your teacher to give you a test; prepare tests of your own, and be sure to place emphasis on your "trouble spots." Also, be sure that you make your test cover everything to date.

10. The Brief Forms, as you know, represent commonly used words and need to become completely "automatized." Practice these over and over again. You will notice that several are grouped to make meaningful combinations when recited. For instance, make a question out of "j" by asking the question, "Just gentlemen?" "N" becomes, "When not in, no know information!" Etc.

11. As with any other skill where instant recall or response is necessary, consistent and repetitious practice is very important. Write words and combinations of words, especially those that may cause you to hesitate, a sufficient number of times to eliminate the hesitation and uncertainty. Just remember how capable athletes have to do the same thing many, many times, some more than others, perhaps, in order to become proficient in their respective skills. Meaningful repetition, even though a bit "boring" at times, will help you to become a better PS writer.

12. Transcription and Vocational Pointers present many useful ideas for making your personal-use notetaking more practical and efficient. Pay close attention to what they say. You may want to discuss some of the "pointers" with your teacher.

13. In addition to learning to read PS notes rapidly, spend considerable time *transcribing*. Use the typewriter, if you have developed that skill; otherwise in longhand ... all the time paying particular attention to spelling and punctuation. Your teacher will counsel with you regarding this type of activity.

14. It is recommended that you equip yourself with *two* notebooks ... one for outside practice work and one for class time. A free-flowing ballpoint pen (medium or fine point) is recommended for writing. Pencil or felt pen create undesirable "drag" on the writing surface. It is a good idea to have a second ballpoint handy, if the one in use runs out of ink.

15. Keep your notebook in a comfortable writing position. This means that your forearm is on the desk surface and remains there throughout the writing time. The free hand should be used to move the notebook when necessary in order to keep it in the correct writing position. If this type of writing stance is maintained, notetaking will be less tiring, your posture will be more attractive, and the PS notes will be more legible and easily read.

16. Pronunication of the same word may vary, depending upon the part of the country in which you find yourself. New Englanders may pronounce the word "law" as "lawr." In every case, however, it should be written as it is spelled and marked in standard dictionaries.

17. Commonly used and well-known longhand "abbreviations," if shorter than the PS words, should be used when taking dictation. You be the judge.

18. A regular stenographic notebook (spiral binding) is recommended. Use your own judgment concerning whether you write down one column at a time or completely across the page. Remember, use the non-writing hand to keep the pad in an effective writing position.

19. Recordings in cassette form have been prepared to provide instructional assistance throughout this textbook. If your school has purchased them, your teacher will devise a procedure by which you can make effective use of them. They will talk to you through the theory in very much the same manner that would be used by a teacher. They can be useful especially for "make-up" and "review" purposes.

Personal Shorthand

CARDINAL SERIES

1.1   *Theory Review:*

1.2

> **Basic Rule No. 1**
> **Never write a silent vowel.**
>   **EXAMPLES:**   kite · *kit*   boat · *bot*

> **Basic Rule No. 2**
> **Even a sounding vowel *within* a word should be omitted**
> **unless it has the long sound of *a, i, o, u,* or *oo*. Normal-**
> **ly, the long sound of *e* may be assigned to any preced-**
> **ing consonant.**
>   **EXAMPLES:**   bet · *bt*   cat · *ct*
> **Note: Treat a half-long vowel as a short vowel and omit**
> **it.**
>   **EXAMPLE:**   more · *mr*

1.3   Preview and practice the more difficult words in paragraph
       1.4 and then see how quickly you can write the entire article
       (60 shorthand words) in PS.

1.4   *Every person who works in an office needs to consult a*
       reference manual at one time or another. Many types of
       manuals are available. They will help you reach correct deci-
       sions on problems ranging from correspondence to office
       housekeeping. Remember to consult these books when you
       need the opinion of an expert. (60 words) (s.i. 1.63)

1.5   Now follow the same procedure for practicing paragraph 1.6.
       Be sure to review any theory principles that cause you to
       hesitate in your writing of PERSONAL SHORTHAND.

1.6   *The goals of business education are two — to provide voca-*
       tional training for those who will not continue on to more ad-
       vanced schooling and to provide general education for all
       persons. The latter goal is designed to make each person an
       intelligent consumer of all the goods and services that busi-
       nesses provide. (60 words) (s.i. 1.65)

1.7   Transcription Pointers: APOSTROPHE

Use the apostrophe: After a noun to show possession.

Add an apostrophe and s *('s)* **in singular nouns and all plural nouns ending in any letter other than** s.

> *The play's chance of success is doubtful.* (Singular noun)

> *The boy's hat was lost.* (Singular noun)

> *The children's lunches were served in the small room.* (Plural noun)

> *Women's hats will be more beautiful next year.* (Plural noun)

Add an apostrophe to form the possessive plural of a noun if the plural ends in s.

> *The secretaries' supplies are kept in the business office.* (Plural noun)

> *The beneficiaries' securities were held in trust.* (Plural noun)

> *Every employee receives two weeks' vacation* (Plural noun)

1.8   The following article contains 120 shorthand words. First practice key words and phrases carefully; then see how fast you can write the entire article in PS.

1.9   *Contrary to what many people think, all secretaries do not sit at their typewriters turning out letters from nine to five. While typing and shorthand are basic skills required of most secretaries, their duties cover a broader field than the work performed by such office workers as file clerks, typists, and stenographers. ¶ Today, secretaries act more like assistants to their employers. They often are entrusted with confidential matters in the office and usually are instrumental in helping avoid delays in the office. In many businesses, the secretary also acts as the office hostess. These are only a few of the secretary's chores. (120 words) (s.i. 1.65)*

1.10   See how quickly you can *read* or *transcribe* this PERSONAL SHORTHAND letter. Always transcribe at the typewriter, if possible; otherwise, use pen or pencil.

1.11 a 35 mlyn (mln) wm r ngagd n homkg n e
Unitd Stats (US). n spit o e xtn o ts
ocpas, e Gvrnm (Gvt.) z b slo t rcgniz
homkg z a vocas. ts i bcs e wrkrs n i
nrml r n pad (pd.) a rglr, dal wag. i i
gnrl agred, wv, t homkrs ctrbut tr sr t
e wrk o e wrld. (P) brd nlg a a mstr o
dfnt skls r nedd b e homkr. tes skls r
agird b trang a pctc--y d n c t wn (1)
b nstnk. n wn (1) sd ntr ts vocas wo
csdrg z/h psnl qlfcass f crg o is duts,
z ts vocas crs w i grat rspnsbls. (P) n
e pblc scols, vwn c w v trang n homkg.
n tes crs, vwn c lrn w t pvid f e fscl
neds o a fml, w t cr f cldrn, a w t
crat e ppr atmsfr f a hom. (180 words)
(s.i. 1.58)

1.12 Vocational Pointers:

Be prepared for dictation at all times. Have necessary materials (shorthand pad, pens, etc.) organized and placed in a standard location — ready to go.

1.13 The sentences in paragraph 1.14 have been taken from a special PS letter, designed to review carefully all theory principles, phonetic abbreviations, and word beginnings. Practice writing these sentences in PS until you can do so without hesitation.

1.14 *Dear Mr. Prentice: We are encountering some unexpected trouble in the construction of our Denver plant. Excavation at one corner of the property has threatened the foundation of a nearby church and may compel a change in plans.*

1.15 Some phrases in the English language occur over and over again, with extremely high frequency. Most of these combine brief forms and other very high frequency words. It is important that you practice such phrases until you can write them automatically. See how well you can do on the phrases in paragraph 1.16.

1.16

	1	2	3
1	about it	about that time	be able
2	can be	day or two ago	each day
3	few days ago	few times	give me
4	had been	has given	I am glad
5	I could have	I did not	less and less
6	many of the	next day or two	of course it is
7	question of time	seems to be	send you
8	thank you for	that can be	that is the

1.17 See how well you can write the special vocabulary terms (accounting) in paragraph 1.18. From time to time, you may need to check one or more dictionaries for proper pronunciation.

1.18

	1	2	3
1	accounts payable	control account	gross
2	accounts receivable	creditor	journal
3	adjusting entry	current assets	ledger
4	amortization	current liabilities	proprietorship
5	audit	deductions	reversing entry
6	balance sheet	depletion	subsidiary ledger
7	capital stock	depreciation	voucher
8	closing entry	earned surplus	withholding

Personal Shorthand

2.1   *Theory Review:*

2.2

Basic Rule No. 3
Always write a sounding vowel whenever it occurs at the very *beginning* of a word.
    EXAMPLES: acre · *acr* abate · *abat*

Basic Rule No. 4
If a word contains a double vowel, write only *one*.
    EXAMPLES: broom · *brom* book · *bok* feed · *fed*

2.3   Now do some analyzing of the more difficult words in the next paragraph (for example: subject, correspondence, etc.); practice writing these in PS several times; and then see how rapidly you can write the entire article.

2.4   *A subject filing system is often set up in offices where there is much correspondence on many subjects between a small number of people. This system is often difficult for employees to handle because it is hard to build up a logical, consistent subject classification and then adhere to it strictly. (60 words) (s.i. 1.65)*

2.5   *You* are the best judge of what you need to practice *most.* If you find yourself hesitating on certain words in the next paragraph, analyze those words — and the related principles — and practice them until you can write them without hesitation.

2.6   *Art appreciation comes from inside the viewer; it cannot be learned. To prepare for this appreciation, however, one must have an understanding of what the artist's purpose is, what medium he is using, and what basic elements compose the work. With this basic knowledge, the viewer can appreciate art more fully. (60 words) (s.i. 1.65)*

2.7   Transcription Pointers: APOSTROPHE

> **Add the apostrophe and s ('s) after proper nouns to show possession.**
>> *Mr. Blaine's bonds*
>> *Mr. Smith's statement*
>> *Mr. Jones's account*
>
> **Add the apostrophe and s after z**
>> *Mr. Perez's letter*
>
> *Add the apostrophe and s after the last name only when showing joint possession.*
>> *Mitchell and Baker's Principles of Advertising is an outstanding text.*
>>
>> *Henry and Harry's equipment is in good condition.* **(Equipment owned jointly)**
>>
>> *Henry's and Harry's equipment is in good condition.* **(Equipment owned independently)**

2.8   In the following letter, there are 120 shorthand words. Scan the letter; determine which words you need to practice; and then see how fast you can write the letter. Try it again and again, if time permits.

2.9   *Dear Doctor Garcia: Your article, "Facts about Distribution," which appeared in the June issue of Economics, was a great contribution to the field. ¶ For many years, I have been interested in this field of study, but have not been able to acquire any professional information on how materials were distributed from wholesale markets to distributors. It is a real tribute to your professional standing that the magazine printed your article, since it presents only the highest quality of material. ¶ If I complete my study with any degree of success, I shall attribute it, in part, to your article. Yours truly, (120 words) (s.i. 1.68)*

2.10   Time yourself (or have someone else time you) and see how long it takes to *read* or *transcribe* the following letter. Make a note of any words that cause you difficulty and try to determine *why*. There are 180 shorthand words in this letter.

2.11   *dm dennis: bcs o m 20 yrs xprn a trang n e scrtrl fld, i m kg e lbrt o aplig f a jb w y frm. i m cvnd t i c b o vlu t y orgnzas. (P) f 5 yrs i z mplyd n e psnl*

dprtm (dept.) o e boeing (bog) cpn (co.)
z scrtr t e psnl mgr a sprvisr o e tipg
pol. tn i movd t e star products company
(str pdks cpn), wr i w hold e sam tip o
pss. i m ntrstd n obtang mplym w y cpn
(co.), z i hr t i oprtunt (oprtont) f
advnm. (P) gd i m data set a cs o rfrn
ls pprd b fmr a psn mplyrs. fel fre t
g n tc w tm, f u sd ned frtr n a m. (P)
u ma ctk m a 333-6678 btwen 8am (a.m.)
a 5pm (p.m.), m tro f. i hop w c arag a
ntrvu. yvt (180 words)(s.i. 1.61)

2.12   Vocational Pointers:

> **Most professional secretaries today prefer a pen to a pencil (the pencil point creates greater writing "drag" and varies too much during a prolonged period of dictation); and that usually means a good ball-point pen. Have several on hand (for emergencies); one with red ink — for "flagging" special notations.**

2.13   Here are more sentences from the special PS letter that was mentioned in Lesson 1. Remember that these carefully review theory principles, phonetic abbreviations, and word beginnings. See how smoothly you can write these more difficult sentences.

2.14   *Is it your belief that we should continue on schedule or phone our regional vice president for advice? From a cost standpoint, it would be much better to continue form construction without delay; which, in turn, would be helpful from a personnel assignment standpoint.*

2.15   Practice writing the phrases in paragraph 2.16 until you can write them without the slightest hesitation.

2.16

	1	2	3
1	up to date	was made	was the
2	we are sure	we are sending	we do not see
3	years ago	we can be sure	about which
4	and I will be	any time	be glad to know
5	before that time	can you give us	cannot have
6	do not have	do that	every month
7	every one of them	few minutes ago	for one thing
8	glad to know	good many of the	has not been able

2.17   Here are some more special vocabulary terms (advertising) that a capable PS writer should know. Practice writing each of them several times.

2.18

	1	2	3
1	across the board	free lance	package
2	association test	forms close	penetration
3	audience composition	frequency	pioneering stage
4	buying space	insertion order	rate card
5	buying time	island position	space schedule
6	contract year	keying an ad	split run
7	coop advertising	make good	time discount
8	copywriter	medium	wait order
9	film order date	one-time rate	zone plan

Personal Shorthand

CARDINAL SERIES

3.1 *Theory Review:*

3.2

> **Basic Rule No. 5**
> Omit silent consonants within a word; and if a word contains a double consonant, write only *one*.
>   EXAMPLES: right · *rit*   planner · *plnr*
>
>
> **Basic Rule No. 6**
> A sounding vowel at the end of a word should be written.
> Exception: The letter *y* at the end of a word is carried by the preceding consonant *unless* it has a long *i* sound.
>   EXAMPLES: idea · *ida*   berry · *br*   cry · *cri*

3.3 See how fast you can write the following article — without first previewing and practicing the more difficult words. Then note the words on which you hestiated, review the theory principles involved, and practice these words carefully before trying the article again.

3.4 *The act of voting, itself, is not difficult; however, it takes a good deal of consideration and thought to determine whom you want to represent you in government. Your conclusion should be made only after careful study of both the personal characteristics and the political beliefs of all the candidates. (60 words) (s.i. 1.68)*

3.5 Compare your "best time" on the following article with your best effort on paragraph 3.4.

3.6 *Deciding which courses to take in high school is a very important decision. The student should think about his/her schedule and also consult his/her counselor and parents. ¶ There generally are two types of courses — college preparatory and vocational. A decision about these two is important and should be made early. (60 words) (s.i. 1.68)*

3.7   Transcription Pointers: APOSTROPHE (Cont.)

Use the apostrophe to replace an omitted letter or figure.

> *class of '55   in the '30s*
> *don't   I'll   it's   you'll   you're*
> *I've   he's*

Do not use an apostrophe with possessive pronouns.

> *its   his   hers   yours   ours   theirs*
> *Its worth cannot be calculated.*

Note: *It's* means it is.

Use the apostrophe to indicate the plurals of letters or figures.

> *There are two b's in the word* Caribbean.
> *The 2's and 5's are not written clearly.*

Omit the apostrophe with figures referring to interest-bearing bonds.

> *U.S. Treasury 3s*

The newer tendency is to omit the apostrophe in other forms.

> *the 1940s*

3.8   The article in paragraph 3.9 is comprised of 120 shorthand words. After evaluating and practicing the more difficult words, see how fast you can write the entire article.

3.9   *Anyone interested in becoming a public stenographer will find that this position provides for varied activities. These workers sometimes are called upon to take dictation involving terms in a variety of fields and to transcribe that dictation rapidly into letter or report form. ¶ Usually, public stenographers do not have a steady routine in any one business. Instead, their calls may range from the businessman who wants to prepare a letter while on a business trip to professionals at a convention who need stenographic services. The rate of activity in this position varies from very active to occasional. (120 words) (s.i. 1.74)*

3.10   How quickly can you *read* (or, if possible, *transcribe* at the typewriter) the following PERSONAL SHORTHAND letter?

3.11 *son u l b fnsd w y fml scol trang f antr yr--phps fv. z e smr mts aproc, my o u r pbbl askg yslvs a y frns a wrk--wr a w t obtan i. o c u d wil stl n scol t hlp u g t frst (1st) jb? w c u ppr f ntrn nt e bsn wrld? (P) u c absrb z mc nlg a lrn z my skls z p. v u mstrd v ofc msen n y scol? v u cpltd y asinms crfl a stsfkrl? e xtra akvts n w u ptcpat nfln y cns f a g jb, t. (P) mplyrs rliz t an psn ho i l-likd b z asosts a ho i a ldr n ofcr n cmps akvts l b a ast t bsn. sc ldrsp trang a coprtv xprns crtnl hlp an ndvdl t bc mr cfdn o hslf a mr csdrt o otrs, t. (180 words)(s.i. 1.61)*

3.12 Vocational Pointers:

See that your shorthand pad is always handy and that there are, at the very least, a sufficient number of unused pages for an extended dictation session. An extra shorthand pad should be readily accessible at all times.

3.13 Paragraph 3.14 consists of more sentences from the special PS theory letter that we have mentioned before. Practice writing these in PS until you can do so with ease.

3.14 *There is a tendency for the local inspector to magnify the seriousness of the matter. It is true, however, that our heavy equipment does interfere with choir singing at the church, and debris fires have singed some trees and shrubs along the south edge of the property.*

3.15   Here are more high-frequency phrases. Say the phrase aloud as you write the PS equivalent for it. For example: "up to date, *u t d*," etc.

3.16

	1	2	3
1	have been able	have not been	have you made
2	I do not think	I have not been able	I hope it will be
3	let us have	let us know	many of these
4	may be able	might have been	next time
5	now and then	of that	of this
6	on our part	quite sure	relation to the
7	several days ago	several months ago	several times
8	that is to say	that it is	that it was

3.17   The following special vocabulary terms have to do with Farming. Learn to write them fluently. Check a dictionary if necessary.

3.18

	1	2	3
1	acreage	insecticide	rhizome
2	aeration	lactation	rotation
3	blight	livestock	row crop
4	candling	mildew	separator
5	culling	mulch	soil conditioner
6	drainage	nitrogen	subirrigation
7	erosion	parasite	subsoiling
8	farm income	pedigree	toxicity
9	fertility	petiole	tractor
10	germination	pollen	vaccination
11	growing season	progeny	vermiculite
12	heifer	propagation	xylem

Personal Shorthand

CARDINAL SERIES

4.1 *Theory Review:*

4.2

> **Brief Forms — a through e**
>
> *a* — a, an, and, at, about
> *b* — be, by, buy, been, but
> *c* — can, come, copy, credit
> *d* — dear, do, due, did, date, would
> *e* — he, the

4.3 Practice writing the next article two or three times. Make a note of any troublesome words and try to determine *why* they were not easy for you to write.

4.4 *Most application forms include a place for you to list hobbies and forms of recreation. The employer is interested in these items because they tell her/him much about your interests, character, ambition, and intelligence. If the application blank does not ask this question, the employer will during the interview. (60 words) (s.i. 1.71)*

4.5 The letter in paragraph 4.6 is composed of 60 shorthand words. Can you write it in 60 seconds or less? Try it several times.

4.6 *Dear Mr. Stein: It is a pleasure to inform you that your essay, "Vocational Business Education," has been accepted for publication by our magazine. The January 7 issue will carry it as our feature story. ¶ We would welcome any opportunity to represent you in the future. Yours truly, (60 words) (s.i. 1.75)*

4.7 Transcription Pointers: APOSTROPHE (Cont.)

> Use the apostrophe to indicate the plurals of compound words. Add the apostrophe and *s* to the last word of compound combinations.
>
> *His father-in-law's car was stolen.*
>
> *Their mothers-in-law's visit occurred in June.*

> **Add the apostrophe and _s_ when plurals of words are re-ferred to as words.**
>
> _The_ **which's** _and_ **that's** _were not used correctly._

4.8　The following article is composed of 120 shorthand words. Preview the article, and make a list of any bothersome words. Then practice writing these words until you can write them without hesitation. Finally, write the entire article, as smoothly as you can, several times.

4.9　_Once you have decided what kind of work you would like to pursue, start compiling a list of concerns which would be logical employers for you. You can locate companies by looking through advertisements and news articles in trade journals and newspapers. Consult listings in telephone directories. Contact trade association secretaries, who can reveal names and addresses of possible employers. ¶ After compiling your list, select several preferred prospective employers. Learn all you can about them. Then, combine this information to help you write an effective application letter and to ask intelligent questions during the interview. (120 words) (s.i. 1.77)_

4.10　Knowing how to _write_ PERSONAL SHORTHAND is very important, of course; but no more important that knowing how to _read_ it. How fluently can you read the next article?

4.11　_bsn educas (edu.) i wn (1) o e most (mst) widsprd aspks o vocasl educas (edu.) n e Unitd Stats (U.S.) i h is bgngs n ts cntr a 150 yrs ag. (P) e frst (1st) bsn tcrs mt w a g dl o opss f e scols a clgs o t i. nvrels, tes piners pstd. n e erl dcads o e 19t cntr (cnr), y trand yg m f psss n bsn--mostl n bokepg. (P) e frst (1st) pctcl tipritr z xhbtd a e cntrl xpss hld n fldlfa n 1876. piner bsn educas (edu.) tcrs plad a lrg pt n kg i p f wm t g trang n srthn a tipritg;_

a, ts, obtan psss n bsn ofs nrl a hnrd (100) yrs ag. (P) i i ftg t w sd onr e piners ho brt bsn educas (edu.) nt xstn. y v l lg sn lft u, b o y strtd lvs o. (180 words)(s.i. 1.74)

4.12   Vocational Pointers:

> **Get into the habit of writing the current date in the lower left corner of the *first unused page* in your short-hand pad. It also is a good idea to insert the initials of the person dictating to you, alongside the date (whether another student, your teacher, or an employer).**

4.13   Here are some more sentences from the theory letter that we have been previewing. Analyze the "key" theory principles involved, as you practice writing these sentences in PS.

4.14   *We trust that members of the congregation hold no grudge against our organization nor the project itself and will act accordingly while construction is in progress. I should mention, too, that several underground utility installations have proved faulty, causing far too many outages in the area, which, in turn, have distressed church members, as well as the minister.*

4.15   Now practice writing these much-used phrases. Notice how many PS brief forms are involved.

4.16

	1	2	3
1	up to the minute	upon the	we cannot be
2	we cannot say	we can see	we could not
3	we feel sure	we have been	we have been able
4	we have not been	we have your order	we hope it will
5	we may be	we may be able	we may have
6	you are not	you can be	you can have
7	you could be	you could have	you could have been
8	you did not	you did not say	you did not see

4.17   Listed in the next paragraph are special vocabulary terms having to do with Arts and Crafts. See how quickly you can adapt PS to the writing of these words.

4.18

	1	2	3
1	air brush	firing chamber	origami
2	alexandrite	flock	overglaze
3	aurora crystal glass	floratape	planishing hammer
4	baguette	flux	pyrometer
5	batik	gem factor	rattan
6	bezel	grommet setter	scriber
7	brayer	grout	skein winder
8	ceramic glass	gummed Holland	sponge painting
9	chat	hydrometer	styrofoam
10	coquille board	kick wheel	template
11	ethlyene dichloride	kiln wash	travertine art glaze
12	fibre adhesive	majolica	wheat paste

Personal Shorthand

CARDINAL SERIES

5.1　*Theory Review:*

5.2

> **Brief Forms — f through j**
> f — for, from, find, if
> g — go, get, good, glad, give
> h — her, him, had, here
> i — I, it, is, time
> j — just, gentlemen

5.3　In writing the letter to Mr. Upton in PERSONAL SHORT-HAND, see how many brief forms are included. The typical business letter averages at least 50 percent brief forms — and often times much higher. See how many brief forms you find in this letter.

5.4　*Dear Mr. Upton: We received your order for three hundred bales of hay. Since we have just finished ¼ baling the last [1] crop of hay, we will forward your order to you next Friday. ¶ In the event you ½ are in need of any more hay, [2] we suggest you send in your order promptly, as we know the supply ¾ on hand will be sold in a short time. ¶ Thank you [3] for the privilege of serving you. Sincerely, (70 words) s.i. 1.27)*

5.5　The next letter, like the letter in paragraph 5.4, is composed of 70 shorthand words. Again determine the percentage of brief forms as you practice writing this letter in PS.

5.6　*Dear Mrs. Cohen: Thank you for your order of fifteen boxes of Boyd writing paper. Due to a ¼ delay in [1] production, we will not be able to ship your order for three weeks. We are holding / your records on file so you will [2] not have to con-tact us. ¶ We are pleased that you have given us your ¾ order, and we will try to get your paper to you as quickly as we possibly can. Sincerely, (70 words) (s.i. 1.29)*

5.7   Transcription Pointers: APOSTROPHE (Cont.)

Use the apostrophe to show possession with Jr. and
Sr.; also in certain expressions of "time."

Jr. and Sr.:

George A. Eyrich, Jr.'s office is on the tenth floor.

Expression of Time

a month's notice   *two month's notice*

a day's drive   *three weeks' vacation*

Note: The apostrophe is omitted frequently in the
names of organizations, unless it is indicated by
general usage.

Citizens National Bank

Northern State Teachers College

The explorers Club

5.8   The following letter to Mrs. Chang consists of 140 shorthand
words. Practice writing it several times; preferably from dictation, if at all possible.

5.9   *Dear Mrs. Chang: The Kentucky Horsemen's Club is planning to repair the horse barns which are used ¼ for their annual ¹ club show each year. However, we do not have the
money to complete the job. ¶ In ½ an effort to raise some
money for this project, the club is offering some bonds for
sale. Since you ¾ are aware of the value of this annual ³
horse show to our state, we hope you will want to buy some
(1) of these bonds at $25 each. ¶ We were surprised ⁴ to hear
that you will not be entering ¼ your horse, Colonel Foster,
in our show this year, especially since he walked ⁵ away with
first place at last ½ year's show. We had hoped to see your
daughter ride him to first place again this year. ¶ Even ⁶
though you will ¾ not be entering the competition this year,
we hope you plan to attend our horse show. Sincerely, ⁷
(140 words) (s.i. 1.31)*

5.10   Determine your shorthand reading rate on the next letter,
dividing the total number of words (210) by the number of
minutes it takes you to complete the letter.

5.11   *d judy: i hop u l b ab t spn y sprg*

vacas w u. sn u r shirley's romat, i d lik v mc t met u; a i hr i i g a lg wa t y hom. w v plny o rom h, a e wtr i butf, s i n u d lik i. (P) shirley ss u v n b t nu yrk; s, f u lik, w cd spn a da r 2 o e vacas n e ct. i m sr u d b ntrstd n sg sm o e fsnatg sits, sc z cnrl prk a e unitd nass bldg. a, o crs, u mst s e ct a nit. l e elctrc lits g i a psnl o is on. mab w c evn lt u pctc y frnc b gg t a rstrn wr u c r n frnc. (P) f ts g wtr keps u, w sd b ab t v svrl pncs; a, o crs, u c g swmg. ts sd nab u t ad t t tn u v b wrkg o. shirley sd l o u v b wrkg v hrd t g a g tn, b most o u v b pgrsg g slol. (P) i d hop u l vst u, a i d b mc fn t v u h; a i n shirley d lik i. vty   (210 words)(s.i. 1.26)

5.12   Vocational Pointers:

Keep a rubber band around the *used* pages of your shorthand pad, so that the *unused* portion of the pad will be available to you at a moment's notice.

5.13   Practice the next few sentences from the theory letter that we have been "previewing."

5.14   ***There is also a large mound of dirt, near their parking lot, which cannot be moved until cement footings have been completed. We may be able to screen this some with a fence; but in all fairness, there is no sense in pretending that this will be completely adequate.***

5.15   Here are some more important phrases. Practice writing them in PS until they become automatic.

5.16

	1	2	3
1	as a result	as it will be	as soon as
2	as soon as possible	as soon as you can	as they can be
3	as they have	as this may be	as we are not
4	before you are	before you can	between the
5	between us	cannot say	cannot see
6	check up	day or two ago	did not
7	do not say	each month	each morning
8	every one of the	ever since	for this

5.17   The next paragraph consists of a cross-section of Art terms. See how quickly you can write these in PERSONAL SHORT-HAND. You may need to check a good dictionary before writing some of these.

5.18

	1	2	3
1	abstract art	fauvism	naturalism
2	abstract expressionism	fixative	opaque
3	achromatic color	fundamental colors	pastel
4	applied art	gesso	pastiche
5	armature	half tone	perspective
6	casein	highlights	primary colors
7	casting	hot colors	primitivism
8	collage	hue	proportion
9	complementary colors	impressionism	realism
10	cool colors	kinetic	shading
11	cubism	mastic	silk screen
12	Dadaism	medium	surrealism
13	dragging	monochrome	tempera
14	eclecticism	motif	wash drawing

5.19   The very high-frequency words listed in the following chart
        are represented by which PS brief forms?

5.20   **Brief Forms:**

	1	2	3	4	5	6
1	can	and	he	gentlemen	thank	just
2	why	copy	credit	would	has	very
3	be	dear	for	her	with	you
4	time	our	kind	make	up	when
5	at	come	by	the	your	letter
6	from	go	it	him	made	am
7	no	of	price	enclose	which	ever
8	know	what	to	they	we	too
9	she	or	please	about	possible	but
10	do	been	if	get	had	due
11	did	date	find	have	good	here
12	give	quite	order	see	not	out
13	that	put	will	wish	well	me
14	on	my	are	there	us	man
15	men	an	is	were	in	return
16	check	was	his	as	receive	so
17	take	sincerely	also	every	under	buy
18	require	glad	all	how	now	information

Personal Shorthand

CARDINAL SERIES

6.1   *Theory Review:*

6.2

> **Brief Forms — k through o**
> **k** — kind, make, take
> **l** — all, also, will, well, letter
> **m** — am, me, my, made, man, men
> **n** — when, not, in, no, know, information
> **o** — out, of, on, what

6.3   As you practice writing PS, you may find it worthwhile to compile a list of words that seem to bother you consistently, so that you can give such words special attention.

6.4   *Dear Mr. Stein: Have you arranged for your vacation yet for this year? It is not too soon to ¼ start planning now [1] for a summer trip to Europe or to the Far East. ¶ By making a reservation ½ now, you can be sure of [2] getting exactly the flight you want. If you desire to go by ship, ¾ it is even more important to sign up soon. [3] Send now for our schedule of sponsored tours. Sincerely, (70 words) (s.i. 1.31)*

6.5   Compare your speed (or time) in writing the following letter to Mr. Sado, with your rate on the letter in paragraph 6.4.

6.6   *Dear Mr. Sado: The women's skirts on our order No. 523, which was sent on July 10, ¼ have not been [1] received. During the two weeks since July 10, we have had many calls for these skirts; and ½ every day we have to wait means [2] that we are losing business. ¶ As sales by us result in orders for ¾ you, we are confident you will rush us the [3] merchandise when you receive this letter. Yours truly, (70 words) (s.i. 1.31)*

6.7   Transcription Pointers: QUOTATION MARKS

Quotations taken word for word from the author require the use of quotation marks.

She said, "I shall see you tomorrow."

He said, "What is the price of this material?"

The quotation mark is placed *after* the period.

He replied, "I have read the book."

The quotation mark is placed *after* the comma.

"Better late than never," he said.

"I shall see you," she said, "as soon as possible."

6.8   See how quickly you can provide PERSONAL SHORTHAND for the next article of 140 shorthand words.

6.9   *Who was the first person to discover that if the seeds of grains or fruits were put into the ground ¼ they would grow and ¹ bear more grain or fruit? Perhaps it was a woman. Some housewife cleaning up after the ½ noon meal may have thrown out ² leftover berries or grain, and months later, in the same spot, she found plants ¾ that had the same kind of food growing on them. ³ It may have occurred to her then that by putting the seeds (1) in the ground, it would be much easier to make foods grow ⁴ where she lived, than to search for them over ¼ wide areas. This astonishing discovery was of great importance ⁵ to humanity, for ½ with this magic secret, people could stop their endless search for food and settle down in one ⁶ locality. ¾ They could now become farmers, as well as hunters, and improve their struggle for existence. (140 words) (s.i. 1.31)*

6.10   Day by day, see how much you can improve your shorthand reading rate. Whether you are reading or writing PS, however, get into the habit of listing troublesome words (perhaps on some kind of "master" list); gradually deleting such words as you master them. Now read (or, if possible, transcribe at the typewriter) the article in paragraph 6.11.

6.11   *don' strt o o a xcrs f e ski i rd a sn-ris, f n smr u ma xpk svrl hrd swrs; n wnr t v likl l b std a hrd ran w wn. t l l b ran n e sn sts bhin a clwd a n i*

*ris n wn. n e wstrn ski a e hrizn i a
sln gra a snst r i bnkd w drk clwds, t
mns ran t. (P) alto clwds ma n trtn, u
sd lok f ran n e wn blos f e est.   a
nrtst wn usul brgs a cold, std ran w
lsts svrl das. (P) f t i a rg arwn e
mon, d n cwn o ctnud fr wtr; nls sm nu
cdss aris, t l b hrd ran wn a da r 2.
(P) n e blu ski bgns t val islf n a lit
gra mst, u ma n t ran i fmg ovrhd a l
son c dwn. (P) n e lvs o e wit pplr so
tr slvr ling, lok o f ran.   alwas j bf
e strt o a ranstrm, a grop o tes tres,
strd b e est wn, trn tr lvs n mss a sem
t bc vrtb tres o brit slvr. (P) finl, n
e cmpfir smok hgs lo r i drvn t e grwn
b wn, u ma l xpk nplsn wtr.   (210
words)(s.i. 1.28)*

6.12   Vocational Pointers:

> **If your employer calls you in for dictation (even if it is
> time for your "coffee break," close to the lunch hour, or
> nearly time for closing), respond immediately —
> regardless of any other project on which you may be
> working. If the job on which you are concentrating is
> critically important, it may be appropriate to tactfully
> ask your employer whether you should complete the
> task before taking dictation.**

6.13   Here are some more writing sentences from the theory letter on which we have been working, lesson by lesson.

6.14   *Recently, the church sent a letter of complaint to the city council concerning the noise problem; and we, in turn, are planning to send the council a letter of explanation. Obviously, such a large construction project is not a pretty sight; and while we have a permit to do what we are doing, noise, smoke, and dust are natural by-products of any such endeavor.*

6.15   Learn to write the following phrases so well that you can write them automatically, without even stopping to think of the individual words involved. If study conditions permit, say the phrase aloud, while at the same time writing the PS.

6.16

	1	2	3
1	for your convenience	for your information	from our
2	from that	from them	from you
3	glad to have	glad to hear	glad to say
4	good many of these	great many of the	have not been able
5	he can be sure	he cannot be	he cannot have
6	he could not	he did not pay	he did not say
7	he is not	he may be	he might have
8	I shall not be able	I should have	I thank you

6.17   Here are more special vocabulary terms — this time Brokerage terminology. Apply your PERSONAL SHORTHAND knowledge to the writing of these combinations.

6.18

	1	2	3
1	above-average yield	capital stock	current yields
2	American Stock Exchange	capitalization	debenture bonds
3	amortization	common stock	diversification
4	bid price	convertible certificates	Dow-Jones averages
5	blue chip	corporate charter	earning capacity
6	board of directors	corporate earnings	exercise of warrants
7	book value per share	cumulative preferred	funded debt
8	brokerage fee	current assets	indemnity bond
9	capital gains	current liabilities	liquidating transaction

Personal Shorthand

7.1   *Theory Review:*

7.2

> *Brief Forms* — *p* through *t*
> *p* — possible, price, please, put
> *q* — quite, require, enclose
> *r* — return, are, our, or, order
> *s* — sincerely, she, so, see, wish
> *t* — that, thank, there, to, too

7.3   The less you have to "think" about your shorthand the more words you can respond to *automatically*, the easier (and faster) you will write PS. In the next article of 70 words, how many can you write without conscious deliberation?

7.4   *If you plan to work in a business office, you should learn how to operate a ten-key adding ¼ -listing machine. [1] You can learn the keyboard on this machine by the touch method, just like you learn the ½ typewriter keyboard. ¶ The touch [2] method enables you to produce more work in less time. Since the ten-key ¾ touch method has worked well, many firms have [3] developed ten-key keyboards for use on other machines. (70 words) (s.i. 1.32)*

7.5   How about the letter in paragraph 7.6. How many of its words can you write automatically?

7.6   *Dear Mr. Capp: The house plan you sent me needs a little additional work. ¶ For instance, you ¼ indicate there is [1] to be a fireplace, but no specifications are included with it. What kind of ½ roof do you plan to have? You [2] have shown crawl space but have not stated if the furnace is to be in ¾ this space or somewhere else. ¶ Please clear up these [3] problems and contact me as soon as possible. Sincerely, (70 words) (s.i. 1.32)*

7.7   Transcription Pointers: QUOTATION MARKS (Cont.)

The quotation mark is placed *before* the semicolon.
A congressman, who is well known, stated that the action was taken as another "political move"; but his opponent claimed that this was not true.
The quotation mark is placed before the colon.
Please remove from the box labeled "stationery": three envelopes, three purchase order forms, and one requisition.

7.8   See how fast you can turn the following sales letter into readable PS notes.

7.9   *Dear Ms. Amalfi: We are trying extremely hard to have a sensational white sale for you this ¼ summer. We have been* [1] *able to get you some of the most popular styles of the year. ¶ Our salespeople have ½ worked long hours, on special* [2] *displays; and if you are pleased with these displays, they will have achieved much of ¾ their ambition. We are sure you will notice* [3] *their hard work as you enter our store. ¶ If you are (1) interested in attending our annual white sale, come to* [4] *our store quickly before the rush starts. If ¼ you get weary, you can ask for a cool drink, which will be available* [5] *in all areas of the ½ store. ¶ You will be surprised when you pay your bill, as our budget prices are easy on* [6] *the purse. You ¾ save because our overhead is low. ¶ Watch our headlines in the evening paper. Yours very truly,* [7] *(140 words) (s.i. 1.32)*

7.10   Check your reading (or, preferably, transcribing rate at the typewriter) on the PERSONAL SHORTHAND article in paragraph

7.11   *w l e trgc tgs w hr a rd a v da, ppl cn hlp b fel t y r lvg n a i o cfus. evns o e nsl a ntrnsl sn r nkd o sc a vst scal t y r byn r ustng. (P) n sc is, w c gan strgt a crg f w ris abv e wrldl tgs o sit a sn t tnk a tgs t brg jy a hpn t r livs--r frnsps w ln clr a sprt t r dal livs. t i a brit sid z l z a drk sid t r livs. o e brit sid r r homs, famls, frns, a e stsfkss w driv f e wrk w d v da. (P) w c l tran rslvs t cmuncat btr n r homs, amg r frns, a n r scols a cls-roms. e lk o cmuncas, z w r told, lis a e btm o mc o e semg mptn o lif. (P) w sd l st u ams f rslvs--e dtrmas t k e most o o w v. w c depn r stsfkss n l r ctks n w met otr ppl mr tn hf wa. my ppl d 6 mc hpr f y h a ltl mr optmsm a mc ls psmsm. (210 words)(s.i. 1.34)*

7.12   Vocational Pointers:

Upon entering your employer's office for dictation, seat yourself where you can hear clearly and where you will provide the least distraction to the dictator. Some dictators like to pace the floor when they are dictating. Others need the entire tops of their desks for their own notes, files, etc.; and, therefore, prefer that you do not use any part of the desk for a writing surface.

7.13   Let's continue to work on the comprehensive theory letter that we have been systematically reviewing. Analyze the theory involved as you write the next few sentences in PS.

7.14   *Large plants are not portable and cannot be moved to the pristine wilderness. I would be quick to admit that there have been problems with this building site, but they are a rarity and nothing that should jeopardize mature relationships.*

7.15   Here are some more important phrases on which you need
       to practice.

7.16

	1	2	3
1	line of business	line of goods	long ago
2	long time ago	many of them	many of those
3	many times	may be sure	might be
4	might not	next day	next month
5	next year	none of the	on request
6	on sale	on that	on the
7	on this	on time	on your
8	one of our	one of the best	one of the most

7.17   Practice your PERSONAL SHORTHAND on a continuation
       of the Brokerage terminology in paragraph 7.18.

7.18

	1	2	3
1	long-term capital loan	over-the-counter market	semiannual dividend
2	management realignment	participating preferred	short-term capital gain
3	market price	par-value stock	speculative stocks
4	municipal bond	proxy	stock certificate
5	National Association of Securities Dealers	receivership	subsidiary companies
6	New York Stock Exchange	round-lot sale	treasury stock
7	no-par-value stock	securities	underwriters
8	Securities and Exchange Commission	odd-lot trading	unlisted securities

Personal Shorthand

CARDINAL SERIES

8.1 *Theory Review:*

8.2

> **Brief Forms — *u* through *z***
>
> *u* — you, up, under, us
> *v* — very, ever, every, have, receive
> *w* — with, which, we, were, how, now
> *x* — check
> *y* — your, why, they
> *z* — as, has, his, was

8.3 Write the article in paragraph 8.4 as quickly as you can. If any words cause you to hesitate, make a point of finding out *why.*

8.4 *When you begin choosing a career, there will be many possibilities open. You should ¼ carefully consider ¹ what type of work you would enjoy. Life could be pretty dismal if you had to face ½ going to work each day at ² a job that you disliked, even if the pay were good. ¶ One who does not ¾ like his work is likely to do a poor job. ³ You will be most successful doing something you enjoy. (70 words) (s.i. 1.34)*

8.5 Are there any "theory questions" in the next article that cause you to slow down in your writing of PS?

8.6 *If you want the post office to forward mail, you must file with the postmaster at your local post ¼ office. ¶ You will ¹ have to fill out a request, signed in writing, giving your present address and the ½ address to which mail is to be ² forwarded. You also need to state the time period during which ¾ this order is to be observed. If you need ³ to cancel this order, notify the post office. (70 words) (s.i. 1.34)*

8.7   Transcription Pointers: QUOTATION MARKS (Cont.)

The quotation mark is placed *after* the question mark if the quoted material is a question.

He asked, "What shall I do about this matter?"

The buyer asked, "When will the shipment be made?'"

Mr. Clayton replied, "I have read the article, 'What Does Business Expect?'"

The quotation mark is placed *before* the question mark if the quoted material is not in the form of a question but the sentence asks a question.

Did he say, "The order will be shipped next week"?

Did John reply, "I don't wish to discuss the matter further"?

8.8   "Preview" the following letter, practicing the more difficult words several times. Then, if at all possible, take the letter from dictation; perhaps at several different speeds.

8.9   *Dear Karim: When we discussed our mutual hobby, hunting, at the dinner party two weeks ¼ ago, you said that [1] you might enjoy spending a week with me and some other sportsmen at my lodge, in the ½ Rocky Mountains, if we could [2] arrange to get away from our desks for a few days. ¶ I find that a ¾ slow period is in sight in my office, [3] and I am planning to take a week's vacation from (1) September 6 through 13. If you could arrange to get [4] away from your office at the same time, I ¼ believe I can make up a party that you will find very enjoyable. [5] If I receive a ½ favorable reply, I shall get busy on the details. ¶ I will get in touch with you [6] again, when ¾ plans are at a more advanced stage. I hope the suggested dates will be satisfactory.   Sincerely, [7] (140 words) (s.i. 1.36)*

8.10   The shorthand letter in paragraph 8.11 consists of 210 shorthand words. Time yourself and see how long it takes you to read it.

8.11   *dm creston: dailey men's shop (dal m's sp) d lik t k ts oprtunt t t u f e n u placd w n nprsntv, mr. floyd (flyd), o a*

18. *w w xtrml hp t v ts r, z ts i e frst (1st) i u v rd gs f r frm. u c b crtn w l srv u t e bst o r abl. (P) nv w opn nu acwns, w alwas ask f a fnnsl statm f e cstmr. ts hlps u k cr o r cstmrs' c gms. n mr. flyd cld o u, e sd e lft a c o r statm fm, w u w t cplt a r a wn. f sm rsn, w v n yt vd ts fm. i mit b n e mal, r phps u r stl cpltg i a l sn i srtl. (P) o e otr hn, f u cn cplt ts fm w, cd u sn u y x t cvr hf y r, s w c sn i a wn. u c tn dscwn e rmang bln n u v r mtl statm. a a latr d, u c cplt e statm fm a r i t u. (P) t u agn f y r. w hop w v e oprtunt t srv u agn son. vty (210 words)(s.i. 1.35)*

8.12 Vocational Pointers:

During dictation it is important to be as unobtrusive as possible, and to distract as little as possible. Experienced secretaries know that the articulate dictation of well organized letters is a very demanding process. As a matter of fact, very few people — executives or otherwise — do it easily or well. Therefore, it behooves you to interfere with the dictator's concentration as little as possible.

8.13 Let's turn our attention again to the theory letter on which we have been practicing from time to time. Don't leave paragraph 8.14 until you can write each word easily and fluently.

8.14 *We have considered the use of a small seismograph* in the hope of better controlling ground tremors during blasting. Most of the excavation faces church property, which, again, tends to complicate our mission.*

*(When practicing this theory letter, we will use the older spelling and pronunciation, sismograph, rather than the more current, seismograph.)

8.15 Practice applying your PS to these important phrases.

8.16

	1	2	3
1	realize that	shall not	shall not be
2	shall not have	she can	she could
3	she could not	she could not be	she is
4	she is not	should be	should be done
5	should be made	should have	should have been
6	that it will	that it will be	that may
7	that may be	that this is	that there are
8	that this	that those	that will

8.17 Starting in paragraph 8.18 is a good cross-section of special vocabulary (Civil Service) terms. Make sure that you can write them easily in PERSONAL SHORTHAND.

8.18

	1	2	3
1	accessible	apportionment	certificate
2	accomplish	arbitrary	chairman
3	according to	assessments	chief
4	accountant	authority	citations
5	adequacy	authorization	civil service
6	adhered	backlog	commerce
7	agencies	benefit	committee
8	alien	blueprint	compensation
9	allocate	board	compensatory
10	alternative	budget	congratulatory
11	amend	bureau	consensus
12	analysis	carbon copy	controversy
13	annual leave	case	corps
14	appeal	category	cost
15	applicant	census	criminal

Personal Shorthand

CARDINAL SERIES

9.1 *Theory Review:*

9.2

> **Days of the Week**
> *sn* — Sunday
> *m* — Monday
> *tu* — Tuesday
> *w* — Wednesday
> *t* — Thursday
> *f* — Friday
> *s* — Saturday

9.3 How many brief forms are there in the next article. How many brief form "derivatives"?

9.4 *When taking notes in class, students tend to take down everything that is being said, rather than just ¼ important points.* [1] *By trying to get down everything, they miss much of the real value of the class and / most of the interest. ¶ The* [2] *best way to take notes is to sit down for a few minutes after class ¾ and put down the principal idea of* [3] *the day, in three or four carefully written sentences. (70 words) (s.i. 1.34)*

9.5 Are there a greater number or lesser number of brief forms in this next article?

9.6 *When it is necessary to place a phone call, it is a good idea to find out if the ¾ person you are* [1] *calling is free to discuss the particular subject in question. It may be that ½ s/he is in a situation* [2] *where s/he cannot talk freely. Give her/him the opportunity to ¾ ask you to call at a later time or to* [3] *offer to return your call when s/he is free to do so. (70 words) (s.i. 1.34)*

9.7 Transcription Pointers: QUOTATION MARKS (Cont.)

> The quotation mark is placed *after* the exclamation point if the quoted material is an exclamation.
>
> *She exclaimed, "What a beautiful sunset!"*
>
> The quotation mark is placed *before* the exclamation point when the entire sentence is the exclamation.
>
> *Stop crying "wolf"!*
>
> *Look at all this "dough"!*
>
> Note: Quotations using the thought, but not the words of the author, are *not* enclosed with quotation marks.
>
> *He said that he was reading the magazine.*
>
> *She remarked that it was a beautiful day.*

9.8 Write the following article in PS as many times as your study schedule will permit. Give special attention to words involving theory principles.

9.9 *If your high school or college does not have a placement bureau, and if you cannot afford to go ¼ to a placement* [1] *agency for a job lead, the "Help Wanted" column of any local newspaper ¼ is perhaps the next best source* [2] *of job leads. Also, the State Employment Service does not charge for ¾ helping you to get a job, and they will gladly* [3] *offer you assistance in locating a position. (1) ¶ If you are applying for a job on your own, you should* [4] *write a letter of application ¾ directly to the firm's employment office, addressing it to the personnel* [5] *manager. State in this ¼ letter what kind of work you want to do and what kind of work you are qualified to* [6] *do. Also, ¾ tell him/her you will call to make an appointment with him/her, thereby, not putting him/her to any extra work. (140 words) (s.i. 1.45)*

9.10 How is your reading rate coming? How many minutes (and seconds) does it take you to read (or, better still, transcribe at the typewriter) the following letter to Mrs. Graham, consisting of 210 shorthand words.

9.11 *dmrs graham: crsms i aprocg, a w hop u l vst r stor a xm e wnrf slcs o crsms gfts w w v o dspla. w blv ts yr's gfts srps n but a vrt tos ofrd n pst urs. w r sr u l*

[Shorthand text]

b ab t f sm nusl tgs f y fml a frns. (P)
f u r n e mrkt f tys f e cldrn, u l f r
ty dprtm i scg gfts t l dliit cldrn o l
ags. brg e cldrn w u, a lt tm sr n e fn.
(P) r bok dprtm z rd my nu boks j f crsms
gg. t i a lrg stk o cldrn's boks a boks
f v otr mbr o e fml, t. my o tm r butfl
ilstratd. (P) w v xtra salsppl o hn t srv
u, a u l f tr srvs crts a efst. u t
crsms da, r stor l b opn m tro f evngs
ntl 9 o'clk, s t e hol fml c c n f y dsir
t d s. (P) y crg acwn l b cvnn t u a ts
i; w hop u l us i. w aprsat y bsn a wan
t srv u. yvt (210 words)(s.i. 1.39)

9.12   Vocational Pointers:

> **Your function as a secretary is to participate in dicta-
> tion as a highly skilled partner — not a distraction.
> Don't tap pencil or pen, finger jewelry or hair, or look
> out the window. The fact that your employer perhaps is
> very prominent and very knowledgeable in his field,
> does not mean that he necessarily is a fluent speaker
> — or dictator. He may find it difficult to organize his
> thoughts; he may pause for a considerable period of
> time; he may repeat or change his mind.**

9.13   Practice writing the following sentences (out of the theory
letter on which we have been working) in PS.

9.14   *Moreover, it is becoming increasingly clear that we need a
physician "on call" 24 hours a day, in order to efficiently protect division personnel. This will enable us to better answer
any question directed to us by state and federal agencies. I*

thought that this, in itself, was of considerable importance because of recent changes in the law.

9.15   Paragraph 9.16 presents more important phrases on which to practice writing your shorthand.

9.16

	1	2	3
1	very glad	very glad to hear	very good
2	very important	very much	very soon
3	we might	we might be	we might be able
4	we might have	we must	we must be
5	we must have	we shall	we shall be
6	we shall be able	we shall be glad	we shall have
7	we shall not	we shall not be able	we should
8	we should be	we should be glad	we should have

9.17   Now let's work on some more special vocabulary (Civil Service) terms. Make a note of any terms that cause you to hesitate in your writing and give these special attention.

9.18

	1	2	3
1	cross-examination	estimate	injunction
2	customs	exercise	intelligence
3	decentralization	expediency	interest
4	declaration	expedite	interstate
5	decree	federal	invoice
6	defense	fiscal	joint committee
7	department	foreign	jurisdiction
8	dependents	general directive	justice
9	dictate	government	labor
10	disclosure	houses	litigate
11	dismissal	hypothesis	living
12	division	impact	local
13	economy	inclusion	magnitude
14	efficiency	income	management
15	election	initiative	military

Personal Shorthand

10.1   *Theory Review:*

10.2

Months of the Year	
jn — January	*jy* — July
f — February	*ag* — August
mr — March	*s* — September
a — April	*o* — October
m — May	*n* — November
j — June	*d* — December

10.3   The letter in paragraph 10.4 incorporates 70 shorthand words. Can you write it in one minute or less?

10.4   *Dear Secretarial Student: How much time do you spend each day in reading? You may wonder what ¼ the reading of [1] good books has to do with your job as a secretary. It will make you a more ½ and a better informed [2] person. ¶ When you are making plans for your time away from the office ¾ — shopping, movies, and the hairdresser — put [3] aside some time for reading a good book.   Sincerely, (70 words) (s.i. 1.36)*

10.5   The following letter to Mr. Chan also is composed of 70 shorthand words. If you can write it faster than the letter in paragraph 10.4, try to determine *why.*

10.6   *Dear Mr. Chan: For only $5 a year, you can have the world's news at your doorstep every ¼ week. Yes, Events [1] Magazine is making this unusual offer for a limited time only. ½ ¶ Just fill out the enclosed card [2] and return it to us today, so that this vital information ¾ may be on its way to you. You do not have [3] to send your check now; we will bill you later. Yours truly, (70 words) (s.i. 1.36)*

10.7   Transcription Pointers: QUOTATION MARKS (Cont.)

The quotation mark is omitted at the end of each paragraph, except the last paragraph. The quotation marks are placed at the beginning of each paragraph and at the end of the last paragraph only.

We quote the following from their letter:

"A careful examination of the duplicator in your office disclosed that a cracked cylinder was causing the trouble. Our serviceman has made the necessary repairs, and we feel certain that now you will find the machine in good working order.

"We sincerely regret the inconvenience this delay has caused you. If we can be of any further service, please let us know."

"..
....·.
"..
....·. "

10.8   The next writing assignment (in paragraph 10.9) is comprised of 140 shorthand words. See how long it takes you to write it in PS.

10.9   *You have heard it stated that all of us learn through experience. No one can possess all the ¼ knowledge and skill in ¹ a given field at the outset; but by the very nature of things, s/he must increase her/his fund of knowledge and find ² growth in her/his skills as the years come and go. S/he does this by varying ¾ her/his experiences, whether it be in ³ the books s/he reads, in her/his original study and (1) research at the very source of information, or in the ⁴ richness and variety of her/his ¼ experience in her/his leisure hours. ¶ No one has ever been a speed typist ⁵ or clever pianist on ½ her/his first day of instruction. There is no other road to success, for in some form or ⁶ other we ¾ must always learn through experience. Therefore, you must agree that experience is the best teacher. ⁷ (140 words) (s.i. 1.40)*

10.10   Even though it usually is easier to read your *own* shorthand than that written by someone else, the important thing is to be able to read PS anywhere, anytime. See how well you can apply this principle to the PERSONAL SHORTHAND in the next paragraph.

10.11 dmrs jenkins: i m ritg ts l t ask a favr o u. ts favr l k onl a fu mts o y i, b i l hlp u a grat dl. (P) rcnl u vd a smpl btl o sped spt rmovr tro e mal. w hop u v h a oprtunt t tri r sped spt rmovr o a dfclt stan s t u cd dscvr f yslf w gkl sped rmovs e hrdst spts a lvs n rg. tri i o bl pyn pn ink r cfe stans a wc e spt dspr lik mgc. (P) x e slvs a y locl spr-mrkt f a btl o sped tda, bf t smpl btl i mpt. f u cn f i n stk, ask y grocr t r sm imdtl. (P) a don' kep y njym o sped t yslf, etr! b sr t tl y frns a i, t! w r sr y l njy e my savd z mc z u d. (P) f w cd k a mt o y i w, w d aprsat y xg e aproprt rspn o e gd post crd a rg i t u. n ts wa, w c mr stsfkrl srv potnsl cst-mrs n y rgn. yvt *(210 words)(s.i. 1.41)*

10.12 Vocational Pointers:

> **When you are taking dictation on the job, be sure that you never look bored, distracted, perplexed, or exasperated. Make a point of studying your notes and concentrating on your *own* job. Regardless of whether your employer is a fluent dictator or finds dictation difficult, try to make your writing as legible as possible; and use every spare moment for checking your shorthand notes, verifying punctuation, etc.**

10.13   Paragraph 10.14 will complete our first complete "preview" of the comprehensive theory letter on which we have been working. Practice writing these sentences in PS until you can do so without hesitating on a single word.

10.14   *Finally, the project engineer is undecided whether to allow further excavation on days when cloud formations indicate possible heavy rain. The soil in which we are working absorbs great quantities of moisture and could pose a hazard for employees. Of course, if we cut back on excavation, we will have to deploy some of our workers elsewhere, in the usual fashion. Sincerely,*

10.15   Here are some more phrases on which to practice your PS.

10.16

	1	2	3
1	you should not be able	you have	you have been
2	you have had	you have not	you have not been
3	you have not been able	you made	you may
4	you may be	you may be able	you may be sure
5	you may have	you might	you might be
6	you must	you must be	you must be able
7	you must have	your order	you shall have
8	you should	you should be	you should be able

10.17   Paragraph 10.18 incorporates the last group of Civil Service terms. Practice writing these carefully before moving on to the brief form review.

10.18

	1	2	3
1	mutual	price	retirement
2	national	private	revenue
3	obstruct	program	secretary
4	office	prohibit	seminar
5	official	protocol	seniority
6	organization	public	service
7	pamphlet	purchase order	specialist
8	party	qualifications	stipulation
9	pending	rebuttal	supply
10	per annum	receipts	testimony
11	per diem	reciprocal	trade
12	personnel	recruit	translation
13	port	relocation	United States
14	precedent	requisition	wage
15	President	resources	Washington, D.C.

10.19   Keep in mind that the high-frequency words in the paragraph 10.20 chart will comprise, on the average, 50 to 51 percent of the words used in general correspondence. See how quickly you can call (or write) the brief forms for these very important words.

10.20   **Brief Forms:**

	1	2	3	4	5	6
1	and	credit	be	possible	at	from
2	no	would	she	do	did	give
3	that	on	men	as	can	why
4	dear	our	come	go	of	what
5	or	been	date	require	put	my
6	an	was	he	check	for	letter
7	by	it	price	to	please	if
8	find	time	will	thank	is	his
9	gentlemen	how	her	receive	the	him
10	enclose	they	about	get	have	too
11	wish	there	make	see	I	know
12	with	up	your	quite	which	we
13	information	had	good	not	well	copy
14	us	in	just	very	you	when
15	now	all	ever	too	but	due
16	here	out	me	man	made	so
17	take	kind	sincerely	order	every	man
18	under	also	buy	has	glad	return

Personal Shorthand

11.1 *Theory Review:*

11.2

> **Phonetic Abbreviations**
>
> In addition to representing their own basic sounds, carrying a long *e* sound, and carrying the final *y* (unless it has a long *i* sound), a number of consonants also are used to represent certain phonetic units or word parts:
>
> **Phonetic Abbreviations:**
>
> *b* — -ble
> *c* — ch-, -ch, com-, -com, con-, -con, (k), (s)
> *f* — ph-, -ph, for-, -for, -ful, -ify
>
> **Word Examples:**
>
> trouble — *trb*
> church — *crc;* compel — *cpl;* continue — *ctnu*
> phone — *fon;* form — *fm;* helpful — *hlpf;* magnify — *mgnf;* magnified — *mgnfd (mgnfid)*

11.3 Are there any words in the following letter that you need to practice before trying to write the letter in one minute or less?

11.4 *Dear Miss Lopez: According to our records, it has been almost sixty days since your last charge purchase.* ¼ *During that time,* [1] *we have not received any payment from you.* ¶ *As you know, our credit policy states* ½ *that customers may charge* [2] *purchases up to sixty days without interest. After that time,1 ¾ per cent will be charged each month.* ¶ *Please send us your* [3] *check for $50 or write us soon. Sincerely yours, (70 words) (s.i. 1.38)*

11.5 Now write the article in paragraph 11.6 (It, too, is comprised of exactly 70 shorthand words.).

11.6 *When dictating, most employers have to stop and spend some time thinking. Make sure you use this time to* ¼ *advantage.* ¶ *Use* [1] *it to read your shorthand notes and fill in needed punctuation. You can also ½ indicate paragraph markings ² to help save time when you transcribe. Finally, try to figure out ¾ any words missed, or make yourself a note to check missing words with your boss before leaving his office. (70 words) (s.i. 1.40)*

11.7　Transcription Pointers: QUOTATION MARKS (Cont.)

Single quotation marks are used to distinguish the in-ner quote from the outer quote.

The sales manager said: "I heard the president say, 'Sales are not high enough in this department.'"

He replied, "I have read the article, 'Business Behavior.'"

To set off titles of articles, lectures, paintings, etc.

She read the article, "Modern Fashions."

His lecture was entitled, "Effects of Taxation."

He replied, "The painting is entitled, 'Issues of Our Time.'"

Note: Titles of books, magazines and newspapers are underscored in typewritten material and italicized in print.

11.8　The letter in paragraph 11.8 is composed of 140 shorthand words. How many of these (if any) cause you to hesitate when you are writing them in PERSONAL SHORTHAND?

11.9　*Dear Mr. Brokaw: I am surprised you have not sent in your payments on your new stove. You have always ¼ been care-ful ¹ about your credit rating, and it would be too bad if something happened to that rating ½ now. ¶ If you are hav-ing ² financial problems, come and speak to us. I am sure we can devise some ¾ workable plan that will be satisfactory ³ to both of us. It is definitely better to (1) let your problem be known than to lose that precious credit ⁴ rating. ¶ A good credit rating should not ¼ be taken lightly. Your business operation depends on this rating ⁵ which gives you the abili-ty / to borrow. We are anxious to help you keep this rating, even if unexpected ⁶ financial ¾ problems have arisen in your business. ¶ Come in now, and let us help you if we can. Yours truly, ⁷ (140 words) (s.i. 1.41)*

11.10   How fast can you read the PS in paragraph 11.11?

11.11   *psnl, wil atng scol, u v a oprtunt t bc pfst n vrs tips o wrk f w e bsn wrld l gl pa u. i i mprtn, tf, t u k crtn u d y dal wrk crkl. (P) u sd rliz t lrng b rot mr won' g u v fr. u mst d sm tnkg a, tb, ariv a e pyn wr u c acpls tgs b yslf. u ned t n u c apli y lrngs t e vrs tsks u l b gd t pfm. (P) t r crtn ppl ho njy gg o da aftr da, wo gg an rl tt t tr acplsms. y atmtcl k o y r told r o y rd, a lt i g a t. i i mprtn t tnk tro y acss. dscvr o i nvlvd n tm. lrn t brg y rdg t br o y wrk. (P) ppl ho rliz tr gols r ndvdls ho c d tgs n a wa t hlps flo mplyes w hom y c n ctk. y r e mplyes ho k pid n tr wrk, dmstratg t y njy tr wrk. i i aprn t ppl ho njy tr wrk r crtn t b scsf n tr cosn flds. (210 words)(s.i. 1.42)*

11.12   Vocational Pointers:

> **Most experienced secretaries advocate keeping the shorthand pad *open* during dictation; that is, do not turn used pages *under*. To do so not only takes time but also is distracting to the dictator. Moreover, keeping used pages readily accessible makes it considerably easier to check your notes, from time to time.**

11.13   Now let's practice writing parts one and two of the comprehensive theory letter on which we started in Lesson 1.

11.14 *Dear Mr. Prentice: We are encountering some unexpected trouble in the construction of our Denver plant. Excavation at one corner of the property has threatened the foundation of a nearby church and may compel a change in plans. Is it your belief that we should continue on schedule or phone our regional vice president for advice? From a cost stand-point, it would be much better to continue form construction without delay, which, in turn, would be helpful from a personnel assignment standpoint.*

11.15 Practice writing the following much-used phrases in PS.

11.16

	1	2	3
1	as we can	as we cannot	as well
2	as yet	as you	as you are
3	as you can	as you cannot	as you do
4	as you do not	as you may	as you may be
5	as you may have	be glad	be glad to see
6	be sure	before it is	before many
7	before that	before the	before they
8	before us	before you	being able

11.17 Practice your PERSONAL SHORTHAND on the Clothing terms in paragraph 11.18.

11.18

	1	2	3
1	accessories	gabardine	pique
2	applique	hemline	petticoat
3	bouffant	herringbone	pongee
4	broadcloth	hosiery	rayon acetate
5	cashmere	iridescent	reversible
6	Chantilly lace	lingerie	sequin
7	chiffon	marquisette	shirtwaist
8	corduroy	mouton	simulated
9	crease-resistant	neckline	sleeveless
10	crinoline	negligee	tartan plaid
11	decollete	nylon	velour
12	denier	organdy	water-repellent
13	dickey	orlon	worsted
14	embroidered	peignoir	wrinkle-resistant

Personal Shorthand

12.1 *Theory Review:*

12.2

> **Phonetic Abbreviations**
>
> *g* — -ng, -ing, -dge, -nge
> *k* — -ct
> *l* — -lity, -lty
> *m* — m-(any nonlong vowel)-m, m-(any nonlong vowel)-n, moun-, -moun, -ment
>
> **Word Examples**
>
> sing — *sg*; singing — *sgg*; fudge — *fg*; singe — *sg*; danger — *dagr*
> act — *ak*; conduct — *cdk*
> utility — *utl*; faulty — *fl*
> member — *mbr;*
> minister — *mstr;*
> mound — *md*; torment — *trm*

12.3 The *more* you write PS, the *faster* you will write PS. Practice writing the next letter until you can do so automatically.

12.4 *Gentlemen: I just received my monthly telephone bill which I believe is in error. I have been ¼ charged for a [1] long distance telephone call to Kansas City, Missouri, on February ½ 19. I know no one in [2] Kansas City, so I am certain that I should not be charged for this call. ¾ ¶ Please check your records to see if they are in [3] error and notify me at once. Very truly yours, (70 words) (s.i. 1.40)*

12.5 Are there any words in the following article that you need to practice — before writing the complete article several times — preferably from dictation.

12.6 *Sometimes a person orders goods and then refuses to take them or pay for them. This might happen ¼ because s/he can [1] get the goods cheaper somewhere else, or for a variety of other reasons. ¶ When ½ this happens, the seller has [2] to consider what can be done to avoid losing money on the ¾ transaction. One avenue open to the [3] seller is to sue the buyer for the price of the goods. (70 words) (s.i. 1.40)*

12.7   Transcription Pointers: QUOTATION MARKS (Cont.)

Use quotation marks to set off technical or unusual words.

The term attempted to "freeze" the ball.

The actor "fluffed" his lines.

The stock issue had the appearance of a "blue-sky" venture.

The railroad adopted the "piggy back" transportation method.

12.8   Quickly scan the following letter for any words that might require special practice; then see if you can write this letter in
two minutes or less!

12.9   *Dear Miss Woo: By an overwhelming vote of the Portland
Business Club, you have been selected ¼ as our speaker [1]
for the June meeting. According to the calendar, our next
meeting will be held on ½ Friday, June 16, at 6 [2] p.m. Will
you be free to speak on that date? ¶ It is a custom for ¾ the
Club to entertain new members at a [3] reception held after
the business meeting. This function (1) normally lasts an
hour. It is also customary [4] for the speaker at our monthly
meeting ¼ to be an honored guest at that reception. Therefore, I have been asked by [5] the president of our Club ½ to
mention the reception at this time, so you may make plans
to attend if you [6] possibly can. ¾ ¶ We would be honored if
you could accept this invitation to be our speaker. Very truly
yours, [7] (140 words) (s.i. 1.41)*

12.10   When you practice *reading* PERSONAL SHORTHAND, make
a point of listing any words that pose a problem. Then practice *writing* such words several times.

12.11   *dms sanchez: cgrtlass! u v hlpd u tro
antr scsf yr n'r bsn. r pdks v bc mr
pplr, a ts pplr z cratd a v ncrsg dmd f
r gs. (P) w a nu yr a nu fld li n watg.
w o e xctv stf v m a rslus t k ts r
bgst yr, w mr sals a btr pdks tn v. u*

c hlp u w e sals, s y n k r rsluss ys.
(P) svrl yrs ag w h t ct r sals fc f
300 ppl t 110 bcs o e por mrkt f r gs.
ts mt ncrsd wrk f e stf w kpt, b w hrd
n a sgl cplan f an o tm, evn n i bcam
nsr t dcrs tr slr. (P) w i h g nus f u.
o jn 1, a 5 pcn (%) ncrs n y slr l bgn.
u v wrkd hrd f u, a w d lik t k ts mns
o sog r grttud. (P) drg e cg yrs, w
hop w l b ab t nlrg r stf t is orgnl
siz, b w ned y ctnud hlp a copras. w
aprsat l y fin hlp n e pst. s
(210 words)(s.i. 1.43)

12.12 Vocational Pointers:

> **Analyze your writing style and determine whether it is more advantageous for you to use a *two-column* pad, a *single* column (perhaps with a narrow column, for changes and corrections), or whether to add an *extra* column, as some writers do. Much depends on the kind of shorthand you are using and whether your notes tend to be quite large or relatively small.**

12.13 Practice writing the next two parts of the comprehensive theory letter.

12.14 *There is a tendency for the local inspector to magnify the seriousness of the matter. It is true, however, that our heavy equipment does interfere with choir singing at the church, and debris fires have singed some trees and shrubs along the south edge of the property. (P) We trust that members of the congregation hold no grudge against our organization nor the project itself and will act accordingly while construction is in progress. (P) I should mention, too, that several underground utility installations have prove faulty, causing far too many outages in the area, which, in turn, have distressed church members, as well as the minister.*

12.15   Here are more important phrases on which to practice your PS.

12.16

	1	2	3
1	could be	could be done	could
2	could have	could have been	could not
3	could not be	could not say	could not see
4	could see	do you	do you know
5	do you mean	do you think	do you want
6	does not	does not have	during the last
7	during the past	during the year	during which time
8	each case	each one	each other

12.17   Here are some Congressional Record terms on which to practice your shorthand.

12.18

	1	2	3
1	accumulate	establish	resolution
2	against	expenditure	senate
3	agriculture	expense	senator
4	amendment	farm	service
5	appropriate	general	system
6	appropriation	given	taxpayer
7	bureau	guarantee	vice-president
8	candidate	investigate	victory
9	chairman	involve	violate
10	committee	legislation	voluntarily
11	community	people	vote
12	compensate	problem	warrant
13	conference	produce	weapon
14	congress	product	whether
15	conversation	provide	withdraw
16	economic	provision	withhold
17	economy	reason	witness
18	election	regulate	yield

Personal Shorthand

13.1 *Theory Review:*

13.2

> **Phonetic Abbreviations**
>
> *n* — ·nc(e), ·ns(e), ·ness, ·nt, ·nd
> *p* — (as word beginnings only) pr·, p·(any nonlong vowel)·r, pro· and por· (either long or nonlong o)
> *q* — qu· (kw)
>
> **Word Examples**
>
> fence — *fn*; sense — *sn*; fairness — *frn*; bent — *bn*; send — *sn*; sending — *sng*
> pretty — *pt*; permit — *pmt*; prod — *pd*; port — *pt*; program — *pgrm*
> quick — *qk*

13.3 As you work to increase your shorthand speed, it often is helpful to compete with other students; but the record you *really* want to "break" is your own *previous* "best" score. See if you can do this in paragraph 13.4.

13.4 *Dear Miss Banks: The dress you ordered arrived in our shop today; however, we have a problem. Even ¼ though we[1] requested one size larger, it seems the additional length required was not met by this ½ size increase. ¶ Since time is of [2] the essence, we suggest sending through a rush order asking for a ¾ size twelve. Alterations can be made upon [3] its arrival. ¶ Please let us know your wishes.   Sincerely, (70 words) (s.i. 1.42)*

13.5 The article in paragraph 13.6 has the same number of words as the letter in paragraph 13.4. Compare your writing speed on these two exercises.

13.6 *Do you like to type numbers? Not many people do, but the age of the computer has made ¼ numbers more important [1] to the typing student than ever before. Businessmen are asking for typists ½ who can type numbers. ¶ Number [2] drills should be stressed until the student is able to type 50*

per ¾ cent of his straight copy speed on them. They should
³ be typed accurately and without watching your fingers.
(70 words) (s.i. 1.42)

13.7   Transcription Pointers: CAPITALIZATION

Capitalize the first letter of every sentence.

> *They may go.*
>
> *We are here.*

Capitalize the first word of every expression represen-
ting a sentence.

> *Not at all.*
>
> *More than that.*
>
> *Will she attend the meeting? Yes.*

Capitalize the first word of every line of poetry.

> *And, if each system in gradation roll,*
> *Alike essential to the amazing whole;*
> *The least confusion but in one, not all*
> *That system only, but the whole must fall.*
> >   *—Pope*

Note: Capitalize unless lower case is indicated. Exam-
ple:

> *"For I dipt into the Future*
> *   far as human eye could see,*
> *Saw the Vision of the world*
> *   And all the wonders that would be . . ."*
> >   *—Tennyson*

13.8   Practice writing words like *dictation, chances, necessary,*
        recipient, explanation, conviction, and *positively* — before
        practicing the following article in its entirety.

13.9   *If you plan to dictate material, you should have all the facts*
        at hand before you begin. You ¼ should not try to ¹ bluff
        your way through the dictation period if you are not fully in-
        formed. Chances ½ are this will cause you to "lose ² face"
        with your reader, and it will make it necessary for the reci-
        pient of the letter to write back for ³ a better explanation. In
        the end, you have to get (1) all the facts anyway, and it is
        much easier to ⁴ write one letter rather than two. ¶ The words
        ¼ in a letter carry power and conviction if the writer talks to
        ⁵ his reader positively ½ and surely, because s/he is in-
        formed on the subject at hand. Everyone respects facts, ⁶

but h/she ¾ quickly loses confidence in anyone who seems unsure of her/his ground due to ignorance or laziness. [7] *(140 words) (s.i. 1.42)*

13.10   The following article consists of 210 shorthand words. How fast can you read it the first time through? The second? The third?

13.11   *a slogn, f rptd ofn enf, ma final bc pt a pcl o r glrs lgg, a i gs wo sag t mc o e vlu o an slogn dpns uo is rpts. b a b, e slogn a e tg advrtisd b i, bc blnd nt 1 (wn) mng a 1 (wn) ks e plac o e otr. (P) n my nstns, e nam o e tg f w e slogn z nvnd bcs almost lst, e slogn kg is plac, z n smwn ks a nu k o srt a f a slogn, us 3 cptl ls w v n vsb rlas t an k o srt. n e crs o i, e slogn bcs s mc a pt o e tg islf t sd u g nt a str w hnls t k o clotg, u mit l g sutd mr gkl b rptg e slogn tn b pvidg a dtald dscrps o e artcl islf. (P) ts i fr f bg a isolated nstn, b i i a cds o tgs cstnl t b fwn. almost v 1 (wn) o r stats z is on slogn, a e cntr islf z 1 (wn) w ma b fwn o j a v pc o my u spn r ern. (210 words)(s.i. 1.43)*

13.12   Vocational Pointers:

> **Set up a system (with your dictator), so that names and addresses are automatically furnished to you, letter by letter, and memo by memo, as the dictation proceeds.**
>
> **Devise two or three symbols or special marks, with which to indicate obvious errors, questions about the**

> dictation, etc. You should not interrupt the dictator
> with these, of course, but quickly review them *with* the
> dictator at the end of the dictation or at the end of a
> thought, if he (or she) prefers.

13.13   Here are two more parts of the comprehensive theory letter,
for writing practice.

13.14   *There is also a large mound of dirt, near their parking lot,
which cannot be moved until cement footings have been
completed. We may be able to screen this some with a
fence; but in all fairness, there is no sense in pretending that
this will be completely adequate. (P) Recently, the church
sent a letter of complaint to the city council concerning the
noise problem; and we, in turn, are planning to send the
council a letter of explanation. Obviously, such a large construction project is not a pretty sight; and while we have a
permit to do what we are doing, noise, smoke, and dust are
natural by-products of any such endeavor.*

13.15   Practice your PERSONAL SHORTHAND on the following
much-used phrases.

13.16

	1	2	3
1	every one of these	every one of those	every other
2	for those	for us	for which
3	for whom	for you	for yourself
4	from him	from his	from it
5	from that time	from the	from these
6	from this	from time	from us
7	from which	gave me	gave us
8	gave you	give us	give you

13.17   Now write these Contract terms in PS — more than once, if
        your time permits.

13.18

	1	2	3
1	accord and satisfaction	injunction	plantiff
2	assignment	interstate	precedent
3	breach of contract	legal consideration	public offer
4	consideration	legal incapacity	qualified acceptance
5	conversion	legal tender	ratification
6	counter offer	liquidated damages	revocation
7	defendant	material alteration	specific performance
8	executed contract	meeting of the minds	tender of performance
9	executory contract	mutual agreement	testator
10	express contract	novation	transfer of title
11	formal contract	operation of law	usurious consideration
12	fraud	oral contracts	valid consideration
13	implied contract	parole evidence rule	voidable contract

Personal Shorthand

CARDINAL SERIES

14.1 *Theory Review:*

14.2

> **Phonetic Abbreviations**
>
> *r* — ·rity, ·ure
>
> *s* — sh·, ·sh, s·(any nonlong vowel)·s, c·(any nonlong vowel)·s (when *c* has an *s* sound), ·sion, ·tion, ·cian, ·shion, ·cien, ·tien
>
> **Word Examples**
>
> rarity — *rr*; mature — *mtr*
> ship — *sp*; dish — *ds*
> sister — *str*; basis — *bas*
> races — *ras*; cistern — *strn (cstrn)*
> mission — *ms*; mention — *ms*; physician — *fss*; division — *dvs*; question — *qss*
> fashion — *fs*; efficient — *efst*;
> patient — *past*

14.3 The letter in paragraph 14.4 incorporates 70 shorthand words. See if you can write it in one minute or less!

14.4 *Dear Mr. Estutaro: We would appreciate it if you would take the time to let us know why your charge ¼ account has [1] remained inactive this year. ¶ We have always been proud of our reputation for ½ efficient, prompt, and courteous [2] service; and we are eager to prevent anything that would threaten our ¼ reputation. ¶ Has there been any failure [3] on our part? If so, please let us know. Very truly yours, (70 words) (s.i. 1.42)*

14.5 Practice writing the words *considered, complicate, present,* and *correspondence,* several times, before testing your skill on the next article.

14.6 *Good filing is an art, and it should be considered as such. It is a simple art unless you ¼ complicate it [1] for yourself. There is only one rigid rule: Read everything you have to file. ¶ Train ½ yourself to find something of [2] interest in every letter you file. Then you will be able to ¾ relate past and*

present correspondence to [3] *future correspondence. That is*
the secret to filing. (70 words) (s.i. 1.44)

14.7   Transcription Pointers: CAPITALIZATION (Cont.)

Capitalize the first word in each division of a topical
outline.
I. Marketing functions
   A. Functions of exchange
      1. Buying
      2. Selling
   B. Functions of physical supply
      1. Transportation
      2. Storage
   C. Facilitating functions
      1. Financing
      2. Risk-bearing
      3. Standardization and grading
      4. Marketing information

14.8   The letter in paragraph 14.9 consists of 140 shorthand
words. Determine how many you need to practice before
seeing how fast you can take this letter from dictation.

14.9   *Dear Mrs. Temple: For the past week I have been attending*
the hearings in your case against the ¼ *moving company* [1]
which damaged your furnishings. It is my opinion that you
are not receiving ¼ *fair treatment and that the public is pre-*
judiced because of the coverage this case has received ¾ *in*
the papers. ¶ I have saved many of the [3] *clippings and have*
studied them carefully. My feelings in (1) this matter are that
you should receive complete compensation [4] *for the things*
that were damaged which should ¼ *be paid from the earn-*
ings of the company and not by the insurance [5] *company. ¶ I*
have practiced ½ *law in this state for many years, and it*
would be my pleasure to consult with you [6] *regarding this* ¾
case. If you wish to avail yourself of my services, please call
me at my office. Sincerely yours, [7] *(140 words) (s.i. 1.42)*

14.10   Be sure to note any troublesome words as you practice
reading the letter to Mr. Mazzi.

14.11   *dm mazzi: y n lnc a advrtisg cmpan o e*
      est cost? w v a sgss w d lik t ofr w d
      d j t. (P) 1 (wn) da lst wek i z tkg w a

frn o min ho i a huswif. s i e mtr o 3 cldrn. 2 o tm l bgn scol n e frst (1st) grad ts fl; a, ntrl, s i ntrstd n tr wlfr. s z j rcnl movd h f dls, tx, t lv w h hsbn, a mplye n ny. (P) bf v lg, r cvrsas trnd t scol a e v-xstg pblm o scol lncs. s usd kl pnt btr wil lvg n dls, b z yt s z n fwn antg t k is plac. in' i rsnb t spos t t r my mtrs o e est cost ho v e pblm n pprg scol lncs? (P) d u spos u cd ppr y pdk f mrktg o ts cost? i s, w d b g t advrtis i ovr r ntwrk. tlvs i gk, i i atrkv, a i i nxpnsv. y cmpan cd b strtd a e frst o nxt yr n w rrag r brdcst scdl. (P) in' ts sgss wrt csdras. yt (210 words) (s.i. 1.43)

14.12   Vocational Pointers:

During dictation, simply draw a line through or circle incorrect notes or portions that the dictator indicates should be dropped. Not only does erasing waste time; but later, the dictator may decide to *use* some of this original dictation. You then can mark it "O.K." or otherwise indicate that it *is* to be transcribed.

14.13   Practice writing the next two parts of the comprehensive theory letter on which we have been working, lesson by lesson.

14.14   *Large plants are not portable and cannot be moved to the pristine wilderness. I would be quick to admit that there have been problems with this building site, but they are a*

*rarity and nothing that should jeopardize mature relation-
ships. (P) We have considered the use of a small seismo-
graph* in the hope of better controlling ground tremors during blasting. Most of the excavation faces church property,
which, again, tends to complicate our mission.*

(*When practicing this theory letter, we will use the older
spelling and pronunciation, sismograph, rather than the
more current, seismograph.)

14.15   Here are more phrases for PS writing practice.

14.16

	1	2	3
1	glad to see	glad to send	good deal
2	good many	good many of them	good time
3	great many	great many of them	have been
4	have done	have gone	have had
5	have made	have not	have not yet
6	have not yet been	have you	he called
7	he came	he can	he can be
8	he can have	he can make	he cannot

14.17   Here are some Cooking terms. Work on them until you can
write them without hesitation.

14.18

	1	2	3
1	a la king	braise	croquettes
2	aspic	brochette	croutons
3	au gratin	canape	curry powder
4	au lait	capon	demitasse
5	basil	chervil	dough
6	baste	chiffon	dredge
7	batter	chives	endive
8	bay leaf	chutney	escarole
9	bearnaise	coddle	flambe
10	bisque	compote	fondue
11	blanch	condiment	fricassee
12	bouillabaisse	crepe	garnish

CARDINAL SERIES

15.1 *Theory Review:*

15.2

> **Phonetic Abbreviations**
>
> *t* — th-, pth
> *w* — wh- (as in where), ou (as in cloud), -ow (as in cow),
>   -aw (as in raw)
> *y* — oi-, -oi, oy-, -oy (as in boil and toy)
>
> **Word Examples**
>
> thought — *tt;* south — *swt*
> whether — *wtr;* cloud — *clwd;* cow — *cw;* straw — *strw*
> boil — *byl;* toy — *ty;* oil — *yl;* oyster — *ystr*
>
> **Note:** If a consonant is representing a phonetic unit, it
> cannot also carry the long *e* sound; so we must write
> this long *e* sound. Example cheat — *cet.*

15.3 Are there any words in the next letter that you need to practice writing, prior to working on the letter for speed purposes?

15.4 *Dear Mr. Kent: We would appreciate it if you would take the
time to let us know why your charge ¼ account has [1] remained inactive this year. ¶ We have always been proud of
our reputation for ½ efficient, prompt, and courteous [2] service; and we are eager to prevent anything that would
threaten our ¾ reputation. ¶ Has there been any failure [3] on
our part? If so, please let us know.   Very truly yours, (70
words) (s.i. 1.42)*

15.5 See if you can write the following article without hesitating
on any word — and without any preliminary "previewing" or
practicing of vocabulary.

15.6 *Dear Mr. Ching: The enclosed folder shows you that you can
now get a copier that's inexpensive, [1] economical, fast —
and reliable. Reliable in terms of copy quality and in [2]
terms of general performance. I am referring to the Cartright 444.
(P) Why not find out what [3] copier quality is? Just fill out the
enclosed card and drop it in the mail today. Sincerely, [4] (70
words) (s.i. 1.44)*

15.7   Transcription Pointers: CAPITALIZATION (Cont.)

Capitalize . . .
The first word of a direct quotation:
The salesman said, "The price is $4.95."
The first word of a direct question within a sentence:
The question is: What time shall we leave?
All Proper Nouns:
John will attend the University of Wisconsin at Madison, Wisconsin.

15.8   The following letter (to Mr. Tivoli) is composed of 140 shorthand words. Can you write the entire letter (preferably from dictation) in two minutes or less?

15.9   *Dear Mr. Tivoli: The next 32 seconds you spend reading this letter may be the most [1] important step you have ever taken to provide for your family's welfare. ¶ You would put up a [2] good scrap, Mr. Tivoli, if you learned that some relative was about to take 18% to [3] 70% of the property you have accumulated without your permission. That's just [4] what can happen to you and the relative referred to is Uncle Sam; the 18% to [1] 70% is the estate settlement costs and taxes. ¶ Our Estate Analysis Service is [2] designed to assist you in your planning and to help you avoid unnecessary settlement costs. [3] ¶ I will call you in a few days to discuss just how our office may be of service. Sincerely yours, [4] (140 words) (s.i. 1.42)*

15.10   Reading shorthand notes will help to alert you to theory and phonetic principles about which you may be slightly uncertain. Make a note of any such points and review those principles carefully.

15.11   *my mplyrs tda g aplcns f tipg psss t k a tst t so tr sped a acrc. f most jbs, 50 t 60 wrds a mt i gd. tipsts sd l v a g bkgrwn n splg, vocblr, pnctas, a grmr. (P) mplyrs ofn pfr t hir hi scol grduts. bsn trang, ncludg e opras o ofc egpm, sc z cg a adg msens, ma b hlpf. l, e fdrl gvrnm w spnsrs trang pgrms f nmplyd a u-mplyd wrkrs f ntr psss z tipsts u pvss o e mpwr dvlpm a trang ak. (P) mprtn apttuds a psnl trats f e tipst nclud figr dxtr, acurc, ntn, a frnl psnl, a e abl t ccntrat n e mdst o dstrkss. trn-scribing msen oprtrs l ned t v g hrg. a tipst ma b pmotd f jnr t snr tipst r t otr clrcl wrk w nvlvs gratr rspnsbl a hir pa. tipsts ho n srthn ma b pmotd t stngrfrs r scrtrs. (220 words)(s.i. 1.90)*

15.12　Vocational Pointers:

Not only do many dictators dictate in a very spasmodic way, with frequent pauses, they frequently are distracted by phone calls and other interruptions. Use this time to improve your notes and be prepared to read back portions of the dictation, at any time.

15.13 Use your PERSONAL SHORTHAND on the following sentences taken from the comprehensive theory letter we have been reviewing.

15.14 *Moreover, it is becoming increasingly clear that we need a physician "on call" 24 hours a day, in order to efficiently protect division personnel. This will enable us to better answer any questions directed to us by state and federal agencies.*

15.15 How quickly can you provide the PS for the phrases in paragraph 15.16?

15.16

	1	2	3
1	he could	he did	he did not
2	he did not see	he does	he does not
3	he felt	he found	he gave
4	he gives	he is	he knew
5	he knows	he lost	he made
6	he may	he may be able	he may be sure
7	he may have	he mentioned	he might be
8	he might have been	he might not	he must

15.17   Here are some more Cooking terms on which to practice your shorthand. Check a good dictionary if you are in doubt about pronounciation.

15.18

	1	2	3
1	glaze	oregano	saute
2	goulash	panbroil	shallot
3	Hollandaise	paprika	skewer
4	hors d-oeuvres	peppercorn	souffle
5	julienne	pilaf	thyme
6	knead	provolone	timbale
7	leek	puree	tripe
8	mace	rissole	veloute
9	meringue	romaine	vichyssoise
10	marinate	rosemary	vinaigrette
11	minestrone	sauerbraten	white sauce

15.19   Call (or write) the PS brief forms for the very high-frequency words in the following chart.

15.20   *Brief Forms:*

	1	2	3	4	5	6
1	on	not	at	we	just	my
2	there	she	also	that	and	is
3	do	out	check	gentlemen	take	been
4	make	require	can	her	to	him
5	dear	credit	under	information	or	see
6	the	go	me	give	know	for
7	his	with	they	about	he	was
8	kind	sincerely	copy	price	are	how
9	find	an	which	ever	well	up
10	have	receive	date	as	every	return
11	very	possible	put	us	it	made
12	good	if	no	here	now	please
13	but	in	come	buy	quite	thank
14	wish	would	time	what	has	were
15	men	get	so	am	due	when
16	from	order	glad	did	letter	of
17	by	man	you	too	be	enclose
18	all	our	your	had	why	will

Personal Shorthand

16.1 *Theory Review:*

16.2

> **Word Beginnings — Shortcuts**
> For *em* — Write *m*, unless a vowel follows the *m*.
> EXAMPLES: embrace — *mbrac*, emit — *emt*
> For *im* — Write *m*, unless the *m* is followed by another *m*.
> EXAMPLES: imagine — *mgn*, immature — *imtr*

16.3 Write the following article as quickly as you can — several times, if your schedule permits.

16.4 *To get the most out of a lecture, you must listen carefully. One must be alert in class in ¼ order to [1] listen well, and the key to staying alert in a class is preparation. ¶ Before attending ½ class, it is a good rule [2] to reexamine the latest reading assignment and your notes on ¾ the preceding lecture. Also, spend a few [3] minutes thinking on what points today's lecture may cover. (70 words) (s.i. 1.44)*

16.5 Scan the letter in paragraph 16.6, make a mental note of any difficult words, and then write it in PS several times.

16.6 *Dear Mr. Thompson: We are happy to send you information on our lawn products. Enclosed are ¼ five folders on [1] products in which you indicated an interest. ¶ I am sure you will find our ½ products surpass anything else [2] on the market today. Although our products cost a little more, you ¾ would be willing to pay twice the price after [3] seeing the results obtained with them. Yours very truly, (70) (s.i. 1.46)*

16.7 Transcription Pointers: CAPITALIZATION (Cont.)

> Capitalize . . .
> Proper adjectives:
> > *French descendants*
> > *New York style*
> > *English books*

> *Italian models*
> **Relationships**
> **When used in connection with names**
> **Brother Harry**
> **Uncle William**
> **Capitalize** *father* **or** *mother* **when used in direct address only.**
> **Yes, Father, I shall be there.**
> **His father was away on a business trip.**

16.8   Are there any words in the next paragraph that you need to preview and practice, before writing the entire article in PERSONAL SHORTHAND — preferably from dictation?

16.9   *If you want to make your filing system work for you, you need to purchase good tools. If you work in* ¼ *a large office,* [1] *chances are your filing equipment will be ordered by the purchasing department.* ½ *Therefore, you will get your* [2] *supplies from the stockroom. If you work in a small office, however, you* ¾ *may have occasion to recommend filing* [3] *supplies and help your employer purchase equipment and (1) supplies. You need to do some careful studying in* [4] *order to help make correct decisions.* ¼ ¶ *Regardless of the size of the office in which you work, you will be more* [5] *efficient if you get to know / the kinds of supplies and equipment used on your job. All businesses require that* [6] *records be stored* ¾ *properly, and it is part of your job to become familiar with your firm's record storage systems.* [7] *(140 words) (s.i. 1.42)*

16.10   What is your reading rate, on the shorthand in paragraph 16.11. If possible, check it several times.

16.11   *f u r a hi scol r clg studn, sz uo e g t c b fwn t. rmbr, u g g b gg i. f u fel t i smtg flt a e plac, u c k i a btr plac b cerfl acplsg y tsks v da, e bst u c. (P) n u acpt a jb w a mplyr, tn u sd rl wrk f h/h. sn s/e pas y wags, u sd stn b h/h a e bsn s/e rprsns. f, wv, u f i nsr t etrnl crtciz h/z v acs, tn u sd rsin y pss. (P) v mplyr i alwas egr t locat ppl ho c hlp h/h. anwn ho i a hnrn, wv, l v t g. ts i e lw o an bsn, a t r rwrds onl f e ndvdl ho hlps. (p) n r t b hlpf, u mst b ustng. mplyes cn hlp tr mplyrs f y xpwn n utons a wsprs, b attud a tt, t e bs i a fol r t h/z pcdrs r n wrkb. b strg u dsctn a strif amg co-wrkrs n a bsn, u r likl t f yslf lokg f antr pss g son. (210 words)(s.i. 1.46)*

16.12　Vocational Pointers:

> Many experienced secretaries use a colored pen or pencil to highlight or emphasize special instructions relating to their shorthand notes or to indicate action to be taken relative to certain letters or memos. Such instructions might include special enclosures, the number of extra copies required, special handling for certain messages, etc.

16.13　Paragraph 16.14 is composed of two more sentences from the comprehensive theory letter on which we have been practicing. The purpose of this letter, of course, is to provide you with a realistic way of reviewing your shorthand theory.

16.14　*I thought that this, in itself, was of considerable importance because of recent changes in the law. ¶ Finally, the project engineer is undecided whether to allow further excavation on days when cloud formations indicate possible heavy rain.*

16.15　Write the following phrases in PS — several times, if your study schedule will permit.

16.16

	1	2	3
1	less than	less than the	let us
2	let us make	let us say	let us see
3	long time	make the	many other
4	may be	may be done	may have
5	men and women	might be able	might have
6	might not be	might not be able	months ago
7	must be	must be able	must be done
8	must have	my time	need not be

16.17　Paragraph 16.18 contains a cross-section of Economic terms. Practice writing these in PS until you can write each one with equal ease. Again, use a dictionary if you are in doubt about any of these terms.

16.18

	1	2	3
1	affluent society	depression	market price
2	automation	devaluation	monopoly
3	balance of trade	disposable income	national income
4	business cycle	exports	oligopoly
5	capital	factor of production	parity ratio
6	capitalism	federal reserve system	progressive tax
7	commodity	foreign exchange	public debt
8	common market	free enterprise	purchasing power
9	conspicuous consumption	free trade	rate of exchange
10	consumer price index	gold standard	recession
11	creditor nation	gross national product	reciprocal trade agreement
12	currency	holding company	socialism
13	debted nation	inflation	standard of living
14	deficit financing	inventory	tariff
15	deflation	labor force	unemployment rate

Personal Shorthand

CARDINAL SERIES

17.1 *Theory Review:*

17.2

> **Word Beginnings — Shortcuts — (Cont.)**
> For *um* — **Write *m***
> **EXAMPLE: umbrella — *mbrla***
> For *in* — **Write *n*, unless the *n* is followed by another *n*.**
> **EXAMPLES: inability — *nbl*, innocent — *incn***

17.3 What word or words do you need to practice on in the next paragraph, before writing the entire article?

17.4 *Today more girls are going into the secretarial field as a career than ever ¼ before. It is a ¹ field that a girl can enter with little or much training and can always find ½ a job. ¶ She will perhaps quit ² working for 10 to 15 years while she is rearing her family. ¾ Then at age 35 to 40, she may ³ reenter the secretarial field and work again. (70 words) (s.i. 1.46)*

17.5 How should these words be written in PS: brochures, effective, expected, expectations, reordering, printing, contract, product. When you can write them easily, apply your skill to the next letter.

17.6 *Dear Niki: Enclosed is our check for $75 for the printing job you did for us. ¼ ¶ The brochures are ¹ more effective than expected. We feel this is due to your unique use of color. ¼ If sales reach expectations, ² we will be reordering soon. ¶ We have never been more pleased with the ¾ results of a printing contract. We now ³ wonder how you will display our next product. Sincerely yours, (70 words) (s.i. 1.46)*

17.7 Transcription Pointers: CAPITALIZATION (Cont.)

> **Capitalize . . .**
> **Names and members of organizations:**
> > ***American Legion***
> > ***Chamber of Commerce***

> a *Republican*
> a *Mason*
> **Democrats**
> **Prohibitionists**
> **Political parties and clubs:**
> **Republican Party**
> *Liberal Party*
> *Rotary Club*
> *Belles Lettres Club*
> **Note: But not "a club of businessmen."**

17.8   Preview the following letter carefully (giving special attention to such words as president, congratulate, recreation, and attractive) and then practice writing it in PS.

17.9   *Dear Dr. Fracasso: It was with a great deal of pleasure that I read about your appointment as ¼ President of [1] the newly established college in Miami Beach. ¶ All of us who have worked with you ½ in the past know your [2] ability, and we feel that we should congratulate the Board of Regents ¼ on its choice, as well as you as recipient [3] of this coveted appointment. You may not know that (1) I had training during the war at the government school [4] which was the seed of this college. ¶ Certainly ¼ there is no more beautiful spot in the country than Miami Beach. [5] To a sportsman like you, the ½ opportunities for recreation in that area must have made the offer [6] seem doubly ¾ attractive. ¶ Good luck to you, Dr. Fracasso, both in your work and in your fishing. Very truly yours, [7] (140 words) (s.i. 1.43)*

17.10   How quickly can you read (or, if possible, transcribe at the typewriter) the following shorthand article)

17.11   *most o u tri t avyd tos ppl ho k tmslvs u ddl srsn l e i. a sn o humr i a mrk o ntlgn. e psn ho z a sn o humr l z a sn o vlus. n l aspks o lif r eql mprtn. u k alwns. u r ab t lok a sm o y on acss a rflk t sm o e tgs u d r o e rdculs sid. (P) e hmrls psn ho i sr s/e i alwas rit a vbd els i rg ks hslf/hslf trol dslikd. f u tri t tk rsnbl t h/h, s/e stks of n agr. w ofn k scrt plsr n dflatg e psn ho ks hslf/hslf t srsl a ho sems nvr t nbn. (P) abrhm lncln pssd a l-dvlpd sn o humr. n drk is, e d rlat sm rdculs str t brok e tns a brt smils a lftr f e mbrs o z cbnt. psr dsprd z f b mgc. (P) i i l t rmbr t a kl smil, a xprs o aprsas, a a smpl wrd o pas, cpld w a sn o humr, l britn v da f u a otrs arwn u. (210 words)(s.i. 1.46)*

17.12 Vocational Pointers:

> **Number each successive letter or memo, during dicta-
> tion; and then be sure to write these same numbers on
> any letters (usually incoming) or memos that are
> related to the dictation. Once you have written a num-
> ber (from your shorthand notes) on the correspondence
> used by the dictator, in the course of dictation, turn
> those letters and memos face down, so that when you
> start to transcribe, they will be in the same order or "se-
> quence" as your shorthand notes.**

17.13 Here are the last two sentences from the comprehensive
theory letter. Make sure you can write them easily in PS.

17.14 *The soil in which we are working absorbs great quantities of
moisture and could pose a hazard for employees. Of course,
if we cut back on excavation, we will have to deploy some of
our workers elsewhere, in the usual fashion. Sincerely,*

17.15　Here are more phrases that you should automatize in your PS practice.

17.16

	1	2	3
1	no doubt	none of them	not only
2	of course	of his	of its
3	of mine	of my	of our
4	of such	of that time	of the
5	of their	of them	of these
6	of those	of time	of which
7	on behalf	on his	on it
8	on our	on such	on that day

17.17　Practice your PERSONAL SHORTHAND on the Educational terms in paragraph 17.18. Keep a good dictionary handy, in case you are in doubt about the meaning of a word or its pronunciation.

17.18

	1	2	3
1	acceleration	curricular	intelligence quotient
2	accreditation	denominational college	inventory test
3	accredited	departmentalization	liberal arts
4	adult education	desegregation	matriculation
5	aptitude test	detention	motivation
6	audiovisual	diagnostic	orientation
7	baccalaureate	discipline	pedagogy
8	certification	dissertation	phonic method
9	coaching	dropout	placement bureau
10	collegiate	educational television	prerequisites
11	comprehension	elective	probation
12	consolidated school	elementary school	proctor
13	continuing education	evaluation	progressive education
14	controlled vocabulary	experimental	psychological
15	cooperative education	extracurricular activities	questionnaire
16	coordinator	filmstrip	released time
17	core curriculum	guidance	scholastic
18	correlation	higher education	secondary school
19	correspondence course	humanities	seminar
20	counselor	individualized instruction	syllabus
21	curriculum	integration	team teaching

Personal Shorthand

18.1 *Theory Review:*

18.2 | ***Word Beginnings — Shortcuts — (Cont.)***
For *un* — Write *n*, unless the *n* is followed by another *n*.
EXAMPLES: unable — *nab*, unnecessary — *unsr*
For *en* — Write *n*
EXAMPLE: entail — *ntal*

18.3 Write the words concentrate, content, complete, and correct several times, before taking the following article from dictation.

18.4 *When writing letters, it is usually smart to start with a rough draft. You can concentrate on ¼ the content of [1] your letter when you draft it this first time. ¶ After you complete the first draft, check the ½ material and make needed [2] revisions. The beginning letter writer may have to revise his ¾ letter several times. Finally, type the [3] letter in good form when it's correct in every detail. (70 words) (s.i. 1.46)*

18.5 See how fast you can write the following letter in PERSONAL SHORTHAND.

18.6 *Dear Mrs. Sang: Do you and your husband really enjoy doing all of your yard and garden work? You can increase [1] your gardening pleasure by letting someone else take care of the routine jobs, such as ½ mowing the lawn and pulling [2] the weeds. ¶ By letting us do all the dirty work, you can concentrate ¾ on the more enjoyable phases of [3] gardening. Our rates are very reasonable. Sincerely, (70 words) (s.i. 1.46)*

18.7 Transcription Pointers: CAPITALIZATION (Cont.)

> **Capitalize . . .**
> **Government, when the word is used in connection with the name of a country.**
>> ***French Government***
>> ***Swiss Government***

> Note: Do not capitalize when not used with a proper adjective and not used in a specific sense.
>
> *Good government will be needed during the present crisis.*
>
> Federal, when referring to the United States.
>
> *He paid the Federal tax.*
>
> *Federal offense*

18.8   Practice writing various words and sentences in the following article, several times; then, if possible, take the letter at least once or twice from dictation.

18.9   *It is amazing to see how just a little more effort made by a person puts him/her ahead ¼ of others. That [1] observation applies even in the physical aspects of life. Here are, let us ½ say, twenty people. One of [2] them is bound to be tallest, even if only by a small ¾ fraction of an inch. It is that fraction, however, [3] which makes the difference. ¶ Students need to be realistic and be aware of the fact that they live in a [4] competitive world. They will have ¼ competition when they apply for jobs. They will also have to compete with [5] other employees when they go ½ to work. For this reason, every student should understand that it will often be just [6] that little ¾ extra something which will account for his/her being promoted to a more responsible position. [7] (140 words) (s.i. 1.45)*

18.10   Reading shorthand, quickly and easily, is just as important as writing it fluently. See how well you can apply your shorthand reading skill to the next article.

18.11   *n nrl v ofc, wtr i i lrg r sml, t i usul a psn ho srvs z a rcpsst f e frm. ts i a v mprtn dut, bcs e rcpsst aks z a g- btwen f e clins a h/z mplyr. e rcpsst c estbls e mod o e ofc b h/z acss. f s/e i efst, past, l-mrd, a nicl gromd, tn s/e i a rl ast t h/z cpn (co.) (P) e rcpsst l c n ctk w l srts o ppl drg h/z wrkg da. sm gsts l b n a hr a l b v rlctn t wat. otr gsts l b v k a ustng*

*n e rcpsst nfms tm t y cn g n t s h/z
mplyr rit awa. (P) i i obvs t a rcpsst
mst v pys, pasn, a tk w h/z gsts. s/e
mst b mprsl a tri n t g spsl favrs t
an 1 (wn) clin. (P) crm i 1 (wn) fkr w
l hlp e rcpsst n h/z wrk w e pblc.
crm i a dfclt atrbut t dscrib. u mit sa
t crm i a ntgb inr pwr t nabs 1 (wn) t
atrk otrs a wn tm ovr. (210 words)(s.i.
1.48)*

18.12   Vocational Pointers:

> **After taking dictation, get to your transcribing as quick-
> ly as possible: There is a tendency for less experienced
> secretaries to "put it off," as long as possible. Procras-
> tination, where transcription is concerned, is a poor
> policy. The *sooner* you transcribe, the *easier* it will be;
> and the longer you wait, the harder it will be.**

18.13   Paragraph 18.14 is comprised of some "key" words from the
comprehensive theory letter on which we have been working. Practice writing these words in PS until you can write
them fluently.

18.14   ***encountering, unexpected, trouble, construction, excavation, property, threatened, foundation, church, compel,
change, continue, schedule, standpoint***

18.15   See how well you can write the following phrases in PS.

18.16

	1	2	3
1	seem to be	send them	send this
2	send us	several days	several months
3	several other	shall be glad	shall have
4	she cannot	she may be	she must
5	she would	should not	should not be
6	should see	since that time	since the
7	since this	so many	so many of the
8	so many of them	so many times	so much

18.17 Put your PERSONAL SHORTHAND to good use in writing the Family Shopping terms in paragraph 18.18.

18.18

	1	2	3
1	adhesive tape	hamburger	razor blades
2	aluminum foil	home permanent	shaving cream
3	ball-point refill	hosiery	shoelaces
4	bath towels	ice cream	shower cap
5	bunch of carrots	instant coffee	skim milk
6	cauliflower	light bulb	snapshots
7	cleansing tissues	margarine	soft drinks
8	curlers	mayonnaise	stationery
9	curtain rods	nail polish	stick cologne
10	deodorant	paper napkins	stuffed olives
11	dress pattern	paper plates	toothpaste
12	flashlight batteries	picnic ham	tuna fish
13	furniture polish	plastic rainboots	washcloths
14	graham crackers	pocket comb	whole wheat bread

Personal Shorthand

CARDINAL SERIES

19.1 *Theory Review:*

19.2

> **Word Beginnings — Shortcuts — (Cont.)**
> For *intro* — Write *ntr* (whether *o* is short or long)
> EXAMPLE: introduction — *ntrdcs*, intricate — *ntrct*
> For *post* — Write *pst*
> EXAMPLE: postage — *pstg*

19.3 How do you plan to write the words interested, variety, qualified, arithmetic, attitude, succeeding, and employee, which appear in paragraph 19.4? Be sure you can write these words fluently, before attempting the material at faster and faster speeds.

19.4 *If you are interested in a banking career, this field offers a variety of ¼ entry jobs for [1] qualified people. Explore this field if you are good in arithmetic and have skill in ½ dealing with people. ¶ If you [2] have a positive attitude, you have a good chance of succeeding ¾ as a bank employee, since the bank's aim is [3] treating the customer right, so it can stay in business. (70 words) (s.i. 1.46)*

19.5 Now write the letter to Mrs. Chan in PERSONAL SHORTHAND (Don't let yourself trip on the word, *inconvenienced.*).

19.6 *Dear Mrs. Chan: Thank you for your order for thirty shorthand textbooks and twenty-six workbooks. ¼ The textbooks are [1] being shipped to you by express today; however, the workbooks will not be sent ½ until the end of next week as [2] they are temporarily out of stock. ¶ We regret the delay in ¾ sending the workbooks and hope that you will not [3] be inconvenienced too greatly.   Yours very truly, (70 words) (s.i. 1.46)*

19.7 Transcription Pointers: CAPITALIZATION (Cont.)

> Capitalize . . .
> Legislatures and Congress:

> *Illinois House of Representatives*
> *British Parliament*
> *Congress of the United States*
> *Seventy-eighth Congress*
> **Note:** Capitalize *Senate* and *House* when used synonymously with the United States Government.
> *The Senate will convene in January.*
> *He is a member of the House.*
> **Constitution of the United States:**
> *The Constitution was adopted in 1789.*

19.8　　What, if any, words do you need to practice in paragraph 19.9 before taking it several times from dictation?

19.9　　*If you examined two magazines, one of the cheap variety and the other top rank, you ¼ would probably [1] find quite a difference in their language. Often the writer who gets paid little for ½ his/her efforts uses many [2] big words. In contrast, the writer who gets paid more for his/her efforts is ¾ more discreet with his/her language. S/He sometimes [3] uses big words for a special effect, but on the whole, s/he (1) writes simply. ¶ This is because the best writers know the [4] power of short words. This does not mean it is ¼ a bad practice to possess a large vocabulary; however, one [5] should never use words of ½ many syllables unless there is a definite reason for it. You should make your [6] message easily ¾ understood by using simple words that retain vitality and interest in your writing. [7] (140 words) (s.i. 1.46)*

19.10　Check your reading rate, from lesson to lesson, and see how much it is increasing. Transcribe shorthand letters and articles at the typewriter, whenever possible. What is your reading or transcribing rate on paragraph 19.11?

19.11　*dm himstreet: i i m plsr t nfm u t u v b elkd z a dlgt t cgrs t xprs e opnns o e ppl o ts ct o e nvgas a irgas lws w n cmte n cgrs. (P) i hop u l n rfus e apynm, bcs u r e onl psn n e ara ho z a grat dl o ts sbjk. n onl v u spn yrs o wrk n ts fld, b l u v e abl t hnl pltcl pblms t ma aris. u l v ab t gss mbrs o e cmte a locat e dfcl w a mm o eft. (P) y v stdd tes bls f 4 weks w, b sem t b cfusd o e isus a v msntrprtd e rslts o e sbcmte's fgs. y r rfusg t sbmt e bl f vot ntl a dlgt f r nabrhod z psnd r vus. ts rfusl i cstg e txpars i a my. (P) f u acpt ts apynm, u l v e grttud o my ppl. u ma b sr t w l pmt u l e fredm u s n hnlg ts pblm. s   (210 words)(s.i. 1.49)*

19.12 Vocational Pointers:

> Keep in mind that no two office vocabu,aries are the same: Even in the same business or industry, even in the same specialized field, this is true simply because no two dictators possess the same vocabulary. Concentrate on the words that are particularly unique to your office, your job; practice these words until you can write them fluently; and until you can virtually "anticipate" their usage.

19.13 Practice your PS on the following words from the comprehensive theory letter.

19.14 *tendency, inspector, magnify, seriousness, equipment, interfere, choir, church, debris, singed, edge, property*

19.15 Practice writing the phrases in paragraph 19.16 until your hand can write them automatically.

19.16

	1	2	3
1	that will be	that will not	that would
2	that would be	that would have	the only thing
3	there are	there has been	there have
4	there is	there may	there may be
5	there might be	there must be	there was
6	there will	there will be	they are
7	they are not	they can	they can be
8	they can have	they cannot	they cannot be

19.17   Paragraph 19.18 includes a cross-section of Furniture terms. Practice writing these in shorthand until you can do so without hesitation.

19.18

	1	2	3
1	antique	footboard	refectory table
2	baroque	gate-leg	room divider
3	buffet	headboard	satinwood
4	ceramic	innerspring	sealer finish
5	chesterfield	laminate	shellac
6	chiffonier	mahogany	stipple
7	chippendale	modern	studio couch
8	colonial	mohair	traditional
9	console	motif	transitional
10	dado	overstuffed	Tudor
11	dovetail	pier glass	upholstery
12	dowel	prima-vera	webbing
13	Early American	room divider	reclining chair

Personal Shorthand

20.1 *Theory Review:*

20.2

> **Word Beginnings — Shortcuts — (Cont.)**
> For *super, supr* — Write *spr (regardless of how the u is pronounced)*
> EXAMPLES: supercilious — *sprcls,* supreme — *sprm*

20.3 Scan the following article quickly, to see if there are any words on which you need to practice; and then, if possible, take the article several times from dictation.

20.4 *A glorious, all-over tan is flattering, but it's a medical fact that overdoses ¼ of sun may wrinkle and age skin and can cause skin diseases, including cancer. ¶ The best trick to ½ browning without burning is to [2] know your skin type! Find out how your skin reacts to sunlight and protect ¾ it accordingly. Ten minutes to start is [3] sufficient. Remember, a little sun goes a long way. (70 words) (s.i. 1.46)*

20.5 Can you write the following letter in one minute or less? How should the word, *accomplishments,* be written in PS?

20.6 *Dear Mr. Levy: Your letter applying for a position as salesman arrived this morning, and ¼ I have read it [1] with interest. ¶ As explained in our advertisement, we plan to increase our sales staff ½ within the next few weeks. Will [2] you call for an interview on Thursday, June 10, between 3 and 5 ¾ p.m.? ¶ Please bring full data on your personal [3] background and sales accomplishments. Yours very truly, (70 words) (s.i. 1.46)*

20.7 Transcription Pointers: CAPITALIZATION (Cont.)

> Capitalize . . .
> **Cabinet:**
> > *He is a member of the Cabinet.*
> > *The President has selected his Cabinet.*

> **Departments of Government:**
> > **Civil Service Commission**
> > **Treasury Department**
> > **Bureau of the Census**
> > **Pennsylvania State Highway Commission**
> > **United States Department of Agriculture**
>
> **Military:**
> > **United States Army**
> > **United States Navy**
> > **United States Air Force**

20.8   If you find yourself hesitating on any of the words in the following article (consisting of 140 shorthand words), make a note of these and analyze the theory principles involved.

20.9   *Obviously, no one should undertake a pursuit for which s/he is not fitted. You should not feel ¼ bad if your [1] qualifications prevent your entrance into some career of which you or your parents ½ have dreamed. You must be honest [2] with yourself. Sometimes it takes courage to admit that you lack certain ¾ abilities, but it is no disgrace to [3] acknowledge that your sphere of activity and service should be that of a tradesman, artisan, mechanic, [4] farmer, or laborer. ¶ What you like to do, ¼ you will do well. Whatever you do well will lead to better things. [5] Society is turning with ½ growing respect toward the skilled person who works with both brawn and brain. It is better to [6] be a skilled, ¾ contented mechanic in overalls than an unhappy second-rater in a white-collar job. [7] (140 words) (s.i. 1.47)*

20.10   How does your reading rate on the following letter (210 words) compare with your rate on Lesson 18? Lesson 15? Lesson 10? Are there any troublesome words that you need to analyze from the standpoint of theory?

20.11   *dms torres: z a bgng scrtr, y l pbbl f t y srthn, tipg, a filg skls r g g. f u d n us tes skls rglrl, wv, u l f t y l n sta wa. (P) f u v ned t mprov y skls n e aras msd abv, w wlc u t k advng o e rvu crs ofrd a talr bsn clg. r pgrm ncluds nstrcs n tipg, srthn, a filg. (P) f u s, tes crs c b tt n y on frm, f enf mplyes r ntrstd n nrolg f e clss. n my artcls a r scol, i z b pynd o t scrtrl pdcs z ncrsd n l cpns (cos.) wr r rvu crs w ofrd. f t i n enf ntrst n y frm, u c k tes crs drg r nit scol pgrm. (P) f u r y cpn (co.) r ntrstd n r pgrm, w d b g t sn u adsl n a r scol. l u ned d i fl o a r e gd crd t v adsl mtrl. w hop w c b o srvc t u n e nr futr. yvt (210 words) (s.i. 1.49)*

20.12   Vocational Pointers:

> In the process of taking dictation on the job, you will find that those words that have extremely high frequency, you will soon learn to abbreviate to the maximum degree. Indeed, the rule of thumb is this: You can abbreviate in shorthand in direct proportion to the *frequency* of the word; if the word has extremely *high* frequency, you can condense or telescope it greatly; if the frequency is lower, abbreviate with care. If the frequency is very low, don't abbreviate at all!

20.13   Here are more words from the comprehensive theory letter. Make sure you can write them fluently in PS.

20.14   *members, congregation, grudge, organization, project, accordingly, construction, progress, mention, underground, utility, proved, faulty, outages, church, minister*

20.15   The next paragraph presents more important phrases on which to practice your PERSONAL SHORTHAND.

20.16

	1	2	3
1	up to the	up to this time	upon request
2	upon such	upon the subject	upon this
3	upon which	very many	very small
4	very well	we made	we mailed
5	we make	we may	we need
6	we realize that	we thank you	we thank you for
7	we thank you for the	we think	we will
8	we will be	we will be able	we will have

20.17 Continuing our study of special vocabularies for shorthand practice: Make sure you can write the following Insurance terms easily.

20.18

	1	2	3
1	actuary	claimant	insurability
2	adjuster	compulsory insurance	interim term insurance
3	annuity	disability insurance	lapse
4	assignee	double indemnity	liability insurance
5	assigner	earned premium	maturity date
6	assured	effective date	ordinary life policy
7	assurer	endorsement	paid-up policy
8	beneficiary	endowment insurance	primary beneficiary
9	benefits	exclusion	riders
10	broker	general agent	surrender value
11	cancellation	group insurance	underwriter
12	cash surrender value	hospitalization insurance	workmen's compensation

20.19 Call (or write — preferably from dictation) the PERSONAL SHORTHAND brief forms for the high-frequency words in the following chart.

20.20 **Brief Forms:**

	1	2	3	4	5	6
1	did	her	our	when	his	have
2	give	thank	dear	to	out	been
3	are	in	the	man	there	too
4	is	him	by	well	under	all
5	would	date	good	return	my	also
6	see	be	letter	has	why	was
7	us	an	get	or	that	of
8	every	no	now	will	they	how
9	check	with	gentlemen	from	your	make
10	wish	you	very	were	information	had
11	we	at	for	he	it	do
12	made	credit	me	enclose	sincerely	know
13	here	what	time	which	just	as
14	up	men	require	put	order	find
15	on	possible	not	come	ever	so
16	if	copy	can	take	and	please
17	am	but	quite	glad	she	due
18	go	price	about	buy	kind	receive

Personal Shorthand

CARDINAL SERIES

21.1   *Theory Review:*

21.2

How Each Letter of the Alphabet is Used in PS		
LETTER	**SOUNDS ACCORDING TO *BASIC THEORY***	**PHONETIC ABBREVIATIONS**
a	long ā (regardless of spelling)	—
b	b, bē-, -by	-ble
c	c (either s or k sound), cē, -cy	ch-, -ch, com-, -com, con-, -con
d	d, dē-, -dy	—
e	long e when the preceding consonant represents more than itself; one of two e's occurring together; short or long e at beginning of word or ending of word	—

21.3   How fluently can you write the next article? Remember: You're the best judge of which words may call for some extra practice.

21.4   *In times when jobs are plentiful, applicants can pick and choose from the jobs available, and ¼ employers are [1] almost helpless to interfere. When jobs are hard to find, however, the employer has ½ a chance to pick and choose from [2] a variety of applicants. ¶ When there is strong competition ¾ for jobs, one must pay attention to details [3] that might have been overlooked when work was easy to find. (70 words) (s.i. 1.46)*

21.5   Analyze the related theory principles and practice writing the following words in PS before taking the letter in paragraph 21.6 from dictation: informed, secretary, saleslady, product, experience, area, position.

21.6　　*Dear Mr. De Nicola: I have been informed by your secretary that you are looking for a good ¼ saleslady to [1] sell your new product, Sweet Clover Cosmetics. I have had experience selling ½ cosmetic products in the [2] Utah area for some time; but I would like to move to Oregon. ¾ ¶ May I talk to you about this position? [3] I will be in town until next week. Very truly yours, (70 words) (s.i. 1.46)*

21.7　　Transcription Pointers: CAPITALIZATION (Cont.)

Capitalize . . .

Countries and Political Subdivisions

　　Commonwealth of Massachusetts

　　New York State

　　City of New York

　　Republic of Mexico

　　British Empire

Capitalize words that refer to a specific country or political subdivision.

　　the Dominion

　　the Lone Star State

　　the State

　　the Empire

21.8　　What is the best way to write the following words in PS: reference, recent, correspondence, railroad, forwarded, fortunately, portion, permit, allowance, directly, considerably, patronizing. After practicing these words carefully, study the letter in paragraph 21.9, and then, if possible, take it several times from dictation.

21.9　　*Dear Miss Bateman: In reference to your recent correspondence regarding rebate on the ¼ unused portion of [1] your railroad ticket, I wish to inform you that a check was made out in your name and ½ was forwarded to you [2] yesterday. ¶ Fortunately, you returned the unused portion of your ¾ ticket soon enough to permit us to make this [3] refund. Many people do not take advantage of this (1) service in time to avail themselves of this allowance. [4] ¶ If, in the future, you wish to return ¼ another railroad ticket, I wonder if you would be good enough to [5] mail it directly to our ½ nearest ticket office. This will expedite matters considerably. ¶ Thank you for [6] patronizing ¾ our railroad, and if we can be of further service to you, please let us know. Yours very truly, [7] (140 words) (s.i. 1.51)*

21.10 Check your reading and/or transcription rate on the next
PERSONAL SHORTHAND letter.

21.11 *dmrs rosalada: drg e nxt 4 weks, w r
ofrg u a a nmbr o otr dpnb fmls n bldgs
e pvlg o usg a c acwn a e pals fod str
n y ara. w r ofrg ts oprtunt bcs w n y
c i g. (P) n e pst, pals fod strs v catrd
t cs cstmrs, b bcs o efst mgm, w c w met
cpttv ps a l g dlvr a tlfon srvc. tro
xprn, w v fwn t w c grn l o ts t tos
fmls ho r rlib a rspnsb. u c b sr tes
adsl srvs l n cst antg xtra. o e ctrr,
w tnk w c hlp u ct dwn y fod csts. (P)
f u d lik t k advng o ts ofr, w d csdr
i a pvlg t srv u. l u ned d i ctk e
pals fod str mgr n an str a g h ts l z a
ntrdcs. e l opn y acwn wo dla r qssg,
xcpt t f o w u s t pa y acwn. (P) w hop
u dcid t k advng o r ofr. yt (210
words)(s.i. 1.50)*

21.12 Vocational Pointers:

> When your employer has finished dictating, ask any
> questions that *need* to be asked — *before* you start
> transcribing. Individual questions, pertaining to any
> particular memo or letter, normally are asked at the end
> of each such letter or memo.

21.13 The words in paragraph 21.14 are from the comprehensive
theory letter on which we have been working. Be sure you
can write them easily; and be especially sure that you under-

stand the theory principles involved.

21.14 *mound, parking, cement, completed, fence, fairness, sense, pretending, completely, adequate, recently, church, complaint, city, council, concerning, noise, problem, explanation.*

21.15 Practice writing the phrases in the next paragraph. Work for speed.

21.16

	1	2	3
1	we will not	we will not be	we will see
2	we will send you	we wish	we would
3	we would be	we would be glad	we would have
4	we would not	we would not be	we would not be able
5	week or two	week or two ago	weeks ago
6	were not	were sure	what are
7	what has been	what is	what our
8	what was	what will	when that

21.17 Practice writing the following Music terms in PS.

21.18

	1	2	3
1	a cappella	double flat	obbligato
2	accidental	dulcimer	oratorio
3	aria	forte	pianissimo
4	arpeggio	fortissimo	prestissimo
5	artificial harmonics	glockenspiel	quaver
6	bass clef	grace notes	ritardando
7	cacophony	grandioso	slur
8	chromatic modulation	harmonic modulation	sotto voce
9	coda	largo	Stradivarius
10	coloratura soprano	legato	tempo
11	concertmaster	maestro	treble clef
12	crescendo	meter	trill
13	decrescendo	mezza voce	triplet
14	diminuendo	mezzo forte	virtuoso

Personal Shorthand

CARDINAL SERIES

22.1   *Theory Review:*

22.2

How Each Letter of the Alphabet is Used in PS		
LETTER	**SOUNDS ACCORDING TO *BASIC THEORY***	**PHONETIC ABBREVIATIONS**
f	f, fē-, -fy	ph-, -ph, for-, -for, -ful, -ify
g	g (hard or soft or zh sound), gē-, -gy	-ng, -ing, -dge, -nge
h	h, hē-	—
i	long i (regardless of spelling)	—
j	j, jē-	—

22.3   Practice your PERSONAL SHORTHAND on the following article.

22.4   *A research paper is a factual presentation of other people's findings on a ¼ subject. It has two [1] basic purposes: 1) It informs the reader, and 2) it gives the writer practice ½ in techniques of scholarship. [2] ¶ The writer will learn how to organize his thoughts, where and how to ¾ locate information quickly, how to use the [3] library, how to take good notes, and how to make footnotes. (70 words) (s.i. 1.48)*

22.5   Carefully check the letter in paragraph 22.6 and see if there are any words that need special attention, before practicing the entire letter several times.

22.6   *Dear Mr. Rosini: In reference to your request, our supply of the pamphlet, Boating in ¼ Coastal Waters, is [1] exhausted. We hope to have a new issue in the future, and a supply will be ½ forwarded. ¶ We are enclosing [2] several other pamphlets in which you might be interested. ¾ If we can be of service to you again, [3] please do not hesitate to write us. Very truly yours, (70 words) (s.i. 1.48)*

22.7   Transcription Pointers: CAPITALIZATION (Cont.)

Capitalize . . .
Administration:
   That law was passed during the Truman Adminis-
   tration.
   The State Administration has spent large sums of
   money for highway construction.
Courts:
   Supreme Court of the United States
   Oregon Circuit Court, Multnomah County
   Pennsylvania Supreme Court
   Fifth Circuit Court
   Federal District Court of the United States
   Superior Court of Alameda County

22.8   Practice writing the following words in PS: appearance, im-
        pression, quality, noticeable, selecting, stationery, avoid,
        cheap, showy, expensive, extremes, unwanted, reactions,
        secretary, arouses, suspicion, contempt.

        The practice writing the entire article in paragraph 22.9,
        preferably from dictation.

22.9   *When you write a letter, a good appearance is vital if you*
        want to make a good first impression. ¼ Since this first [1] *im-*
        pression is often the lasting impression, you should take
        great pains with the looks of ½ your letters. Use good quali-
        ty [2] *paper; see that the typing is neat, free from noticeable ¾*
        errors, and well spaced; and let no errors slip through. [3] ¶
        When selecting your paper, choose good stationery. You (1)
        should avoid using cheap paper, as well as showy, [4] *expen-*
        sive paper. Using either of these ¼ extremes may bring
        about unwanted reactions from your readers. Cheap [5] *paper*
        may cause a secretary ½ to place your letter into the pile for
        "second" instead of "first" reading. Showy, [6] *expensive ¾*
        paper often arouses negative reactions and may cause feel-
        ings of suspicion or contempt. [7] *(140 words) (s.i. 1.53)*

22.10   Time yourself (or have someone else time you) and see how
        long it takes to read or transcribe the next letter.

22.11   *dm scofield: w r crtn u d pfr t dl w*
        pnrs opratg f lrg plns ho c g u e mtrls

[shorthand text]

22.12 Vocational Pointers:

> **Once you have clarified any questions or doubts, per-
> taining to dictation, leave your dictator's office quickly
> and quietly, making certain that you take all cor-
> respondence, writing instruments, and other supplies
> with you. As soon as you return to your desk, make sure
> that you are ready for the *next* dictation session
> (whenever it may be), *before* you start transcribing.**

22.13 In the next paragraph, there are additional words from the
comprehensive theory letter. Analyze the theory principles
involved and then practice writing these words until you can
do so without the slightest hesitation.

22.14 **construction, obviously, project, pretty, while, permit, noise,
by-products endeavor, portable, pristine, wilderness.**

22.15   Here are more speed phrases. Make sure you can write them
         easily.

22.16

	1	2	3
1	you should have	you should not	you think
2	you want	you wanted	you will
3	you will be	you will be able	you will be glad
4	you will be sure	you will find	you will have
5	you will not	you will not be	you will not be able
6	you will not have	you will see	you would
7	you would be	you would be able	you would be glad
8	you would be sure	you would have	you would have been

22.17   Practice writing the following Office Supply terms.

22.18

	1	2	3
1	angular	composition books	duplicating stencils
2	appointment books	construction paper	offset paper
3	art gum	copyholders	onionskin
4	atlases	corporate seals	opaque ink
5	auxiliary guides	daters	perforators
6	calculators	denatured alcohol	postal scales
7	calendar refills	dictionaries	posture chairs
8	carbon paper	duplicator fluid	pressboards
9	cellophane tape	electric typewriters	rotary files
10	cement adhesives	erasing shields	spirit masters
11	check protectors	featherweight	stencil styli
12	chronologic	hectograph	transfer binders
13	clasp envelopes	insertable	keyboard
14	collating trays	ledger sheets	type cleaners
15	columnar pad	liquid duplicators	watermark

Personal Shorthand

23.1   *Theory Review:*

23.2

How Each Letter of the Alphabet is Used in PS		
LETTER	**SOUNDS ACCORDING TO *BASIC THEORY***	**PHONETIC ABBREVIATIONS**
k	k, kē-, -ky	-ct
l	l, lē-, -ly	-lity, -lty
m	m, mē-, -my	m- (any nonlong vowel) -m; -ment; m- (any nonlong vowel) -n; moun-, -moun
n	n, nē-, -ny	-nc(e), -ns(e), -ness, -nt, -nd
o	long o and oo	—

23.3   Practice your PS on the article in 23.4. Take is several times from dictation, if at all possible.

23.4   *Swimming is a very good skill to have. It is not only a very enjoyable sport, but ¼ it could help you* [1] *save the life of someone else. ¶ Today, with more time for recreation and leisure ½ activities, there are more* [2] *people on the lakes and beaches. An urgent call is made for capable ¼ watchguards and swimming instructors in an* [3] *attempt to make these recreational areas safer. (70 words) (s.i. 1.48)*

23.5   Make a mental note of how you plan to write the proper nouns, in practicing the following letter.

23.6   *Dear Mr. Higaki: We are planning a Career Day at Wilson High School on September 10. We ¼ would like very* [1] *much to have you on a bookkeeping panel. Mr. Paul Roberts will be the other ½ member of the panel. You* [2] *can contact him at the New York Life Insurance office in Seattle. ¾ ¶ If for any reason you cannot help* [3] *us, please notify me immediately. Yours truly, (70 words) (s.i. 1.48)*

23.7   Transcription Pointers: CAPITALIZATION (Cont.)

Capitalize . . .

Names of Laws:

Federal Food, Drug, and Cosmetic Act

Public Law 591

Social Security Act

Titles:

General William D. Smith

Mayor J. Richard Donohoue

Honorable William A. Boyd

Reverend John Henry Anderson

Note: Capitalize both parts of compound titles of distinction.

Vice President   Rear Admiral

23.8   How quickly and easily can you "translate" the following words into PS: attitude, develop, inclination, friendly, encourage, anybody, stability, morale, determining, factor, aspect, specialized, technical, knowledge, important, necessarily, possessor, opportunities, people, happily, congenially, effectively. When you can write each of these words without hesitation, practice the article in paragraph 23.9.

23.9   *The right attitude means that we can be of good cheer; that we hold our heads high; that we take the time and ¼ develop the ¹ inclination to be friendly, smile, and encourage others; and to carry on our ½ own work in good spirits. ² Anybody who thinks and works in that attitude, day by day, will ¾ develop courage, stability and morale. ³ ¶ It is thus our attitude which is the determining (1) factor in every aspect of our lives. Over and ⁴ over again it has been shown that specialized ¼ skill and technical knowledge, important as they may be, do not ⁵ necessarily bring to their ½ possessor the opportunities which should be his. It is sad, but true, that too ⁶ many people ¾ never really learn to work happily, congenially, and effectively with other people. (140 words) (s.i. 1.53)*

23.10   See how quickly you can read (or, better still, if your class schedule and facilities permit, *transcribe* at the typewriter) the following PERSONAL SHORTHAND letter.

23.11   *dm browning:* w w v hp t v y n 1 (wn) r
f 3 dzn 5-drwr filg cbnts n gren, a wn t
advis u t y r z alrd b p nt pdcs. r cpn
(co.) hil rcmds ts 5-drwr siz cbnt, a w
n u l f t ts ptclr cbnt l esl a cpltl
flfl y filg qms. (P) w v h my ls o pas
rtn t r cpn n rgrd t e drbl o r filg
cbnts, a w v n trb w r fils n lvg u t
tr 5-yr grnte. l, w v vd my favrb cms
f scrtrs a filg clrks, ho sa r fils sav
tm i a trb bcs o e mtl glids a stel bl
brgs w k e fils s es t opn a clos. (P)
n r idho salsm, frnk anrsn, cld uo u n
o, u msd u w ntrstd n mtl dsks t mc e
filg cbnts. r cpn i j brgg o a nu lin
o mtl dsks ts mt, a w hop u l lt mr.
anrsn brg u n t vu e lin son. yt
(210 words)(s.i. 1.51)

23.12   Vocational Pointers:

> **From time to time, you may be asked to take dictation
> on the typewriter. If you are fortunate, this will not hap-
> pen until you are well acquainted with the dictator's
> dictation habits and, even more important, the vocabu-
> lary to be used. If you are well acquainted with the
> vocabulary (and the general content of such dictation),
> you soon can virtually *anticipate* much of the dictation,
> which makes any dictation much easier, whether taken
> on the typewriter or written in shorthand.**

23.13   Here are some more practice words from our old, familiar
theory letter. Practice writing them in PS until you can write
them without hesitation.

23.14 *quick, problems, building, rarity, nothing, jeopardize, relationships, considered, seismograph*, controlling, ground, tremors, excavation, church, property, tends, complicate, mission.*

  *Remember to use the older pronunciation, sismograph, with this word.

23.15 See if you can write the phrases in 23.16 without having to "worry" in the slightest about any of the words. Make a special note of any that might cause you to pause in your writing.

23.16

	1	2	3
1	as you might	as you might be	as you might have
2	as you must	as you must be	as you must have
3	as you will	as you will be	as you will find
4	as you will have	as you will not	as you will not be
5	as you will see	as you would	as you would be
6	as you would be able	as you would have	as you would not
7	as your	at a loss	at a time
8	at least	at length	at such a time

23.17 Here are some Photography terms on which to practice your shorthand. If you are in doubt about any of them, check their pronunciation in a standard dictionary.

23.18

	1	2	3
1	aberration	cable release	desensitizer
2	abrasion	candle power	diaphragm
3	actinic	carbonates	double exposure
4	Adurol	cassette	ejector
5	anastigmatic	circle of confusion	emulsion
6	angstrom unit	color temperature	ferrotype
7	aperture	coma	fixed focus
8	barrel mount	complementary colors	flat
9	bayonet	concave	fluorescent
10	baryta	convertible lens	focusing scale
11	blow up	curtain aperture	foot-candle
12	bounce light	densitometer	gradation

Personal Shorthand

24.1 *Theory Review:*

24.2

How Each Letter of the Alphabet is Used in PS		
LETTER	SOUNDS ACCORDING TO *BASIC THEORY*	PHONETIC ABBREVIATIONS
p	p, pē-, -py	(as word beginnings only) pr-; p-(any nonlong vowel)-r; pro- and por- (either long or nonlong o)
q	q (k)	qu- (kw)
r	r, rē-, -ry	-rity, -ure
s	s (s or z or zh sound), sē-, -sy	sh-, -sh; s-(any nonlong vowel)-s; c-(any nonlong vowel)-s; (c has s sound) -sion, -tion, -cian, -shion, -cien, -tien
t	t, tē-, -ty	th-, -th

24.3 Preview the vocabulary and then practice writing the next paragraph.

24.4 *The best way to convince people that they should not use drugs is through education. We must demonstrate ¼ that there are better and more lasting ways to experience fullness and variety in life ½ than by taking these harmful ² chemicals. ¶ Adults and students alike, in their use of drugs, are ¾ reacting to conditions which negate human ³ values and human worth. We must help find meaning for them. (70 words) (s.i. 1.48)*

24.5 Compare your writing speed on paragraph 24.6 with your best "time" on paragraph 24.4.

24.6 *At some time in your office career, someone may ask you to put together an office handbook. ¼ In order to ¹ do this, you will have to assemble company policies, ideas, and rules that ½ are important. ¶ Through the use ² of drawings and writings, you will have to describe and explain office ¾ procedures in detail. When finished, you will ³ have a valuable tool for all office employees. (70 words) (s.i. 1.51)*

24.7   Transcription Pointers: CAPITALIZATION (Cont.)

Capitalize . . .

Academic Degrees
> *Arnold J. Gordon, Ph.D.*
> *Mary Jane Smith, M.A.*

Holidays
> *Fourth of July*   *Christmas*

Historic Events
> *World War II*   *Civil War*

24.8   Quickly preview the letter in paragraph 24.9, giving special attention to such words as expanded, experienced, secretaries, personalities, etc. Then see if you can establish a new record for yourself in the writing of this letter to Mrs. Collins.

24.9   *Dear Mrs. Collins: Our business has expanded so rapidly the past few months that we now have ¼ openings for ¹ two experienced secretaries in our main office. The women we want should be ½ up to thirty years of age ² and should have a few years' experience where they used their typing and ¾ shorthand skills. ¶ We want people with pleasing ³ personalities who can get along with fellow employees (1) and with company customers. They should have the ⁴ ability to write neatly and clearly ¼ as they will be asked to prepare a number of monthly reports for the ⁵ firm. ¶ The positions have a ½ wonderful future, and the salary is quite attractive. Our Personnel Department ⁶ would be ¾ happy to arrange interviews for anyone you can recommend for these jobs. Yours very truly, ⁷ (140 words) (s.i. 1.54)*

24.10   Time yourself (or have someone else time you) as you read (or transcribe at the typewriter) the next letter:

24.11   *dm asparro: w r hp t anwn e spynm o ms nny brin z drkr o r psnl dprtm. u pbbl l rmbr h z trang sprvisr o nu mplyes a r but ofc. (P) nny z b w r cpn f 15 yrs;*

[shorthand text — 210 words (s.i. 1.52)]

24.12 Vocational Pointers:

> **Don't let dictation at the typewriter worry you: While it does call for considerable typing skill and good control of spelling (since there is no time to check the dictionary for spelling), taking dictation on the typewriter *does* have its *advantages*. No transcribing is necessary; and, when dictation is over, the letters or memos involved are ready for signing.**

24.13 Let's continue to work on our theory review letter: Here are some more practice words in paragraph 24.14.

24.14 *moreover, becoming, increasingly, physician, efficiently, protect, division, personnel, enable, answer, question, directed, agencies.*

24.15 See if you can automatize your writing of the following phrases.

24.16

	1	2	3
1	by it	by mail	by myself
2	by that	by that time	by the
3	by the time	by the way	by them
4	by themselves	by these	by this
5	by this time	by those	by us
6	by which	by which it is	by which time
7	by which you can	by which you may	by you
8	can be done	can be sure	can have

24.17   Now let's work on some more special vocabulary terms in the field of Photography. Don't hesitate to use your dictionary if you are in doubt concerning the pronunciation of these words.

24.18

	1	2	3
1	halation	opaque	sensitometry
2	helical	panchromatic	shutter release
3	imbibition	panorama	spectroscope
4	infinity	perspective	splicing
5	infrared	photoflood	split image
6	macrophotography	photomicrography	still life
7	magenta	planar	stop bath
8	Metol	processing	strob
9	microfilm	rangefinder	translucent
10	montage	resolving power	transparency
11	negative	rheostat	ultraviolet
12	neutral density	scenario	visibility

Personal Shorthand

25.1 *Theory Review:*

25.2

How Each Letter of the Alphabet is Used in PS		
LETTER	**SOUNDS ACCORDING TO *BASIC THEORY***	**PHONETIC ABBREVIATIONS**
u	long u (also ōō if spelled with u)	—
v	v, vē-, -vy	—
w	w, wē-	wh-, ou (as in cloud), -ow (as in cow), -aw (as in raw)
x	x, -xy	—
y	y, yē-, (ending y when no consonant available to carry it)	oi-, -oi, oy-, -oy (as in boil, toy, and oyster)
z	z (z or zh sound), zē-, -zy	—

25.3 See if you can write the following letter without the slightest hesitation. Make a particular point of mastering any words that cause you to hesitate.

25.4 *Dear Mr. Arnst: Please send me your latest price list quoting the prices of various brands of fishing ¼ gear. I am [1] particularly interested in gear suitable for trout fishing. My son will be ½ fourteen next month, and I would [2] like to give him a suitable rod and reel for his birthday. ¶ I shall ¾ appreciate any recommendations [3] you can give me before I place my order. Yours truly, (70 words) (s.i. 1.51)*

25.5 If possible, take the next article from dictation at 70, 80, and even 90 wpm.

25.6 *Young men and women of today are faced with a world which becomes more complex daily. The increased ¼ communication [1] facilities make them aware of the problems of all the peoples of the world. ½ ¶ They are also called upon [2]* *to understand and cope with an explosion of knowledge that has ¾ increased at an accelerated pace during ³ the past decade, and no letup is currently in sight. (70 words) (s.i. 1.51)*

25.7   Transcription Pointers: CAPITALIZATION (Cont.)

Capitalize . . .

Periods of History:
     Colonial Period
     Renaissance
     Stone Age
     Middle Ages

Days of the Week and Months:
     Sunday
     Monday
     November
     December

Note: Do not capitalize seasons of the year.
     spring   summer   autumn   winter

25.8   Do not take the article in paragraph 25.9 from dictation until you are sure you can write these words easily and without hesitation: pigeons, mankind, Noah, messages, ancient, conveyed, Olympic, messengers, history, Crusades, telegraph, telephone, television, communications, available, patrol, occasion, reporting, assistance, trouble.

25.9   *The use of homing pigeons in the service of mankind is very old. Ever since Noah sent ¼ out the dove which ¹ returned with an olive leaf, these birds have been used for delivering messages. The ½ ancient Greeks conveyed names of ² Olympic victors to their cities by this means, and Roman leaders ¾ used pigeons as messengers during their wars. ³ History tells us that during the time of the Crusades, (1) there was a pigeon postal service. ¶ Even in our day ⁴ of radio, telegraph, telephone, ¼ and television, the homing pigeon is useful where modern ⁵ communications are not ½ available. The forest patrol has had occasion to use homing pigeons for reporting ⁶ fires, and ¾ in several cases, fishing fleets have used them to send back for assistance when they were in trouble. ⁷ (140 words) (s.i. 1.54)*

25.10   Make a special point of timing yourself on reading (or, better still, transcribing at the typewriter) the letter to Mr. Walters, in the next paragraph.

25.11 *dmr walters: e ofcrs o e ntrnsl rlass clb v askd m t xprs t u tr aprsas f y adrs lst nit. dzns o cls v c t u f mbrs o e adn, statg w mc nsit y msg brt tm o e ntrct pblm o e nr est. (P) alto u nstd u w n a xprt, vwn flt t e cbnas o y rcn trp tro t trbd ara a y lif-lg std o e hstr o e cntrs nvlvd pprd u v l t dscs wisl a wo bis e vrs pblms nvlvd. crtnl v-wn ho hrd u lft e metg w a btr ustng a a nu aprsas o e sosl a pltcl gsss facg r cntr n is dlgs w e cntrs u dscs. (P) a nmbr o psns v sgstd w ask wtr u v a lst o rcn boks r artcls w d b hlpf t tos ho d lik t ncrs tr nlg a e mdl est. w sd b most gratf f u cd sn u sc a lst. (P) agn, r mst sncr ts f a nrcg xprn. vty (210 words)(s.i. 1.53)*

25.12 Vocational Pointers:

> **Just as you need to have supplies ready for *dictation* (at all times), you should have certain *transcription* supplies ready and waiting, too: letterhead paper (perhaps in several sizes), carbon paper, manifold paper, second sheets, envelopes, erasers, correction tape, correction fluid, and at least one or two good reference books and spelling aids.**

25.13 Practice your PS on some additional words from the theory letter on which we have been working, lesson by lesson.

25.14 ***thought, itself, considerable, importance, because, recent, changes, finally, project, engineer, undecided, whether, allow, further, excavation, cloud, formations, indicate, heavy.***

25.15   Make sure you can write the following phrases, without any pauses or hesitations.

25.16

	1	2	3
1	can say	can see	can you
2	can you give	cannot be	cannot be done
3	cannot be sure	cannot pay	days ago
4	do it	do not	do not pay
5	do not see	do so	do the
6	do this	each time	every minute
7	every one	face to face	few days
8	few minutes	few moments	few moments ago

25.17   Now practice your PERSONAL SHORTHAND on the Political terms in paragraph 25.18.

25.18

	1	2	3
1	absentee voting	disenfranchisement	parity
2	acclamation	electoral college	plebiscite
3	alderman	filibuster	precinct
4	amendment	flexible tariff	pressure groups
5	blue laws	fusion candidate	quorum
6	boondoggling	gerrymander	recall
7	bourgeoisie	Hatch Acts	referendum
8	bureaucracy	House of Representatives	sectionalism
9	"clear and present danger"	impeachment	Senate
10	closure	incumbent	subsidy
11	comity	indemnification	tariff
12	defacto government	jingoism	trust busting
13	de jure government	lame duck	veto
14	democratic socialism	logrolling	ward
15	direct primary	muckraker	white paper

25.19   Call (or write) the PS brief forms for the high-frequency words in the following chart:

25.20   **Brief Forms:**

	1	2	3	4	5	6
1	so	there	will	quite	from	take
2	information	good	you	be	find	did
3	why	it	has	which	on	know
4	buy	return	go	ever	thank	not
5	the	would	of	put	about	me
6	they	by	in	too	come	copy
7	all	price	well	receive	see	were
8	have	when	do	him	and	an
9	every	been	glad	make	or	what
10	time	under	can	that	man	made
11	gentlemen	is	letter	he	to	require
12	at	am	had	just	please	was
13	date	sincerely	check	kind	due	out
14	possible	she	credit	up	with	us
15	enclose	now	but	we	very	no
16	also	men	my	his	here	wish
17	our	order	dear	her	give	for
18	get	are	as	if	how	your

Personal Shorthand

26.1 *Theory Review:*

26.2

> *General Writing Aids for PS —*
>
> Use *u* for the *oo* sound when the longhand spelling is with a *u* — it is usually more natural and much easier to transcribe.
>
> Use *k* for *c·t* whenever feasible — even within words: dictation — *dktas* — and so on.
>
> Use *b* for *bal, bel,* and *bol,* as well as the *ble* ending: tribal — *trib*; label — *lab*; gambol — *gmb*

26.3 Try taking the following letter at 70 wpm, without practicing or previewing any of the words. Should you hesitate on any of the vocabulary, be sure to make a note of such words.

26.4 *As a typist, it is your responsibility to see that all correspondence you send out ¼ is appealing [1] to the eye. This means it should be free from strike-overs and obvious erasures. It ½ should also be neatly [2] arranged on the page. ¶ If you are ever required to write any of the ¾ letters you type, you are also responsible [3] to follow and apply essentials of good writing. (70 words) (s.i. 1.51)*

26.5 If your class procedure permits, take the following letter at 70 wpm; and then, if possible, at even higher speeds.

26.6 *Dear Ms. Accuardis: Your note asking for a description of the retailing courses that Olympic ¼ College offers [1] has been given to me. ¶ Olympic College offers two courses that are taught by ½ Mr. Frank Jones. A description [2] of the courses appears on page 15 of the catalog I am ¾ sending you. ¶ Olympic College would be [3] happy to have you join its retailing classes. Yours truly, (70 words) (s.i. 1.53)*

26.7 Transcription Pointers: CAPITALIZATION (Cont.)

> **Capitalize** . . .

Geographic Areas:

Capitalize points of the compass when designating certain parts of the country.

He returned from a trip through the East.

Industrialization is increasing in the South.

Note: Do not capitalize points of the compass when used in a descriptive manner.

southern cooking   western mountains

26.8   See if you can take the following letter from dictation at 70 wpm — without any special "previewing" or "practicing" of vocabulary.

26.9   *Dear Mr. Zapata: Recently one of your clients, Raymond Price, President of Price Brothers, reported ¼ the skillful [1] manner in which the efficiency engineer supplied by your company handled some problems in his office. [2] Therefore, I decided to ask you to investigate a problem ¾ which has defied solution in our firm. ¶ Would [3] you ask one of your engineers to make an appointment (1) with me so that I may present our problem? Since Miss Long [4] personally handled the Price Brothers ¼ investigation, I should prefer that she consult with me on this [5] matter if she is free to do ½ so now. ¶ So that you may obtain some background regarding our company before our [6] consultation, ¾ a number of reports on our activities are being enclosed with this letter. Yours truly, (140 words) (s.i. 1.56)*

26.10 Your ability to *read* (or *transcribe*) shorthand is just as important as your ability to *write* it. How does your reading skill on the following article measure up with your writing skill?

26.11 *e finst stsfcs u c g o o lif i dg tgs t v pmn t tm. wrkg mrl f my z n pmn, f my c b swpt awa ovrnit. b a rputas f bg k, gnrs, a stdfst t idls lvs o aftr l els i fgtn. (P) w a tn u l met smwn ho blvs t "vwn i o f o e c g f hslf." n u hr sc a statm, u mit l wndr f e spkr i dscribg z on attud. (P) i i mprtn t e ctnud usfn bsn educas ks t r socit b rcgnizd. alwas t l b lrg nmbrs o yg ppl ho l f tr strt n bsn. l u v t d i lok a e wn ads. bsn educas i wrkg f gratr ecmc grot. mr bsn mns mr ppl t d wrk cld f n bsn ofs. (P) n 1 (wn) c argu awa e drk, imdt vlu o bsn educas t mlns o yg ppl. a sld fwnas z b blt f bsn educas--wn t asrs is pmn n r socit. (210 words)(s.i. 1.53)*

26.12 Vocational Pointers:

> **Transcription is not unlike many other areas of en-
> deavor: First things come first. And by that we mean, of
> course, the *most* important should come before the
> *less* important. Especially important letters and
> memos, those that warrant air mail and special de-
> livery, telegrams, etc. should be transcribed *first*, un-
> less otherwise instructed by your dictator.**

26.13 Here are some more words on which to practice from our important theory letter.

26.14 *soil, absorbs, quantities, moisture, employees, excavation, deploy, elsewhere, usual, fashion.*

26.15 Brief forms and high-frequency phrases probably comprise 60% of more of the average letter. It therefore is exceedingly important that you completely master such vital words and word "units." See how well you can apply your PS to the phrases in paragraph 26.16.

26.16

	1	2	3
1	few months	few months ago	for a few days
2	for a few months	for a long time	for his
3	for it	for me	for my
4	for myself	for next month	for next year
5	for one	for our	for so long a time
6	for some years	for that	for the
7	for the last	for the present	for the purpose
8	for the time	for them	for these

26.17   Even Psychology terms are becoming more and more com-
         monplace in our daily lives. See how well you can write the
         ones listed in paragraph 26.18.

26.18

	1	2	3
1	abnormal psychology	fixation	morbidity
2	aggressivity	frustration	neurologist
3	amnesia	hallucinatory	neuropsychiatric
4	antisocial	hyperkinetic	neurotic
5	behavior deviation	hypersensitiveness	paranoia
6	borderline case	hypomanic	phobic
7	case histories	hysterical	prognosis
8	compulsive	illusion	psychiatrist
9	defense mechanism	inhibitions	psychology
10	delirium	intrapsychic	psychosis
11	delusional	investigative therapy	psychosomatic
12	dementia praecox	libido	regression
13	deviant	maladjusted	retardation
14	disorientation	manic quality	schizophrenia
15	egocentricity	maturation	symptomatic
16	exhibitionism	Mongolism	verbalize

Personal Shorthand

27.1   *Theory Review:*

27.2

> **General Writing Aids for PS —**
>
> Use the ampersand (&) rather than the letter *a* for the word *and* — many writers find it much easier and faster to transcribe.
>
> Use *p* for the *p-r* and *pr* combinations, even within words, if transcription is not impaired: apart — *apt*; important — *mptn*; surprise — *srpis*
>
> Use *f* for *ify* even with suffixes: testified — *tstfd*; testifier — *tstfr*

27.3   How do you plan to write the word, *motorcycle,* in paragraph 27.4? How fast can you write the entire letter in PERSONAL SHORTHAND?

27.4   *Dear Mr. Thomas: We are about ready to make some very extensive changes in the ¼ design of the ¹ motor on the Honda. ¶ Since you have owned a Honda for the past several years, we would ½ appreciate your advice ² as to any improvements you feel would be beneficial which would ¾ help us make the Honda the outstanding ³ motorcycle on the market today. Yours very truly, (70 words) (s.i. 1.53)*

27.5   Are there any words that you need to practice in the next letter, before working on the letter for speedbuilding purposes?

27.6   *Dear Mr. Chin: I am sending to you an electric iron, which has been returned to us by a ¼ customer. Our ¹ records show she purchased the iron from us on March 5. This leaves nine months remaining ½ on the one-year guarantee. ² ¶ The connection inside the handle appears to be the difficulty. ¾ We would appreciate your repairing ³ or replacing the iron for us. Thank you. Sincerely yours, (70 words) (s.i. 1.53)*

27.7   Transcription Pointers: CAPITALIZATION (Cont.)

Capitalize . . .
Personification:
> *The long arm of the Law caught up with him.*
> *It is a story of a man for whom Time stood still.*

The Deity:
> *God*
> *Jehovah*
> *Almighty*
> *Son of God*
> *Supreme Being*
> *Saviour*

27.8   The following letter, to Mr. Yen, consists of 140 shorthand words. If someone is available to dictate it, take it several times, at increasing speeds; finally dropping back to 70 or 80 words per minute. In any event, make sure that you can write all of the words in the letter, without hesitation.

27.9   *Dear Mr. Yen: Have you heard of the bill being considered by the Senate saying that all ¼ imports from now on [1] will have to be taxed an extra duty of $10? We feel that this is not ½ only impossible but also an unfair and improper imposition. We are going to ¾ file a complaint. ¶ We cannot encourage our [3] customers to invest their money in our company (1) if taxes continue to rise. Indeed, we are [4] considering asking our friends to write their ¼ congressmen, suggesting that they insert a clause making an exception of [5] our products. This would encourage ½ the congressmen to confer with their voters before proposing any more [6] legislation ¾ of this type. ¶ Will you please let me know immediately how you feel about this matter. Yours truly, (140 words) (s.i. 1.56)*

27.10   Many students can *write* shorthand, of one kind or another; but many of these same students cannot read or transcribe it easily or accurately. Make sure that you can both *read* and *write* PS.

27.11   *dms roberts: t u f y l o m 10 (tn) a e ntrst u v n obtang a ofc pss w u drg e cg smr mts. y l z b trnd ovr t r ofc mgr, ho fels t e z e tip o smr pss u d lik. (P) ofc mplyes ho v b w u mr tn 5 yrs v a 3 weks' vacas, a tos ho v b h ls tn 5 yrs r gn a 2 weks' vacas. e vacass o r pivt scrtrs r stgrd troo e smr; csgnl, i i nsr f u t mply 1 (wn) adsl scrtr f ts prd. (P) i i mprtn t ts psn b ab t adpt hslf/hslf gkl t a nu stas a t s/e b lg a rd t lrn r ofc rotn. ts tip o jb d g u my vrd xprns t d b v wrtwil. (P) mr. smt d lik t ntrvu u ts wek. etr w r t aftrnon d b most cvnn. n u ariv n stl, p fon h a 228-0946 f a dfnt apynm. w sl xpk y cl nxt wek. sy (210 words)(s.i. 1.53)*

27.12 Vocational Pointers:

> **Give *special* attention — even extra time — to the handling of names and titles. Few things antagonize as much as the misspelling of a name, and running a close second is the use of an improper title — whether Mister, Miss, Mrs., Ms., Dr., Col., or whatever it may be. Any good reference book will be a considerable help in the handling of names and titles.**

27.13 Practice writing (*very* carefully) the first paragraph from our theory letter. Make sure you can write every word of it without hesitation.

27.14 *Dear Mr. Prentice: We are encountering some unexpected trouble in the construction of our Denver plant. Excavation at one corner of the property has threatened the foundation of a nearby church and may compel a change in plans. Is it your belief that we should continue on schedule or phone our regional vice president for advice? From a cost stand-point, it would be much better to continue form construc-*

tion without delay, which, in turn, would be helpful from a personnel assignment standpoint.

27.15   Practice writing the following phrases until you can do so automatically.

27.16

	1	2	3
1	he must be	he must have	he needed
2	he needs	he said	he saw
3	he says	he seemed	he should
4	he should be	he should be able	he should have
5	he should not	he told	he took
6	he wanted	he wants	he was
7	he will	he will be	he will be able
8	he will be glad	he will find	he will have

27.17   Now use your shorthand on these Radio and Television terms in paragraph 27.18.

27.18

	1	2	3
1	acoustics	documentary	newsreels
2	adaptation	dolly man	outlet
3	amplifiers	electromagnetic	photosensitive
4	antenna	electronic	remote control
5	audimeter	emcee	round-table discussion
6	audition	fade-out	sequel
7	backdrop	frequency modulation	simulcast
8	cabinet	iconoscope	stand-by
9	cameramen	kilocycle	superimpose
10	circuits	listeners	tape recorder
11	coaxial	loud-speaker	telegenic
12	commentator	master of ceremonies	telethon
13	continuity	megacycle	travelogue
14	cowcatcher	mike-boom operator	turntable
15	cyclorama	moderator	ultrahigh frequency
16	dialogue	modulation	very high frequency
17	disk jockey	multipath transmission	video
18	distortion	newscaster	wavelength

Personal Shorthand

CARDINAL SERIES

28.1 *Theory Review:*

28.2

> **General Writing Aids for PS —**
>
> Use **s** for all *shun, zhun,* and *shen* sounds, regardless of the spelling (*tion, sion, shion, cien, tien, clan*): division — *dvs*; efficient — *efst*; patient — *past*
>
> Use **s** for *shus:* delicious — *dls*; precious — *ps*
>
> Use Brief Forms for syllables within words; this is a good shortcut as long as words can be easily transcribed: adjustment — *ajm*; justify — *jf*; justice — *jc*; notetaking — *notkg*; almost — *lmost*; altogether — *ltgtr*; already — *lrd*; although — *lto*; always — *lwas*; alternative — *ltrntv*; mistake — *msk*; welcome — *lc*

28.3 How fast can you write the following article in PERSONAL SHORTHAND? See if you can set a new record for yourself.

28.4 *If you are going to write to a business requesting printed material or samples ¼ offered by that firm, ¹ take time to determine what the receiver of your letter needs to know. If you ½ merely ask for "a copy of ² the pamphlet your company sends out," you haven't given enough ¾ information. ¶ If you want to receive the ³ proper material, you must identify it well. (70 words) (s.i. 1.56)*

28.5 See if you find the next article easier or more difficult to write in shorthand. Analyze its content and try to determine *why* it seems one way or the other.

28.6 *The aroma of good cooking coming from a kitchen is a smell unequaled anywhere in ¼ the world. The ¹ kitchens of the world create many fine dishes, such as Italian spaghetti, ½ Mexican tacos and refried ² beans, French cream sauces and pastries, lamb from the Baltic countries, curry ¾ dishes from India, and fresh fruit dishes ³ from the Pacific Islands. ¶ Oh, the joy of good eating! (70 words) (s.i. 1.56)*

28.7   Transcription Pointers: CAPITALIZATION (Cont.)

Capitalize . . .

Books of the Bible:

Genesis   St. John   Revelation

Note: The word *Christian* and its derivatives — *Christianity*, etc.

School Subjects:

Capitalize the names of school subjects when derived from the proper nouns or when used with numbers to specify a particular course.

English

French

Chemistry 227

He is studying marketing, advertising, and English.

Neither biology nor psychology is required.

He studies Marketing 344 and Advertising 451.

28.8   The article in paragraph 28.9 is composed of 140 shorthand words. In other words, it is twice as long as the articles in paragraphs 28.4 and 28.6. How well can you maintain your speed on a letter of this length?

28.9   *Business subjects, usually considered of value only to persons undertaking ¼ business careers, [1] also have much value for those who will use them for either personal use or in a ½ career that is not strictly [2] business in nature. High schools should make every effort to include ¾ certain commercial subject matter which may serve [3] those students who are not strictly vocational students. (1) ¶ Leading the field of personal–use business subjects is [4] typewriting. Much progress has been made in ¼ promoting typing for its personal-use value. Some schools have gone so [5] far as to require all of ½ their students to take a short course in typing. All high school graduates, whether [6] continuing their ¾ education or entering a field of employment, will find typing a useful personal aid. [7] (140 words) (s.i. 1.58)*

28.10   The shorthand article in paragraph 28.11 is made up of 210 shorthand words. If possible, read or transcribe it several times; and then compare your rate with previous letters or articles of this length.

28.11   *scs n dvlpg tipg skl dpns t a lrg xtn uo e mtl attud e lrnr z trd z/h wrk.*

eft crats abl, b n r t elmat wastd
movms a t rc e hist dgre o skl n e srtst
i, e studn mst v a ustng o e wrk e/s i
dg a mst brg t i ec da a dtrmas t k t
da's wrk btr tn e lst. (P) b ng o s/e
i strivg f, s/e l ustn e ned f dg l z/h
wrk z acrtl a sklfl z p. l-drkd eft lds
t e dvlpm o hi skl n tipg. ec lin o
tipg mst b rtn w crk tcng. e studn mst
g dfnt atns t e dtals o strokg, evnn o
tc, a acrc o ritg. t mst b n crls,
ndfrn wrk. (P) n e pctc prd, e sam dgre
o eft mst b m z i gn t e wrk hnd n f c.
hbts dvlpd drg pctc prds r e wns w ma
hlp r hndr e studn's pfsc. crls pctc
aks z a dtrm t stg u crk hbts.
(210 words)(s.i. 1.54)

28.12   Vocational Pointers:

> In the process of transcribing, when you encounter questions pertaining to spelling, word division, involved punctuation, and various vocabulary nuances, don't guess — use your secretarial reference books; or, if appropriate, ask your employer for verification, if you are in doubt about the meaning of a sentence, a technical word that is not available in your dictionary, etc.

28.13   Now practice your PERSONAL SHORTHAND on the next three paragraphs from the theory letter that we have been studying.

28.14   *There is a tendency for the local inspector to magnify the seriousness of the matter. It is true, however, that our heavy equipment does interfere with choir singing at the church, and debris fires have singed some trees and shrubs along the south edge of the property. (P) We trust that members of the congregation hold no grudge against our organization nor the project itself and will act accordingly while construction is in progress. (P) I should mention, too, that several underground utility installations have proved faulty, causing far too many outages in the area, which, in turn, have distressed church members, as well as the minister.*

28.15   See if you can perfect your PS on the following phrases.

28.16

	1	2	3
1	I should	I should be	I suggest
2	I talked	I think	I thought
3	I told	I took	I want
4	I want to see	I wanted	I was
5	I will	I will be	I will be able
6	I will have	I will not	I will not be
7	I will not be able	I will see	I wish
8	I would	I would be	I would have

28.17   Use your PS on the Real Estate and Building terms included in paragraph 28.18.

28.18

	1	2	3
1	abstract of title	escrow	mortise
2	appraisal	fire insurance	niche
3	architecture	foreclose	option
4	assessments	gable	patios
5	balcony	grantee	portico
6	basement	grantor	premises
7	bedroom	insulation	quitclaim deed
8	blueprint	joint tenancy	real estate
9	broker	lease	real property
10	building and loan	lessee	realtors
11	commission	lessor	realty
12	contract	lien	residence
13	cross-ventilation	living room	sheathing
14	depreciation	market price	specifications
15	dining room	market value	surety bond
16	down payment	mortgage	tenant
17	easement	mortgagee	title
18	encumbrance	mortgagor	warranty deed

Personal Shorthand

29.1 *Theory Review:*

29.2

> **General Writing Aids for PS —**
>
> Use the zip code state abbreviations. Use either all caps, initial caps, or all lower case; probably all caps or initial caps would be the easiest to transcribe, particularly within sentences. It is wise to have these abbreviations memorized, anyway, for use when typing addresses.
>
> Use initial caps for a person's name to aid in transcription. Using initial caps for other proper nouns is also helpful in transcribing.
>
> Saluations: Dear Sir — *d s;* Dear Mr. — *d m;* Dear Mrs. — *d mrs.;* Dear Miss — *d ms;* Dear Ms. — *d ms.* or *d mz* (be sure to use period).
>
> These could also be written together: *ds, dm,* etc.

29.3 See how fast you can supply the shorthand for the 70-word letter in paragraph 29.4.

29.4 *Gentlemen: We are enclosing our check for $63.70 in payment of ¼ your invoice of [1] May 2 for $65 less 2 per cent. ¶ Do you have sufficient stock on hand ½ to supply us with ninety [2] units of No. 60 bolts? We will need the units by June 1. ¾ ¶ We would appreciate receiving your new [3] stock catalog if it is off the press. Sincerely yours, (70 words) (s.i. 1.58)*

29.5 Compare your shorthand speed on paragraph 29.4 with your best effort on the following article.

29.6 *The letters FBLA stand for a club called the Future Business Leaders of America. ¼ This is a high [1] school business club which combines learning with service and enjoyment. ¶ The many benefits ½ derived from participating [2] in club activities help students advance in their field of ¾ work after they graduate from high school. [3] FBLA helps you, your school, your future; and it is fun. (70 words) (s.i. 1.58)*

29.7   Transcription Pointers: CAPITALIZATION (Cont.)

Capitalize ...
Names of Companies:
    Acme Supply Company
    National Steel Corporation
    Allied Publishers, Inc.
Capitalize *Company* when referring specifically to the particular company being represented.
    The Company will publish the manuscript.
Usually *The* is capitalized *only* if it is the first word of the name.
    The First National Bank

29.8   Again put your shorthand to work and see how fast you can write the next article. Keep in mind that it incorporates 140 shorthand words; in other words, it is exactly twice as long as either paragraph 28.4 or 28.6.

29.9   *Most of the cooking and a good deal of the sewing for the average home is done by the ¼ housewife. Therefore, most [1] home economics courses stress these two subjects. Students are taught correct ½ preparation and the most [2] advantageous and pleasing ways of serving foods. They also are instructed ¾ in the relative values of foods and [3] the proper balancing of individual diets. (1) ¶ Likewise, students study the designing and making of [4] garments. Some of the elements which they ¼ are taught to consider, in addition to the mere cutting and fitting [5] of the clothing, are color ½ selection and harmony, recognition of different kinds of materials [6] and the ¾ numerous purposes for which each is best adapted, and the most economical use of each. [7] (140 words) (s.i. 1.61)*

29.10   The shorthand article in the following paragraph embodies 210 words. See how fast you can read it; or, if possible, transcribe it at the typewriter.

29.11   *wn u v mstrd e notkg stm o srthn, u mst lrn w t p e pncpls nt pctc. (P) t r 2 was t orgniz nots. u c rit tm n nrtv smrs r orgniz tm n olin fm. e fmr i pbbl e most efkv f lctr nots sn orgnizg*

y nots n olin fm g u t rli o e orgnzas
usd b e spkr. (P) e spkr l ofn g u cus
t l hlp u orgniz y nots. f xmpl, e ma
sa, "t r 3 ruls f ritg btr bsn ls; b
brf, b clr, a b crts." ts clu nabs u t
grop e spkr's pyns u 3 man hdgs. (P) f
e lctrr ds n psn mtrl n a mr sutb f:
oling, u sd, a a latr d, rrgniz y nots
nt olin fm. ritg y nots n olin fm
hlps u orgniz y tnkg a ks y nots mr
usf f std a rfrn. ts rrgnzas o nots
c b a vlub lrng xprn n islf. (P) g
notkg ofn dtrms y scs r falr n a crs,
a g notkg strts w g lsng. (210 words)
(s.i. 1.54)

29.12   Vocational Pointers:

If the **executive with whom you work has given you permission to do so, improve syntax, where you feel it is
necessary; insert — or delete — punctuation marks,
etc. But do *not* exercise this prerogative on your own,
without permission.**

29.13   Here is another paragraph from the theory letter that we are
striving to master. Make sure you can write it easily.

29.14   *There is also a large mound of dirt, near their parking lot,
which cannot be moved until cement footings have been
completed. We may be able to screen this some with a
fence; but in all fairness, there is no sense in pretending that
this will be completely adequate.*

29.15   Again apply your shorthand to the following high-frequency
phrases.

29.16

	1	2	3
1	on the part	on the question	on the subject
2	on these	on this case	on which
3	once a month	once or twice	one of the
4	one of them	one of these	one or two
5	one thing	one time	one way
6	only one	only one of these	reach us
7	reach you	so that	so well
8	some of our	some of that	some of the

29.17   Write the following Religious terms in PS.

29.18

	1	2	3
1	abbess	aureole	Christian
2	abbey	baptism	Christianity
3	abbot	bar mitzvah	clergyman
4	absolution	beatitude	cloister
5	altar	benediction	commandments
6	Anglican	blasphemy	communion
7	Apocrypha	Calvary	congregation
8	apostasy	canon law	consecrate
9	apostle	catechism	conversion
10	apostolic	cathedral	crucifixion
11	archbishop	celestial	deacon
12	Ascension Day	chancel	disciple
13	atheism	chaplain	divine wisdom

Personal Shorthand

30.1　*Theory Review:*

30.2

> **General Writing Aids for PS —**
>
> In complimentary closings, join the letters together: very truly yours — *vty*; sincerely yours — *sy*
>
> In writing the word, "period" — the *r* is needed to carry the long *e* sound of the *i*; so it is written *prd*. However, it may be written *pd* if it can be transcribed easily. Some writers use a period with a circle around it for this word.

30.3　Practice your shorthand on the following letter to Miss Wall. Do not go on to the next letter until you can write this one with ease.

30.4　*Dear Miss Zantigo: Thank you for your subscription to our magazine. We are delighted to have you as ¼ a regular [1] reader. ¶ New readers create more commotion around our offices than at the ½ offices of other magazines [2] because the reader is our only interest. We carry no ¾ advertising; therefore, nothing draws our [3] attention away from the job we do for you. Yours truly, (70 words) (s.i. 1.58)*

30.5　From the standpoint of "difficulty," do you consider the next letter to be easier, more difficult, or about the same as the letter in paragraph 30.4?

30.6　*Dear Mr. Jackson: Your application for credit has been received by our credit department. ¼ Since you have been [1] with your present employer less than six months, we must request the name and address of ½ your previous employer, [2] how long you were employed, and the kind of position held. ¶ Upon ¾ receipt of this information, we shall give your [3] application further consideration. Yours truly, (70 words) (s.i. 1.58)*

30.7   Transcription Pointers: CAPITALIZATION (Cont.)

Capitalize . . .

Departments of Business Firms:

Departments may be capitalized only when referred to specifically within a company.

  Sales Department

  an accounting department

School Departments:

Schools and colleges of a university are capitalized.

  School of Business Administration

  College of Arts and Sciences

The names of school subjects are capitalized if the departmental name represents a particular department in a particular school.

  The New York University Department of Business Education is well known.

  Many schools have a department of business education.

30.8   Compare your shorthand speed on the following 140-word letter to Miss Yoshida, with your best speed on the 140-word article in paragraph 29.9.

30.9   *Dear Miss Yoshida: Did you know that over 5 million people read our magazine regularly? We ¼ have been serving ¹ the public for over a hundred years. ¶ Everything we publish meets the strict demands ½ of reader interest, and ² we have never had any complaints or criticism from customers ¾ about our policy. By serving the ³ people of Denver, we feel we are serving our country in (1) bringing before the public an objective analysis ⁴ of current political events. ¼ ¶ If you consider yourself well-informed on government and international ⁵ affairs, you will find ½ this magazine well worth the subscription rate of $10 a year. Why not try our ⁶ free offer. ¾ Just return the enclosed card for an introductory issue of our magazine. Sincerely yours, ⁷ (140 words) (s.i. 1.63)*

30.10   Don't forget to make a note of any words that cause you difficulty in the shorthand reading exercise in paragraph 30.11. If you encounter such words, practice writing them several times.

30.11 *n kg nots f rdg, i i mprtn f u t slk e cnrl ida n o u rd. h r sm gnrl ruls t l hlp u f e cnrl ida. (P) t i usul onl 1 (wn) ida n a pgrf. e ke ida i 1 (wn) tg n e pgrf t c stn alon. usul e frst stn n e pgrf gs u e ke t o e pgrf i a, b ocasl e lst sntn i usd z e ke. sm pgrfs ctan 2 r mr cnrl ids, a u mst f bot o tm a g tm egl pmn n y nots. (P) n kg g nots, u mst b ntrstd n mr tn e cnrl ida n o u rd. u mst b alrt f fks, n, xmpls, a otr ids t xplan, dvlp, a sprt e cnrl ida. tes sprtg ids r a mprtn pt o g nots. (P) slkg e cnrl ida a rlatd ids, fks, n, a xmpls gs jgm z t o i mprtn a o i nmprtn. g nots r n t cplt; y r j cplt enf t srv z tols f lrng. (210 words)(s.i. 1.54)*

30.12 Vocational Pointers:

> **When you finish transcribing a letter, a memo, or an entire page of shorthand, draw a diagonal line through your shorthand notes — but be doubly sure that the material *has been transcribed*.**

30.13 Paragraph 30.14 includes another paragraph from the important theory review letter on which we have been working. Keep practicing it until you can write the material smoothly in PS.

30.14 ***Recently, the church sent a letter of complaint to the city council concerning the noise problem; and we, in turn, are planning to send the council a letter of explanation. Obviously, such a large construction project is not a pretty*** *sight; and while we have a permit to do what we are doing, noise, smoke, and dust are natural by-products of any such endeavor.*

30.15   Put your PERSONAL SHORTHAND to work on the following phrases.

30.16

	1	2	3
1	some of them	some of these	some of this
2	some of those	some time	some time ago
3	some years	some years ago	suggest that
4	they cannot have	they can't	they come
5	they could	they could not	they did
6	they did not	they do	they do not
7	they have	they may	they may be
8	they may be able	they might	they might be

30.17   Practice your shorthand on the Religious terms that are continued in paragraph 30.18.

30.18

	1	2	3
1	divinity	Heavenly Father	Mormon
2	dogma	humility	mosque
3	ecclesiastical	immortal	muezzin
4	ecumenical	immortality	Nazarene
5	edification	Islam	neophyte
6	evangelist	kosher	nirvana
7	excommunication	laymen	offertory
8	exhortation	Lent	omnipresent
9	friar	matzos	omniscient
10	Godhead	mediator	ordain
11	Golden Rule	Messiah	orthodox
12	gospel	missionary	parable
13	heaven	monotheism	parsonage

30.19   Call (or write) the PERSONAL SHORTHAND brief forms for the very high-frequency words in the following chart.

30.20   **Brief Forms:**

	1	2	3	4	5	6
1	make	is	due	also	give	to
2	on	ever	go	price	she	how
3	every	what	as	him	see	of
4	quite	get	which	if	for	have
5	under	by	in	an	we	us
6	copy	receive	about	please	possible	or
7	take	did	they	it	and	has
8	wish	well	return	why	buy	me
9	put	check	not	that	come	just
10	had	order	kind	there	letter	now
11	require	good	date	know	information	were
12	the	been	our	men	when	made
13	out	your	glad	from	enclose	will
14	are	at	but	too	do	was
15	her	my	dear	he	gentlemen	thank
16	very	find	here	would	man	with
17	time	his	so	up	be	credit
18	you	can	all	no	sincerely	am

Personal Shorthand

31.1 *Theory Review:*

31.2

> *General Writing Aids for PS —*
>
> The shorthand writer must be able to distinguish be-tween similar words. A few such problems are illus-trated here:
>
> Between *patient* and *patience*: Use *past* for patient and *pasn* for patience.
>
> Between *interstate* and *intrastate: Use ntrstat* for in-terstate and *ntrastat* for intrastate (or abbreviate *ntrst.* and *ntrast.*)
>
> If the writer finds a need to distinguish between *have* and *receive,* it might be well to retain the *v* brief form for receive and use *hv* for have.
>
> Between similar words, such as *shirts* and *shorts —* if there is a need to distinguish, insert the vowel in *one* of them — probably in the one used less frequently.

31.3 Practice writing the following words in PERSONAL SHORT-HAND: imagine, elegant, period, manufacturing, practically, non-existent, extremely, enhance, beauty, potions, beauties, painted, cheeks, recommended. Then see how fluently you can write these words in the next article.

31.4 *Imagine that you lived in the elegant period of kings and queens when cosmetic ¼ manufacturing was [1] practically non-existent, but ladies were extremely lovely. ¶ What would you do ½ to enhance your beauty? What [2] did they do? Made their own potions, of course. Great beauties of that period ¾ did not believe in lipstick or painted [3] cheeks. For lovely eyes, they recommended keeping good hours. (70 words) (s.i. 1.58)*

31.5 Can you write the letter to Mr. Rand, in the following para-graph, as fluently and as fast as you wrote the article in para-graph 31.4 — but this time *without* previewing and practic-ing any of the vocabulary?

31.6   *Dear Mr. Rand: We wish to correct the mistake that you recently found on your June statement. ¼ Because of an [1] error in our bookkeeping department, you were billed twice for a set of golf clubs. ¶ Enclosed ½ is a credit memorandum [2] for $250 to cover this overcharge. We ¾ regret this error and hope you will accept [3] our apologies for this oversight. Sincerely, (70 words) (s.i. 1.58)*

31.7   Transcription Pointers: CAPITALIZATION (Cont.)

Capitalize . . .

Whereas and Resolved:

The word immediately following *whereas* and *resolved* is capitalized.

> *Whereas, The local chapters are affiliated with the National Council . . .*
>
> *Resolved, That the treasurer shall . . .*

Hyphenated Words:

Capitalize only those words that would ordinarily be capitalized if standing alone.

> *Thirty-fourth Street*
>
> *pro-American*

31.8   Preview vocabulary in the following article carefully, before attempting to build up your shorthand speed on it.

31.9   *The invention of the printing press, in 1450, laid the foundation for the modern ¼ publicity and [1] advertising of today, but the change from handwriting to printing was very slow. ½ As time went on, some handbills [2] came from the printing presses, along with pamphlets and "news books," which would ¾ carry occasional advertisements. ¶ It [3] was unfortunate that at this early period, the (1) patent-medicine makers, cure-all quacks, and other [4] swindlers used advertising to present their ¼ extravagant claims and gave it such a bad reputation that most [5] merchants came to distrust it. ½ However, as industry advanced and the circulation of newspapers and magazines [6] increased, ¾ businessmen came to realize that they could no longer ignore the great power of advertising. [7] (140 words) (s.i. 1.68)*

31.10   The following shorthand article has a particularly good cross-section of vocabulary. Can you read it in 3 minutes, 2½, 2; how fast?

31.11 studns ma, w a tn, g e rg ida t e us o
lg wrds i a ndcas o hi educas a dep nlg.
a pfsr n a clg wn gotd a sntn f a trm
papr rtn b a studn n e clg. h i e sntn.
s o u c k o i. (P) "i i obvs f e dfrn n
elvas, w rlas t e srt dpt o e fld srvad,
t e ctr i sc z t peclud an rsnb dvlpml
ptnsls f ecmc utlzas." a rl nlgb psn
cd xprs ts sam ida n j 7 wrds o onl 1
(wn) sylb ec. i cd b rstatd ts: "e fld
i t step t plw." (P) n ritg ds an g f i
cn b rdl ustod b e rdr. wrds r ofn usd
t mstf nstd o t nfm. sm spkrs g 1 (wn)
e mprs t f y tkd n a smpl, ustnb wa, y
d smw dmn tmslvs. (P) lncn's gtsbrg
adrs z lg sn bc a clsc bcs o is smpl
lgg, is srs ntns, is onst emos, a is
apl t e min a hrt. (210 words)(s.i.
1.55)

31.12 Vocational Pointers:

> The firm or organization for which you work may recommend thin sheets of colored paper (frequently called manifold paper) for carbon copies; and in many cases, the color of the paper dictates the file or "assignment" of the carbon copy. With the tremendous proliferation of photocopy equipment, however, more and more firms are finding that photocopies of correspondence (and other documents) are less expensive than carbon copies. As you will learn (if you have not already done so), correcting errors, on a set of carbon copies, can be very time consuming; moreover, out of habit, you may make *more* carbon copies than some letters, memos,

> or other documents may demand; whereas, photo-
> copies can be made as needed.

31.13   Here are two more paragraphs from the comprehensive theory letter on which to practice your PS. Remember, that in this theory letter we are using the older pronunciation of seismograph (as if it were sismograph), rather than the newer pronunciation, with a long i sound.

31.14   *Large plants are not portable and cannot be moved to the pristine wilderness. I would be quick to admit that there have been problems with this building site, but they are a rarity and nothing that should jeopardize mature relationships. (P) We have considered the use of a small seismograph in the hope of better controlling ground tremors during blasting. Most of the excavation faces church property, which, again, tends to complicate our mission.*

31.15   Now practice your PS on these much-used phrases.

31.16

	1	2	3
1	when the	when they	when this
2	when those	when you	when you are
3	which does	which has	which have
4	which is	which may	which may be
5	which means	which must	which they have
6	which was	which way	which we are
7	which you can	which you cannot	who are
8	who are not	who can	who can be

31.17   Complete your practice of Religious terms in paragraph 31.18.

31.18

	1	2	3
1	Passover	Quaker	saint
2	patriarch	rabbi	salvation
3	penance	Redeemer	scripture
4	Pentateuch	Reformation	secular
5	Pentecost	reincarnation	seminary
6	Pesach	remission of sins	synagogue
7	polytheism	requiem	tallith
8	pontiff	resurrection	transubstantiation
9	predestination	revival	Trinity
10	Prince of Peace	rosary	Unitarian
11	profane	Rosh Hashana	unleavened bread
12	prophet	sacrifice	vestry
13	purgatory	sacrilege	worship

Personal Shorthand

32.1   *Theory Review:*

32.2

> **General Writing Aids for PS —**
>
> **Numbers — ordinals: first — 1ˢ second — 2ⁿ third — 3ᵈ fourth — 4ᵗ (& so on)**
>
>   for hundred — *h./hnrd*
>   for thousand — *t./th.*
>   for million — *m./ml./mil./mln*
>   for billion — *b./bl./bil./bln*
> $100 — $1 h./1 hd
> $1,000 — $1 th./1 td
> $1,000,000 — $1 m./1 md
>   one billion dollars — *$1 b./1 bd*

32.3   If your classroom, lab, or other facility can provide you with dictation, take the following article at 70, 80, and 90 wpm; and then, if time permits, drop back to 80 wpm.

32.4   *Since about 90 percent of all business is conducted over the telephone, employers ¼ arrange ¹ situations for prospective office workers where they will be required to talk over the ½ telephone. It is then ² possible to determine if the applicant has a warm, pleasing ¾ telephone voice. ¶ People who have pleasing voices ³ on the telephone help build good will for their companies. (70 words) (s.i. 1.63)*

32.5   If possible, use the same speedbuilding sequence suggested in paragraph 32.3 in writing the letter in paragraph 32.6. Be sure to master the writing of any troublesome words before moving on to the next paragraph.

32.6   *Gentlemen: Recently I attended a business convention and heard Dr. Klein speak on ¼ methods and techniques ¹ of teaching shorthand. ¶ I am enclosing my check for $6.75 ½ for a copy of his book, Shorthand Methods. If the amount I enclose is not sufficient to ¾ cover the cost of the book, plus mailing fees, ³ please bill me for the additional expense. Sincerely, (70 words) (s.i. 1.63)*

32.7   Transcription Pointers: CAPITALIZATION (Cont.)

Capitalize . . .
Newspapers:
  Chicago Daily News
  New York Times
Note: *The* is not capitalized when not part of the title.
  the New York Times
I and O:
  Shall I send the package?
  O Lord, we know Thy power.
Salutations and Complimentary Closings:
Dear is capitalized only when it is the first word of the salutation.
  My dear Sir
  Dear Mr. Hays
  My dear Professor Clark

32.8   Use your PERSONAL SHORTHAND on the following letter; if possible, practicing it at increasingly higher speeds — noting, as the speed increases, which words cause you to hesitate. Be sure to give these words special attention.

32.9   *Dear Mr. Chen: I understand there is a vacancy in your secretarial staff, and I would ¼ like to place my [1] application with you. ¶ I graduated from Southern Oregon College in ½ 1968 and until [2] May of this year was employed by the Ace Finance Company, in ¾ Portland, Oregon. For two years I acted as [3] receptionist and was later appointed private (1) secretary to the President of the firm. ¶ In May I [4] underwent a serious operation ¼ and was unable to return to my job. My doctor has released [5] me now, and I am able ½ to take up my secretarial work. ¶ My record will show that I am a competent, [6] efficient ¾ secretary. I would appreciate an interview at your convenience. Sincerely yours, [7] (140 words) (s.i. 1.69)*

32.10   Here is another letter for reading or transcribing purposes. See how quickly you can go through it the very first time.

32.11   *dm elgin: u mit b ntrstd n a l w vd [1]*
f e prc cwnt (co.) c buro ccrng bd xs
rtn b jams wgnr. (P) aftr y vd r l o a

3, y adrsd a rgstrd l t mr. jams wgnr a z lst non adrs n rdwod ct, b i z rd mrkd, "movd, no adrs." y l ctkd z brtrs n sn frncsco, bn psn adrs cd b obtand f tm. (P) i sems t u t phps smwn n rdwod ct, pl e rtal mrcns' asosas, sd n wr mr. wgnr wn. e str mgr wr e wrkd t ss n z l t z rltvs tnk e i n r nr ls agls. w sgst u k 1 (wn) mr eft t locat mr. wgnr a tn, f nscsf, t u clos y fil tmprrl o e mtr. (P) crtnl e amt o $600 i t lrg t lt g, wo kg v p eft t clk. wv, nzmc z w v e addrss o mr. wgnr's brtrs, w fel rsnbl sr t sonr r latr i l b p t rlocat h. sy (210 words)(s.i. 1.56)

32.12   Vocational Pointers:

If you have not already done so, get in the habit of proofreading carefully *before* you remove a typed page from your typewriter. It is much, much easier to correct an error while the page is still *in* the machine, than to reinsert the page later and try to make a perfect correction.

32.13   Let's practice our PS on another part of the theory letter. Be sure to master each part before moving on to another.

32.14   ***Moreover, it is becoming increasingly clear that we need a physician "on call" 24 hours a day, in order to efficiently protect division personnel. This will enable us to better answer any question directed to us by state and federal agencies.***

32.15   Here are some more high-frequency phrases, on which to practice your shorthand. Be sure you can write them fast and fluently.

32.16

	1	2	3
1	you would not	you would not be	you would not be able
2	you would not have	your inquiry	your name
3	your order	you are	you are sure
4	you can	you can get	you can give
5	you can make	you cannot	you cannot have
6	you cannot pay	you cannot see	you could
7	you could see	you could not	you could not have
8	you couldn't	you desire	you did

32.17 Practice your shorthand on the Retailing terms in paragraph 32.18.

32.18

	1	2	3
1	advanced dating	flow-process analysis	perpetual inventory
2	brand name	gridiron pattern	physical inventory
3	cash dating	industrial goods	promotion calendar
4	cash discount	initial markup	proximo terms
5	charge accounts	invoice retailing	purchase order
6	C.O.D.	job lot	quota bonus
7	conditional sales	last-in/first-out	R.O.G. dating
8	contract	leader pricing	retail trading zone
9	conventional billing	maintained markup	seasonal discounts
10	cost codes	markdown	seasonal staples
11	cycle billing	multiple-unit pricing	specialty goods
12	departmentizing	never out	stock turnover
13	explicit costs	one-price policy	trading stamps
14	first-in/last-out	open stock	want slip

Personal Shorthand

CARDINAL SERIES

33.1 *Theory Review:*

33.2

> **General Writing Aids for PS —**
> For dollars, write $ sign with just the one vertical line through it.
> **Measurements:**
> pound — *lb.* or #
>   pounds — *lbs.* or #
>   percent — just % sign
>   hour/hours — *hr.*
>   o-clock — *o' (10 o')*
>   dozen — *dz./doz.*
>   dozens — *dzs./dz./doz.*
>   mile/miles — *mi.*

33.3 Here is another 70-word article for both shorthand speed-building and transcription practice. Make a point of mastering each such article and letter before moving on to the next one.

33.4 **The Wall Street Journal** *offers its readers a wealth of information. The* **Journal** *carries daily* ¼ *information* [1] *on the activities of various corporations and the trading that is* ½ *carried out in the Stock Exchange.* [2] ¶ *Advertisements in the* **Journal** *are of a business nature. One* ¾ *portion of the Journal is devoted* [3] *to the current news of interest from around the world. (70 words) (s.i. 1.66)*

33.5 See if you find the following letter easier or more difficult, faster or slower to write in shorthand.

33.6 *Gentlemen: Salmon fishing in the Pacific Northwest is a sport that is a challenge to* ¼ *outdoorsmen. The* [1] *Pacific Northwest is the greatest salmon fishing area in the world.* ¶ *We are* ½ *taking this opportunity* [2] *to invite members of your lodge to visit our salmon fishing* ¾ *area this summer. All equipment is ³ available for rent at a modest cost. Yours truly, (70 words) (s.i. 1.66)*

33.7   Transcription Pointers: CAPITALIZATION (Cont.)

Capitalize . . .

Books, Magazines, Manuscripts, and Themes.

All words should be capitalized except prepositions, articles, and conjunctions.

> *A Tale of Two Cities*
>
> *The Lady of the Lake*

Capitalize the first letter in each word of books and magazines.

> *Saturday Evening Post*
>
> *Circular A*

Titles of books and names of magazines may be underscored or typed in upper-case letters in typewritten manuscripts.

> <u>Life</u>
>
> *GONE WITH THE WIND*

33.8   Can you take the next article from dictation at 70 wpm? 80 wpm? 90 wpm? How does your writing speed on this one compare with your speed on previous articles or letters of this length?

33.9   *For someone who seeks a position in the small office, special attention should be given to ¼ the development ¹ of characteristics that make one's personality shine out. Here, the office ½ worker becomes the shock absorber ² between his/her employer and his/her patrons, and he/she must always take ¾ care to exercise diplomacy and tact. ³ ¶ Many large manufacturing concerns or department (1) stores do not employ wholly inexperienced ⁴ stenographers, although sometimes an ¼ inexperienced typist is given a trial. However, anyone who has ⁵ had from one to two years' ½ training in active business fields finds a short cut here to the enviable ⁶ secretarial ¾ positions that lead to the doors whereupon are inscribed the names of directors of big business concerns. ⁷ (140 words) (s.i. 1.69)*

33.10   Compare your reading or transcribing "time" on the next shorthand article with your best "score" on previous articles or letters of this type. Keep in mind that the following article is comprised of 210 shorthand words.

33.11 *e rtal fld pvids opngs a my edcasl lvls.
t r sm v scsf n a wm n rtalg ho l tl u t
y strtd wrkg n strs z ygstrs, j o o grmr
scol a t y gt ahd b a cbnas o ambs a hrd
wrk. tda, wv, hi scol grduas i e stnrd
mm gm. (P) rlizg e mprtn o e rtal fld,
sm pgrsv hi scols r ofrg crs n dstrbtv
edcas, n w tr studns std rtalg, salsmsp,
a rlatd crs a scol a wrk pt i n locl
strs. wil ts trang i hlpf, i i n esnsl.
(P) t r my ppl erng splnd slrs ho cam t
tr jbs w n spsl glfcass r tcncl trang,
b y w lg t lrn o e jb. n sm cas, e lrg
strs pfr t tran tr on psnl. sc trang
ma cst o a fu weks' ntnsv nstrcs u e
drks o a xprnd xctv, r i ma k e fm o a
aprncsp, n w e nu mplye i asind t a
oldr wrkr f trang. (210 words)(s.i.
1.61)*

33.12   Vocational Pointers:

> **As you complete transcribing each letter, memo, or report, make a point of assembling each letter with its respective envelope, along with any necessary enclosures. Check enclosures carefully, to make sure that they are the ones indicated in the letter. It can be very embarrassing to include enclosures that should *not* be included — or, vice versa, fail to include one or more that *should* be enclosed.**

33.13   Let's continue to carefully practice additional material from the comprehensive theory letter on which we have been working.

33.14   *I thought that this, in itself, was of considerable importance because of recent changes in the law. (P) Finally, the project engineer is undecided whether to allow further excavation on days when cloud formations indicate possible heavy rain.*

33.15   Continue to practice the writing of phrases in PS until you can write them automatically. See how well you can do on the list in paragraph 33.16.

33.16

	1	2	3
1	at that	at that time	at the
2	at the time	at these	at this
3	at this time	at which time	able to say
4	about my	about that	about the
5	about the matter	about the time	about them
6	about this	about this time	about those
7	after that	after that time	after the
8	after these	after this	among the

33.17   Now apply your shorthand to the Supervision and Management terms in the next paragraph.

33.18

	1	2	3
1	absenteeism	disciplinary action	leadership
2	account executive	down time	management
3	administration	empathy	mediation
4	administrative assistant	executive	merit system
5	area manager	feasibility study	output
6	budgeting	fiscal policy	promotion
7	command	fiscal year	public relations
8	communication	foreman	purchasing
9	compulsory arbitration	grade	quality control
10	convene	human relations	queuing theory
11	coordination	incentives	recruitment
12	current assets	interview	staffing
13	current liabilities	job description	turnover
14	depth interview	job specification	unit cost
15	directive	just cause	wages

Personal Shorthand

34.1   *Theory Review:*

34.2

> **Optional Shortcuts —**
>   accommodate — *acmd*
>   afternoon — *afon/afn.*
>   application — *apcas*
>   appointment — *apy*
>   bankrupt — *bkrp*
>   bankruptcy — *bkrpç*

34.3   Give some thought to these words before you start to practice the next article: advantages, secretary, variety, assignments, probably, supervision, responsibility, challenging.

34.4   **There are advantages for the secretary who works in a small office. Usually he/she ¼ has more ¹ variety in his/her duties and assignments. There probably will be less supervision ½ of his/her work with ² responsibility given to him/her sooner than if he/she worked in a large ¾ office. Jobs in small offices are often more ³ challenging, and this appeals to many secretaries. (70 words) (s.i. 1.66)**

34.5   Practice the following words before writing the article in paragraph 34.6 several times: typewriter, chance, demonstrate, ability, previously, handled, success, stenographers, secretaries, businesswomen, positions, function.

34.6   **The typewriter gave women a chance to demonstrate their ability in jobs that had ¾ previously been ¹ handled by men. ¶ The success of these first women typists, stenographers, and secretaries ½ paved the way for today's ² businesswomen to assume the many positions of ¾ responsibility they now hold. Business as we know ³ it now could not function without the secretary. (70 words) (s.i. 1.72)**

34.7   Transcription Pointers: NUMBERS

Write in figures, numbers having to do with . . .

Dimensions, Weights, Distance, Measurements, Temperature

Write in figures.

15 *by* 21 *feet*

10 *feet long*

72 *degrees or* 72°

167 *pounds*

3 *tons*

The room is 11 *by* 13 *feet.* (Spell out *by*).

Note: Use *x* for specifications only. 35′ × 5′ × 3′2″

34.8 Carefully practice and preview; and then see how fast you can write the following 140-word letter.

34.9 *Dear Employee: Because of the numerous requests for hospital and medical insurance ¼ we have recieved* [1] *from our employees, we are initiating a group policy with an easy-½ pay plan. ¶ This pian permits* [2] *complete coverage for your entire family at the inexpensive ¾ rate of $90 a year, and the* [3] *premiums can be made in ten convenient pay-ments of* (1) *$9 each. This family hospital policy* [4] *is available to all employees ¼ of our company. ¶ If you are interested in obtaining such a* [5] *policy, please notify ½ our business man-ager as soon as possible, and the proper deductions will be* [6] *made from your ¾ pay check. If you have further questions, please contact Mr. Baker in the business office. Sincerely,* [7] *(140 words) (s.i. 1.71)*

34.10 Time yourself (or have someone else time you) on the read-ing — or transcribing at the typewriter — of the following shorthand article. Keep pushing, lesson by lesson, to im-prove your speed.

34.11 *c tda i a pvlg grnd grassl a opnl b strs. wv, t z a i n onl a favrd fu w csdrd sutb f e pvlg. (P) csumr c d n c nt is on ntl e bgng o e 20t cnr. bf t, i z n es t opn a crg acwn. mrcns usl rstrkd e pvlg t e wlty r t frns. c z csdrd a nusn a z xtndd rlknl r w msggs.*

e cstmr ho pad (pd.) f pcs b nstlms z lokd dwn o b z/h nabrs, z e ak z asosatd w e frwnd-o pctc o hn-t-mwt lvg. (P) f ts stag, a grat cag z kn plac. dvlpm z b rpd. tda's crg acwn i csdrd b e rtalr z a grat dvic f bldg sals vlm. c z bc a nst, a crg acwns r w slctd. (P) c trnscss tda ad u t a hug sm. totl rtal sals n e unitd stats rg cs rgstrs t e tun o ovr $200 bln anl, o w a sizb pcng i c. (210 words)(s.i. 1.63)

34·12   Vocational Pointers:

> When you are transcribing, if "enclosures" are not enumerated or in some way noted at the bottom of the letter, make a list of them on the carbon copy (or photocopy) and use *this* as your initial point of reference in checking off things to be enclosed. It still may be wise, however, to review the letter for any enclosure reference that you may have missed.

34.13   Here are some more sentences from the shorthand theory letter on which we have been concentrating. Make sure that you can write each word fluently — without the slightest hesitation.

34.14   *The soil in which we are working absorbs great quantities of moisture and could pose a hazard for employees. Of course, if we cut back on excavation, we will have to deploy some of our workers elsewhere, in the usual fashion. Sincerely,*

34.15   Here are more phrases on which to practice your PS. As you practice such phrases, it is often helpful to incorporate each phrase in a longer phrase, clause, or even a short sentence. Learn to "think" in shorthand.

34.16

	1	2	3
1	and are	and have	and his
2	and hope	and I will	and is
3	and let us	and let us know	and our
4	and see	and that	and the
5	and they	any one	any one of our
6	any one of the	any one of them	any other
7	any way	are not	as if
8	as it has been	as it is	as it will

34.17   Here are some more special vocabulary terms; this time from the field of Transportation. Practice writing them in PS.

34.18

	1	2	3
1	aggregate charge	common carrier	embargo
2	airline	compartments	exportation
3	apportioning	compensation	fabrication in transit
4	arbitrary	concession	fiberboard containers
5	automobile	consignee	fragile
6	auxiliary	consignor	f.o.b. destination
7	backhaul	coupler	freightage
8	blanket rate	crosshauling	freight forwarders
9	boxcar	cubic capacity	gondola
10	bulk carrier	demurrage	hangars
11	car floatage	depot	helicopter
12	cargo	destination	hundredweight
13	carload rate	deterioration	intercoastal
14	claimant	diesel engine	Interstate Commerce Act
15	coastwise shipping	domestic	interurban
16	commerce	drayage	intrastate
17	commodities	dunnage	less than carload

Personal Shorthand

35.1 *Theory Review:*

35.2

> *Optional Shortcuts —*
> book — *bk*
> booklet — *bklt*
> handbook — *hnbk*
> Christmas — *xms*
> circumstances — *crcstns/crcm*
> committee — *cte*
> comprehensive — *cphnv*

35.3 See how your speed on the next letter compares with your shorthand speed in Lessons 30, 25, and 20. Remember that shorthand writing speed is achieved by shaving fractions of a second off of your "reaction time" to each word you encounter.

35.4 **Dear Mr. Gazzolino: I wish to accept my contract with Spokane School District No. 52 ¼ for the [1] 1982-83 school year. ¶ I enjoyed working in the district this past ½ year, and I appreciated [2] the cooperation I received from you for improving the ¾ business department. ¶ I trust my work will [3] continue to meet with your approval. Very truly yours, (70 words) (s.i. 1.72)**

35.5 The article in paragraph 35.6 also includes 70 shorthand words. Compare your writing speed on this exercise with your speed on the letter in paragraph 35.4. Try to practice each such writing assignment two or three times, if possible.

35.6 **A problem cited by many "degree seekers" is that of the necessity of constantly ¼ studying to [1] fulfill requirements at the expense of cultural improvement. ¶ "To dream the ½ impossible dream" is to imagine [2] total freedom in selecting courses for one's enlightenment ¾ and education. The pendulum [3] may swing in that direction with increased innovation. (70 words) (s.i. 1.85)**

35.7   Transcription Pointers: NUMBERS
        Write in figures, numbers having to do with . . .

Money:

Sums of money usually are expressed in figures. Round sums are typed in figures without the decimal.

    $120 *not* $120.00 $10 $1

When typing cents alone, use figures and spell out cents.

        50 *cents*   1 *cent*   75 *cents*

In legal documents and in other statements where un- usual emphasis and clarity are desired, sums of money are written out as well as placed in figures.

        In consideration of Forty Dollars and Sixty-Three Cents **($40.63)**

Sums of money are written in checks as follows:

                                    $120.50
One hundred twenty and 50/100   *Dollars*

                                    $65
Sixty-five and 00/100   *Dollars*

                            $ only 50 cents
Only fifty cents   *Dollars*

35.8   Practice writing the following letter (preferably from dicta-
        tion, if at all possible); and then compare your best speed
        with previous writing exercises of this length (140 words).

35.9   *Dear Mr. Steinberg: I wish to submit my application for the*
        position of legal typist ¼ in reply to [1] *your advertisement in*
        the San Francisco Times. ¶ I have completed the clerical ½
        course in the Business Department [2] *at Salinas Junior Col-*
        lege and have completed a legal ¾ secretarial course at
        Marshall Business [3] *School. I have also done part-time work*
        during my college (1) *years for the Franklin Law Offices at*
        350 Star [4] *Avenue, Salinas, California, ¼ and for the Adams*
        Law Offices, 164 Broadway Avenue, [5] *Oakland, California. ½*
        ¶ My record will show that I am a competent and efficient
        typist. I would [6] *appreciate ¾ an interview in order that I may*
        state my qualifications more fully. Very truly yours, [7] *(140*
        words) (s.i. 1.73)

35.10   Check your reading/transcribing speed on the following
        210-word shorthand article. How does your present reading
        rate compare with earlier lessons?

35.11 *n my hi scols troo e stat o orgn, a n my otr stats z l, drivr edcas z bc a rglr pt o e hi scol crclm. e crs usl csts o 30 t 45 hrs. o clsrom nstrcs, psl a 15 hrs. o akl drivg xprn. (P) e studns lrn e esnsl pts o e atmobl, n a ustn e drivrs' ml, v vsl ads a osid spkrs o mprtn, a k tr tst f a lrnr's pmt f y v n alrd obtand 1 (wn). e man pt o e drivr edcas pgrm, wv, wrks w e studns n dvlpg ppr attuds trd a drivr's rspnsbls. (P) y l striv t dvlp n studns a attud o rspk trd e otr drivr. y tc studns t bc dfnsv drivrs a t dvlp cm crts. e md psn bhin e wel, bcs o smtg t z hpnd a hom, scol, wrk, r n sm otr hum tip o rlass, bcs a ptnsl klr n a atmobl. ts, attuds r a v mprtn pt o drivr edcas pgrms. (210 words)(s.i. 1.70)*

35.12 Vocational Pointers:

> **Frequently, problems arise when it is mentioned in a letter that one or more items will be sent *separately* — and then, all too often, they are forgotten. Here, again, a separate "check off" system, on a carbon copy or photocopy, can be a help. If you personally have control of the items to be mailed separately, the most convenient "reminder" is to actually type the shipping label, as soon as you have transcribed the outgoing letter. However, normally items of this type are processed either by the Accounting Department or the Shipping**

> Department; and you therefore may have to make spe-
> cial arrangements to type such labels — and then fol-
> low through to make sure the shipment is made.

35.13 Before practicing more complete segments of the comprehensive theory letter, let's make one more quick "overview"
of some key words from this letter.

35.14 *trouble, church, compel, continue, phone, form, helpful,
magnify, singing, singed, grudge, act, mention, utility, faulty, members, minister, mound, cement, fence, fairness,
sense, sent, send, pretty, permit, product, portable, quick,
rarity, mature, relationships, seismograph,* faces, mission,
physician, efficiently, division, question, thought, law,
whether, allow, cloud, soil, deploy, fashion (*Remember to
use the* old *pronunciation, sismograph.)*

35.15 Put your PS to work on this next group of phrases.

35.16

	1	2	3
1	as many	as much	as soon as the
2	as that	as that is not	as the
3	as there was	as there will be	as these
4	as they	as they are	as they can
5	as they cannot	as they did	as they will
6	as this	as this is	as this may
7	as those	as though	as to
8	as to that	as to the	as to these

35.17 Complete your practice of Transportation terms in
paragraph 35.18.

35.18

	1	2	3
1	liability	omnibus rate	tariff
2	litigation	peddler cars	teamsters
3	livestock	per dium charge	terminal
4	locomotive	phantom freight	timetable
5	maintenance	port of entry	tonnage
6	manifest	port-to-port	tracer
7	merchant marine	quayage	traffic density
8	misrouting	reciprocity	trainload rate
9	mixed-carlot rates	reconsignment	transit
10	multiple car rates	refrigerator cars	transshipment
11	National Mediation Board	revenue	triplicate
12	natural shrinkage	seagoing	variable
13	navigable	seaport	warehouseman
14	negotiable	shipowner	warehouse receipt
15	nonnegotiable	shipper's manifest	waterway
16	nonperishable	straight bill of lading	waybill
17	nonstop	subrogation	wharfage

35.19 Again call or write the PERSONAL SHORTHAND brief forms for the very high-frequency words in the following chart.

35.20   **Brief Forms:**

	1	2	3	4	5	6
1	and	credit	be	possible	at	from
2	no	would	she	do	did	give
3	that	on	men	as	can	why
4	dear	our	come	go	of	what
5	or	been	date	require	put	my
6	an	was	he	check	for	letter
7	by	it	price	to	please	if
8	find	time	will	thank	is	his
9	gentlemen	how	her	receive	the	him
10	enclose	they	about	get	have	too
11	wish	there	make	see	I	know
12	with	up	your	quite	which	we
13	information	had	good	not	well	copy
14	us	in	just	very	you	when
15	now	all	ever	too	but	due
16	here	out	me	man	made	so
17	take	kind	sincerely	order	every	am
18	under	also	buy	has	glad	return

Personal Shorthand

CARDINAL SERIES

36.1 *Theory Review:*

36.2

> **Optional Shortcuts —**
>   conclude — *clud*
>   conclusion — *clus*
>   congratulate — *cgrt*
>   congratulations — *cgrts*
>   congratulating — *cgrtg*
>   disappoint — *dspy*
>   efficient/ciency — *efs*

36.3 The article in paragraph 36.4 is composed of 80 shorthand words, rather than the 70 that we have been working with in previous lessons. See if you can write the entire article in one minute — or less. If possible, take it from dictation several times.

36.4 **When you apply for a job, you may be asked to take some form of employment test given by the person who will** [1] **¼ *interview you or one of his staff members. This test is not given to determine how smart you are. Instead, it* [2] *½ is used to determine the job which would suit you best in that company. ¶ Most times you will find that the work you* [3] *¾ prefer and the test results are much the same. Remember that on most of these tests, there is no failing or passing mark.* [4] *(80 words) (s.i. 1.24)***

36.5 Here is another 80-word article for shorthand writing practice. See how your best "time" on this one compares with your best on paragraph 36.4.

36.6 ***When dining at first-class restaurants, a good guide to follow is to allow 15 per cent of the bill for the* [1] *¼ waiter's tip. If the bill is small, you should pay 20 per cent of the check or a minimum of 25 to* [2] *½ 50 cents a person. If the bill is quite large, you may cut the tip to 10 per cent of the total. ¶ Usually,* [3] *¾ head waiters are not tipped unless they perform a***

special service. Then their tip should not be less than $1. [4]
(80 words) (s.i. 1.29)

36.7   Transcription Pointers: NUMBERS

Write in figures, numbers having to do with . . .

Insurance Policy, Serial, and Telephone Numbers
Write in figures.

> *Policy No. 78396*
>
> *Serial No. HF247891*
>
> *Telephone HAstings 5-2478*

Note: Do not separate hundreds from thousands by commas in these figures.

Street and Apartment Numbers:

Write in figures except when the number is *one*.

> *444 College Avenue*
>
> *29 Windsor Road*
>
> *109 De Witt Place*
>
> *One University Place*
>
> *One Fifth Avenue*

Note: Do not add *th* or *st* to street names.

> *23 West 45 Street*

***Spell out street names up to eleven.* Use figures for street names over *eleven*.**

> *45 West Tenth Street*
>
> *345 Fifth Avenue*

36.8   The longer letter that follows is comprised of 160 shorthand words, rather than the 140, with which we have been working in earlier lessons. Test your PS; see how well you can handle this greater number of words.

36.9   *Dear Miss Skaji: It is possible that we will have the goods you ordered by June 1. ¶ I know Mr. Price is due to* [1] *¼ return on May 10, but it is almost certain he will be delayed due to the strike in Utah. His plans were to* [2] *½ bring some orders back with him, but he tells me that he does not see how he can do so now. ¶ The strike has delayed all* [3] *¾ orders. I know he would not wish you to wait for your order. He had hoped to ship it soon. I made a check to see* [4] *(1) why the goods were delayed and to find out what could be done. ¶ My assistant, Miss Zen, said she lost her copy of the* [5] *¼ order and did not locate it under a packaging list until too late for the 5 p.m. mail. There was no* [6] ½ *one in my office at the time. We wish you to know that Miss Zen is no longer with us.* ¶ *We are sorry for this* [7] ¾ *delay and will make every effort to see that this situation does not recur in the future. Sincerely,* [8] *(160 words) (s.i. 1.20)*

36.10 The following shorthand letter to Mr. Page incorporates 240 words, rather than the 210 words, in previous articles and letters of this type. If time permits, read (or transcribe) the letter at least twice. Compute your speed (your words per minute) for each reading.

36.11 *dm page: z u ma n, w v a cwnt (co.) frz v yr, a w alwas ask svrl bns t mrc n e pad. e pad l b j 14 ts yr, a w d lik t v y fzn bn apr n ts pad. (P) w l met o e hi scol cmps a 9 a.m. a tn lin u f t. e pad rot i sc a srt 1 (wn)--a 2 mils lg-- t e musss sd n b t tird a e en o e pad. (P) a non, l e bn mbrs l v a fre lnc n e scol cftra. ts l smplf tr trig t f a plac t et, z most o e rstrns l b g crwdd. (P) w d lik t v y bn g a srt odor pgrm n e aftrnon, a 4 o'clk. sm lit musc sc z mrcs r so tuns d p e mjr o e ppl. e bn mbrs d pbbl lik t ntr nt e fn o e frn e aftrnon, pir t plag tr musc, s i m gg a pgrm o evns. u l notc t r svrl dsplas, a crnvl, a my pgrms t b gn o e stret stag. nstrms c b lft n e bn rom, aftr e pad; a, f u lik, u c us e rom t pctc bf y pgrm. (P) i hop u l f i p t pla a r fr. p notf m o y dcs, z son z p. yt*

(240 words)(s.i. 1.31)

36.12   Vocational Pointers:

> **After an envelope is typed, the flap should be placed over the left edge of the corresponding letter or memo, with the addressed side of the envelope *underneath* the letter, so the top part of the letter remains visible; and, so assembled, all materials should be placed, *face down,* on your employer's desk, awaiting the necessary signatures.**

36.13   In our previous lessons, we have been practicing on various words, sentences, and paragraphs taken from a comprehensive theory letter — designed especially for the systematic review of theory principles and phonetic abbreviations. Now let's see how well you can write the first one-fourth of this letter in PERSONAL SHORTHAND.

36.14   *Dear Mr. Prentice: We are encountering some unexpected trouble in the construction of our Denver plant. Excavation at one corner of the property has threatened the foundation of a nearby church and may compel a change in plans. Is it your belief that we should continue on schedule or phone our regional vice president for advice? From a cost standpoint, it would be much better to continue form construction without delay, which, in turn, would be helpful from a personnel assignment standpoint. (P) There is a tendency for the local inspector to magnify the seriousness of the matter. It is true, however, that our heavy equipment does interfere with choir singing at the church, and debris fires have singed some trees and shrubs along the south edge of the property. Sincerely,*

36.15   Here are more phrases on which to practice your shorthand. Give special attention (and put in extra practice) on any that cause you to hesitate.

36.16

	1	2	3
1	he will not	he will not be able	he will see
2	he wished	he would	he would be
3	he would be able	he would be glad	he would have
4	he would not	he would not be	hear from him
5	hear from you	help us	help you
6	here are	here is	here is the
7	hope that	hope you will	hours ago
8	how many	how many of the	how many of them

36.17　Now let's do some reviewing of special vocabulary terms, selected at random from the preceding lessons. Feel free to go back and review these terms at any time.

36.18

	1	2	3
1	accounts payable	general directive	pier glass
2	audience composition	government	primary beneficiary
3	blight	houses	quaver
4	baguette	hypothesis	rotary files
5	capital gains	iridescent	scenario
6	common stock	legislation	sensitometry
7	dependents	material alteration	subsidy
8	dismissal	oregano	symptomatic
9	efficiency	panbroil	tape recorder
10	expedite	parity ratio	tenant
11	federal	pedagogy	transubstantiation
12	foreign	picnic ham	Trinity

Personal Shorthand

37.1 *Theory Review:*

37.2

> **Optional Shortcuts —**
> emergency — *mrgnc/mrgny/mrgn/emgn*
> enthusiasm — *ntusm*
> enthusiastic — *ntustc*
> folder — *fldr*
> guarantee — *grnt/gnt*
> legislature — *lgtr/lgstr*

37.3 Write the following letter in PS several times, checking your speed each time. Be sure to use your shorthand whenever and wherever you can — in school, at meetings, on the job.

37.4 **Dear Miss Teppan: We are pleased to tell you that your account with us is now open. We hope you will use the** [1] **¼ account whenever you wish to purchase any item of women's wear. All of our many services are** [2] **½ available to you, and the employees in our store are eager to be of help in any way they can. ¶ When you are** [3] **¾ shopping downtown, be sure to have lunch at our Rose Room. We hope you will enjoy shopping at Smith's. Very truly yours,** [4] **(80 words) (s.i. 1.30)**

37.5 The following article also has exactly 80 shorthand words. Can you write it in one minute or less?

37.6 *Many firms give training courses during work or after work. Show an interest in these courses, and if you can do* [1] *¼ so, attend them. It may be that you will be required to attend. In that case, don't resent the requirement, but* [2] *½ welcome the chance. ¶ Let your employer know that you do want to increase your knowledge and skill, and ask his advice about* [3] *¾ how to do it. He may be able to open your eyes to ways of doing things that had never occurred to you.* [4] *(80 words) (s.i. 1.30)*

37.7　Transcription Pointers: NUMBERS
Write in figures, numbers having to do with . . .

Time:
Use figures with *a.m.* **and** *p.m.*
　　He works from 9 a.m. to 5 p.m.
When *o'clock* **is used, spell in full.**
　　They will arrive at ten o'clock.
Dates:
Use figures to express days and years.
　　January 25, 1956
　　I received your letter of January 25.
When the day of the month stands alone or when it precedes the month, use *d, st,* **or** *th* **following the number.**
　　I received your letter of the 10th of December.
When the day does not precede the month, it is written alone.
　　I received your letter of December 10.

37.8　Compare your shorthand speed, on the following article, with your speed on the letter in paragraph 36.9, in the preceding lesson.

37.9　*Have you recently observed what the well-dressed business-woman wears? Does she display at her desk her knowledge of the [1] ¼ most recent fashion trends, or must she stick to a drab wardrobe? How does she know what is suitable for office wear? [2] ½ ¶ The girl behind the desk need not look like a drab winter morning. If she uses good taste, she may select many [3] ¾ of the colors worn by her friends who are not office workers. Glaringly bright or gaudy colors are not [4] (1) recommended. Basic colors or shades of them are best. ¶ The chic lady need not always wear a suit. She may find [5] ¼ coordinate outfits to her liking and in good taste. Generally, busy, flowery patterns or very bold [6] ½ plaids are not recommended. ¶ Straight skirts are better than full skirts, because of the danger of catching a heel in the [7] ¾ hem of a wide skirt. Stockings should be worn, and a basic heel of a comfortable height is a very wise choice. [8] (160 words) (s.i. 1.37)*

37.10　The shorthand reading/transcribing assignment in paragraph 37.11 is made up of 240 words. How fast can you read or transcribe it?

37.11   f u pln t g y frst fl-i jb z son z u
grduat f scol, u ma g a ltl nrvs tnkg a
i rit w. u sd tri t rlx, wv, a njy y nu
jb z mc z u c. cagg f e clsrom t e ofc
sd b a xcitg xprn f u. (P) y frst gol o
t nu jb sd b t k crtn y aprn i a is bst.
n u r l gromd, ts l hlp p u a es, a u l
f i mc esr t fac y nu jb cfdrl. bsids a
g aprn, u wn t k sr t y skls r a tr hist
p lvl. tn u l b ab t pfm w es a ec o e
msens w u r xpkd t us. (P) u l f t tgs
a wrk r usl mr fml tn y r a hom. ts
atmsfr l vr f cpn (co.) t cpn, wv. j
rmbr t b plit a ttf, a u l g alg l wrv
u wrk. (P) f u v e abl t k otrs fel a
es arwn u, tn u l ft rit n w y flo
mplyes. so y dsir t jyn n, a alwas g o
o y wa t hlp otrs n u s t y ned astn.
f u l trt otrs n e ofc z u d lik tm t
trt u, u sdn' v an pblm ftg n o t frst
jb, wrv i ma b. (240 words)(s.i. 1.31)

37.12   Vocational Pointers:

**Completed letters, memos, and reports also may be
placed "face up" on your dictator's desk, but with a
paper to cover the work, so that the document on top
could not be read by the wrong person. After you have
been on the job for a reasonable length of time, it is
very unlikely that your employer will often suggest — if
ever — that you have transcribed or typed something
that was not dictated (be it a word, a phrase, or sen-**

> tence); but if it does happen occasionally, *don't be of-fended* — simply accept the responsibility and change the letter as requested.

37.13   Here is the second one-fourth of the comprehensive theory letter. See how quickly and easily you can supply the PS for it.

37.14   *We trust that members of the congregation hold no grudge against our organization nor the project itself and will act accordingly while construction is in progress. (P) I should mention, too, that several underground utility installations have proved faulty, causing far too many outages in the area, which, in turn, have distressed church members, as well as the minister. There is also a large mound of dirt, near their parking lot, which cannot be moved until cement footings have been completed. We may be able to screen this some with a fence; but in all fairness, there is no sense in pretending that this will be completely adequate. (P)*

37.15   Paragraph 37.16 presents more phrases for shorthand speedbuilding purposes.

37.16

	1	2	3
1	how many of these	how many times	how much
2	had not	had not been	has been
3	has been able	has been done	has come
4	has done	has made	has not
5	has not been	has not yet	has not yet been
6	has that	has the	has this
7	has to	has written	I would not
8	I wrote	I wrote you	if it

37.17   It's time to do some more reviewing of special vocabulary terms. Go back and review the different terms as often as necessary.

37.18

	1	2	3
1	advanced dating	cross-examination	general agent
2	area manager	customs	grace notes
3	automobile	decentralization	insertable
4	auxiliary	denier	macrophotography
5	balance sheet	economy	montage
6	buying space	conversion	muckracker
7	candling	crepe	neurologist
8	ceramic glass	croquettes	photosensitive
9	collage	currency	premises
10	complementary colors	curriculum	rabbi
11	convertible certificates	deodorant	reincarnation
12	corporate charter	footboard	requiem

Personal Shorthand

CARDINAL SERIES

38.1   *Theory Review:*

38.2

> **Optional Shortcuts —**
>   local — *lcl*
>   locate — *lcat/loc*
>   localities — *lcls*
>   memorandum — *mo/memo*
>   mortgage — *mtg*
>   newspapers — *nusprs/npps*

38.3   Practice writing several words from the following letter (such as, anything, haven't, something, overlooked, straighten) before taking the letter several times for speed-building purposes.

38.4   **Dear Mr. Keith: Very likely you have a good reason for not having paid anything on your account since ¹ ¼ August. In fact, I am sure of that. However, you haven't told us what the reason is. Is something wrong, or have you ² ½ just been so busy that you overlooked your payments? ¶ If there is anything wrong, I am sure we can quickly ³ ¾ straighten it out. Whether you send a check now or later, I do hope you will write and let us know. Very truly yours, ⁴ (80 words) (s.i. 1.30)**

38.5   Compare your shorthand speed on this next letter with your best speed on the letter to Mr. Keith, in paragraph 38.4.

38.6   **Dear Miss Thanh: Thank you for your reservation. We shall reserve a pleasant, comfortable room for you on the third ¹ ¼ floor, as you requested. ¶ Our dinner hour is from 6 p.m. to 8 p.m. If you can arrive on the 7 ² ½ p.m. train, we shall be glad to meet you at the depot, so you can join the other guests at dinner. ¶ We shall strive ³ ¾ to make your stay with us most pleasant. We will be looking forward to seeing you next weekend. Yours very truly, ⁴ (80 words) (s.i. 1.30)**

38.7   Transcription Pointers: NUMBERS
        Write in figures, numbers having to do with . . .

Pages and Parts of a Book:
page 754
Chapter 20
Part II
Volume III
Whole Numbers and Fractions:
Express whole numbers and fractions in figures when written together.
2-5/8
24-3/5
Note: Use the diagonal key on the typewriter to indicate the division of fractions. 3/5.
Type fractions uniformly.
½ *and* ¼ *or* 1/2 *and* 1/4
Spell out common fractions and hyphenate them when they are used alone in the text.
One-third of the sales, or 33-1/3 *per cent of the sales.*

38.8 Compare your shorthand speed on the following longer article, with your speed on the shorter letters in paragraphs 38.4 and 38.6. Normally, the longer the dictation, the more difficult it is to maintain your top speed.

38.9 *Being a new employee often gives one a lonely feeling. No matter if the job is right, if* [1] ¼ *the desk is your first or your tenth, you're still new. You're the person who doesn't know the people, the building, or the* [2] ½ *angles. You're probably excited, and you may be nervous. ¶ Being the new employee can also be rewarding.* [3] ¾ *It can even be fun when you know the rules. Promptness is important. That morning whistle is your first test. Fail it* [4] (1) *more than once during your career, and you're in trouble. Next in importance on the company timetable is a* [5] ¼ *quick lunch and a slower exit at night. ¶ Be courteous. This covers being polite to everyone from the* [6] ½ *janitor on up. It doesn't hurt to say "Nine, please" when you get on an elevator or "Thank you" when you get off.* [7] ¾ *¶ These are just a few of the many rules a new employee should follow. Above all, remember to be yourself.* [8] *(160 words) (s.i. 1.38)*

38.10 If your schedule permits, read (or transcribe at the typewriter) the following letter several times. Try to increase your speed significantly on each reading.

38.11 *dmrs sanchez: z u v b a cstmr o rs f svrl yrs, w r pd t psn u w y on psnl c crd. w r sr ts l b a grat cvnn t u. ts nul dsind crd l ad gratl t y bg plsr. i l l ad t e sped a efsc o y dal spg n an 1 (wn) o r strs locatd troo e slt lak ct ara. (P) f u s a adsl crd f an otr mbr o y fml, j fl o e gd crd a mal i t r c ofc. y l s t adsl crds r mald pmptl. (P) w e nstlas o r nu c crd pln, w r kg a spsl ofr t l o r crg cstmrs. w l alw u a $2 dscwn o an crg pcs o $20 r mr t u k o r bf d 10 o ts yr. w v j vd r nu lin o sprg clotg a sos, w w r sr l p u a e mbrs o y fml. ps v b rducd o ts nu lin f e nxt 2 weks, s y n b w a sav. (P) w hop u a e mbrs o y fml l stp n t s u son. i i a plsr srvg u, mrs. sncz. f t i an astn t w c g u, p fel fre t g n tc w u a r bsn ofc. yvt (240 words) (s.i. 1.34)*

38.12 Vocational Pointers:

> To an experienced secretary, it merely goes, without saying, that all letters, memos, and reports that are ready for signing should be neat and free of errors. Corrections, if any, should be made in such a way that they are not noticeable. A final but important check is to *compare* envelope and letter — that is, the name and inside address on the letter itself — with that on the envelope.

38.13   Paragraph 38.14 consists of part three of the comprehensive theory letter. Preview, practice, and review it, until you are sure of each word.

38.14   *Recently, the church sent a letter of complaint to the city council concerning the noise problem; and we, in turn, are planning to send the council a letter of explanation. Obviously, such a large construction project is not a pretty sight; and while we have a permit to do what we are doing, noise, smoke, and dust are natural by-products of any such endeavor. Large plants are not portable and cannot be moved to the pristine wilderness. I would be quick to admit that there have been problems with this building site, but they are a rarity and nothing that should jeopardize mature relationships. (P) We have considered the use of a small seismograph* in the hope of better controlling ground tremors during blasting.*

(*When practicing this theory letter, use the older pronunciation, sismograph, rather than the current, seismograph.)

38.15   Practice your PS on the next group of phrases.

38.16

	1	2	3
1	if it is	if it was	if it will
2	if it will be	if my	if not
3	if so	if that	if the
4	if there are	if there is	if they
5	if they are	if they are not	if they can
6	if they cannot	if they may	if they would
7	if this	if this is	if we
8	if we are	if we can	if we can be

38.17   Paragraph 38.18 provides another "cross-section review" of the special vocabulary terms on which we worked through Lesson 35. See how well you can do on these.

38.18

	1	2	3
1	brand name	injunction	traditional
2	budgeting	intelligence	underwriter
3	bulk carrier	lingerie	Unitarian
4	car floatage	problem	unleavened bread
5	closing entry	public offer	verbalize
6	contract year	puree	vestry
7	culling	rissole	video
8	ethylene dichloride	socialism	virtuoso
9	fauvism	strob	wages
10	funded debt	syllabus	want slip
11	indemnity bond	tariff	warranty deed
12	initiative	toothpaste	watermark

Personal Shorthand

39.1   *Theory Review:*

39.2

> **Optional Shortcuts —**
>   points — *pys*
>   probably — *pbl*
>   prompt — *pmt*
>   promptly — *pmtl*
>   question — *qs*
>   questions — *qss*

39.3   Compare your shorthand speed, in writing the following letter, with your speed on paragraphs 38.4 and 37.4.

39.4   **Dear Miss Morse: It has been six months since we received your last payment on account. We have written you five letters** [1] **¼** *reminding you of our credit policy. We have received neither payment nor answer to our letters. ¶ If we do* [2] *½ not hear from you in ten days, we will have to turn your account over to a collection agency. We do not* [3] *¾ want this to happen, but we have no choice. Please send us your payment or explain why you cannot do so. Sincerely,* [4] *(80 words) (s.i. 1.32)*

39.5   Are there any words that you need to practice in the next letter, before writing it several times for speedbuilding practice.

39.6   *Dear Miss Cisco: We are happy to welcome you as a member of our Budget and Save Credit Club. Your charge plate,* [1] *¼ which is enclosed, is your key to extra savings and values. This charge plate is good at any one of our twenty-* [2] *½ five stores throughout Oregon and Washington. In case your charge plate is lost or stolen, do not hesitate to* [3] *¾ notify us at once. ¶ If we can be of assistance to you, at any time, please call on us. Very truly yours,* [4] *(80 words) (s.i. 1.32)*

39.7 Transcription Pointers: NUMBERS
   Write in figures, numbers having to do with . . .

Adjoining Numbers:
Using a comma to separate two numbers, or write the smaller one in full.
  In 1956, 385 students enrolled in the College of Business.
  He bought 30 three-cent stamps.
Connected Groups:
Treat all numbers in connected groups alike. If the largest is one hundred or more, use figures for all.
  The merchandise was sent in lots of 50, 100, and 150.
Age:
Use figures to express exact age.
  Mary is 3 years, 6 months, and 2 days old today.
Decimals and Percentages:
Use figures to express decimals and percentages.
  0.0067 inch tolerance
  0.3 of an inch in thickness
  The answer is 4.5567
  Discounts: 40% and 10%
Market Quotations:
Use figures to express market quotations.
  National Products opened at 64-3/8 and closed at 65-1/8 today.
    Imperial Motors 17-7/8
    U.S. Treasury 3s
    Otis Oil 22-5/8

39.8 The next letter is twice as long as the letters in 39.4 and 39.6. Even though it calls for greater endurance, see if you can maintain your speed on this longer effort.

39.9 *Dear Mr. Taylor: Thank you for your letter of March 21 in which you requested prices on our line of* [1] *¼ equipment and furniture for school classrooms. We would like to help you make the new Lincoln Senior High School one of* [2] *½ the best equipped schools in Dallas. ¶ We feel that our equipment and furniture is able to help provide quality* [3] *¾ education for your students. By reading the enclosed price lists, you will find that our line of products are both* [4] *(1) high* in quality and medium in price. By acting promptly, you can still take advantage of our special [5] ¼ back-to-school sale, which lasts for two more weeks. ¶ We would like to have you and your staff come in and visit our display of [6] ½ classroom furniture so that you can see the variety and quality of our merchandise. Our office is [7] ¾ open from 9 a.m. to 5 p.m., Monday through Saturday. ¶ We hope to serve you in the near future. Sincerely, [8] (160 words) (s.i. 1.39)

39.10   How fast can you read the shorthand article in paragraph 39.11: In 4 minutes, 3½, 3, 2½, 2? Try it several times.

39.11   n erasg a crkg errs o a set o tipg papr,
t r svrl pcdrs u sd flo t nsr e bst lokg
crks p. (P) frst, u sd rmbr t dprs e
mrgn rls ke a mov e tipritr crg t 1 (wn)
sid, s e erasr crms d n fl nt y msen. f
y err i o e rit sid o e papr, mov y crg
t e rit. f i i o e lft sid o y papr,
mov y crg t e lft. (P) f u k a msk
(mstak) nr e btm o e pag, i i btr t trn
y papr bkwrds n e msen, nstd o fwrd. ts
pvns e papr f cg o o y tipritr. (P) u sd
tn eras e err w lit stroks--d n scrb e
err. i i hrdr t dtk a erasr f u us srt,
lit erasr stroks, bcs u l n rf u e fibrs
o y tipg papr z mc. u sd tn brs e crms
ot y tab, awa f y msen. (P) f u v a nu
rbn o y msen, u sd us sm tip o clnr t k
of most o e ink mprs o y papr bf u u y
tipg erasr. (P) aftr u v erasd e err,
tip e crk l r ls. b crtn u d n us t mc
fc n tipg n e crk l, r i l stn o f e

rst o e tipg o e pag. (240 words)(s.i. 1.34)

39.12 Vocational Pointers:

> Although you probably are well acquainted with the importance of zip codes and accepted state abbreviations, it is well to keep in mind that these will become *more* important, as time goes on, rather than *less*. Keep in mind, too, that most reference books, typing authorities, and U.S. Postal spokesmen recommend two spaces between the two-letter state abbreviations and the zip code itself.

39.13 Paragraph 39.14 contains part four of the comprehensive theory letter. Keep working with it until you can write each word with ease.

39.14 *Most of the excavation faces church property, which, again, tends to complicate our mission. (P) Moreover, it is becoming increasingly clear that we need a physician "on call" 24 hours a day, in order to efficiently protect division personnel. This will enable us to better answer any question directed to us by state and federal agencies. I thought that this, in itself, was of considerable importance because of recent changes in the law. (P) Finally, the project engineer is undecided whether to allow further excavation on days when cloud formations indicate possible heavy rain. The soil in which we are working absorbs great quantities of moisture and could pose a hazard for employees. Of course, if we cut back on excavation, we will have to deploy some of our workers elsewhere, in the usual fashion. Sincerely,*

39.15 Here are more good phrases for shorthand writing practice.

39.16

	1	2	3
1	if we cannot	if we could	if we do
2	if we have	if you	if you are
3	if you are sure	if you can	if you can be
4	if you cannot	if you could	if you did not
5	if you do	if you do not	if you give
6	if you have	if you know	if you may
7	if you must	if you need	if you think
8	if you want	if you will	if you will be

39.17 Let's continue our "cross-section review" of the special vocabularly terms on which we have been working in this course. Don't hesitate to review specific vocabularies, when necessary.

39.18

	1	2	3
1	aggregate charge	cashmere	inhibition
2	airline	committee	jingoism
3	accounts receivable	defendant	libido
4	across the board	demitasse	megacycle
5	aeration	dough	mortgage
6	air brush	exports	mosque
7	applied art	extracurricular activities	muezzin
8	bid price	furniture polish	Nazarene
9	blue chip	Early American	one-price policy
10	blueprint	group insurance	promotion
11	budget	harmonic modulation	quayage
12	bureau	hectograph	reconsignment

Personal Shorthand

40.1   *Theory Review:*

40.2

> **Optional Shortcuts —**
> statistics — *ststcs*
> statistical — *ststcl*
> sufficient/ciency — *sfs*
> suggestion — *sgs*
> suggestions — *sgss*
> vacation — *vcas*
> verdict — *vdk*
> Chamber of Commerce — *CC/cc.*

40.3   Do your best to set a new shorthand speed record on the following article. If at all possible, take it at least two or three times from dictation.

40.4   **When we stop to think, we realize that we all live in two worlds — the world around us and the world within us. The [1] ¼ world around us consists of things that we use and people with whom we make contacts. The world within us is our [2] ½ attitude and way of thinking. Out of that attitude and thinking we build morale. ¶ Morale can be communicated. [3] ¾ Good morale on the part of a firm can be communicated to build good will on the part of employees. [4] (80 words) (s.i. 1.33)**

40.5   See how your shorthand speed on the following letter compares with your speed on the article in paragraph 40.4.

40.6   *Gentlemen: Today I received a notice from your company that I am behind in my car payments. If you [1] ¼ will check my payment record, you will find that I made two payments in October and November. This was done [2] ½ because I knew I would be laid off this spring for two months. ¶ I am returning to work in two weeks and will make my next [3] ¾ payment when due, on July 15. If you have any questions, please do not hesitate to write. Sincerely yours,* [4] *(80 words) (s.i. 1.33)*

40.7   Transcription Pointers: NUMBERS

Spell in full — — —

Indefinite Numbers

Spell out the numbers when they refer to indefinite numbers.

> *about three hundred people*
>
> *two thousand miles or so*
>
> *five or six years ago*

Spell out approximate age in years:

> *Mary will be seventeen or eighteen years old in November.*
>
> *John was twenty-one years old when he took out his first policy.*

A Number Beginning a Sentence:

Spell out a number that begins a sentence.

> *One hundred fifty new accounts were opened last month.*

Note: *Not* "1955 was a profitable year for the company." *But* The year 1955 was a profitable one for the company.

40.8   The letter in paragraph 40.9 embodies 160 shorthand words. How fast can you write it. Can you take the entire letter at 80 words per minute? 90?

40.9   *Dear Shari: This year the Alumni Association is going to hold its annual meeting at the Ridpath* [1] *¼ Hotel in Spokane. The date for the meeting is Friday evening, July 28. The dinner will start at 6* [2] *½ p.m., and the meeting and dance will follow. ¶ We hope this year's party will be one of the biggest and best yet.* [3] *¾ Therefore, we have reserved one entire floor of the hotel for our use. We have hired a well-known band that will provide both* [4] *(1) the dance music and some additional entertainment. ¶ In order to properly accommodate our guests and* [5] *¼ leave room for dancing, we have had to limit the number of tickets sold to 600. Therefore, it is important* [6] *½ that you get your order for tickets in early. ¶ We hope you can make it to this gathering, as this is the* [7] *¾ tenth anniversary of our class. You will want to see all your old friends again, so be sure and come. Yours truly,* [8] *(160 words) (s.i. 1.39)*

40.10   As you read the following shorthand letter, make a listing of any words that puzzle you unduly; then analyze (and practice) the respective theory or phonetic principles involved.

40.11   *dm chambers: w rcnl lrnd f a frn o rs t u v j movd t so fls. w d lik t k ts oprtunt t lc u t r ct, a w hop u l lik i h. w r crtn u l f r ctzns frnl a lg t hlp u n an wa p. (P) u l, o crs, b tnkg a opng xg a savgs acwns n so fls. w wn u t n t w d lik t srv u n tes ars. r bnk alws u t opn savgs acwns f z ltl z $5. u c dpst u t $10,000 n ec acwn. ntrst i pad (pd.) o tes svgs acwns f e da o dpst, a w c i t y acwn 4 is a yr. (p) f u wrk r f sm otr rsn cn k y dpsts n psn, i i p t hnl l o y bnkg bsn b mal. lt u n f u r ntrstd n ts srvc; a w l b g t sn u l e qd fms. (P) sn w r a fl-srvc bnk, w ofr my otr srvcs t r cstmrs. r nvstm dprtm c hlp u w y scrts. w l v saf-dpst bxs w u ma rn f a sml fe. (P) w hop u l lt u k cr o l y bnkg neds. w d lik t b o srvc t u a t y fml. yt (240 words) (s.i. 1.36)*

40.12   Vocational Pointers:

> Be sure to write the month, day, and year on the cover
> of your shorthand pad, when you *start* to use that pad;
> and then the month, day, and year, when you *complete*
> the use of that pad. Many organizations require that
> shorthand pads be kept on file for several years.

40.13   Paragraph 40.14 includes the *complete* comprehensive
theory letter, parts of which we have used, again and again,
for theory review purposes. Go through the letter carefully.
Make sure that you can write each and every word with complete assurance.

40.14   *Dear Mr. Prentice: We are encountering some unexpected
trouble in the construction of our Denver plant. Excavation
at one corner of the property has threatened the foundation
of a nearby church and may compel a change in plans. Is it
your belief that we should continue on schedule or phone
our regional vice president for advice? From a cost standpoint, it would be much better to continue form construction without delay, which, in turn, would be helpful from a
personnel assignment standpoint. (P) There is a tendency
for the local inspector to magnify the seriousness of the
matter. It is true, however, that our heavy equipment does interfere with choir singing at the church, and debris fires
have singed some trees and shrubs along the south edge of
the property. (P) We trust that members of the congregation
hold no grudge against our organization nor the project
itself and will act accordingly while construction is in progress. (P) I should mention, too, that several underground
utility installations have proved faulty, causing far too many
outages in the area, which, in turn, have distressed church
members, as well as the minister. There is also a large
mound of dirt, near their parking lot, which cannot be moved
until cement footings have been completed. We may be able
to screen this some with a fence; but in all fairness, there is
no sense in pretending that this will be completely adequate. (P) Recently, the church sent a letter of complaint to
the city council concerning the noise problem; and we, in
turn, are planning to send the council a letter of explanation.
Obviously, such a large construction project is not a pretty
sight; and while we have a permit to do what we are doing,
noise, smoke, and dust are natural by-products of any such
endeavor. Large plants are not portable and cannot be
moved to the pristine wilderness. I would be quick to admit
that there have been problems with this building site, but*

they are a rarity and nothing that should jeopardize mature relationships. (P) We have considered the use of a small seismograph* in the hope of better controlling ground tremors during blasting. Most of the excavation faces church property, which, again tends to complicate our mission. (P) Moreover, it is becoming increasingly clear that we need a physician "on call" 24 hours a day, in order to efficiently protect division personnel. This will enable us to better answer any question directed to us by state and federal agencies. I thought that this, in itself, was of considerable importance because of recent changes in the law. (P) Finally, the project engineer is undecided whether to allow further excavation on days when cloud formations indicate possible heavy rain. The soil in which we are working absorbs great quantities of moisture and could pose a hazard for employees. Of course, if we cut back on excavation, we will have to deploy some of our workers elsewhere, in the usual fashion. Sincerely,

(*Use the older pronunciation, sismograph.)

40.15   Practice your PS carefully on this last group of phrases.

40.16

	1	2	3
1	*if you will have*	*if you wish*	*if you would*
2	*if you would be*	*if you would have*	*in a few days*
3	*in a few minutes*	*in a few months*	*in a position*
4	*in addition*	*in addition to the*	*in behalf*
5	*in case*	*in fact*	*in his*
6	*in it*	*in order*	*in order that*
7	*in order to be*	*in order to be able*	*in order to obtain*
8	*in order to see*	*in our*	*in our opinion*

40.17 This completes our "cross-section review" of the special vocabulary terms.

40.18

	1	2	3
1	adjusting entry	fondue	Redeemer
2	association test	foreign exchange	Reformation
3	aurora crystal glass	guidance	remission of sins
4	casein	hamburger	retail trading zone
5	corporate earnings	headboard	staffing
6	corps	hospitalization insurance	straight bill of lading
7	cost	largo	subrogation
8	criminal	ledger sheets	subsidiary ledger
9	dickey	magenta	time discount
10	election	parity	toxicity
11	executed contract	phobic	travertine art glaze
12	flambé	quitclaim deed	wash drawing

40.19 See how fast you can call or write the PS brief forms for the high-frequency words in the following chart.

40.20 **Brief Forms:**

	1	2	3	4	5	6
1	can	and	he	gentlemen	thank	just
2	why	copy	credit	would	has	very
3	be	dear	for	her	with	you
4	time	our	kind	make	up	when
5	at	come	by	the	your	letter
6	from	go	it	him	made	am
7	no	of	price	enclose	which	ever
8	know	what	to	they	we	too
9	she	or	please	about	possible	but
10	do	been	if	get	had	due
11	did	date	find	have	good	here
12	give	quite	order	see	not	out
13	that	put	will	wish	well	me
14	on	my	are	there	us	man
15	men	an	is	were	in	return
16	check	was	his	as	receive	so
17	take	sincerely	also	every	under	buy
18	require	glad	all	how	now	information